TEENAGE KICKS

THE STORY OF

MANCHESTER CITY'S

1986 FA YOUTH CUP TEAM

PHILL GATENBY & ANDREW WALDON

EMPIRE
PUBLICATIONS

First published in 2013

EMPIRE PUBLICATIONS
1 Newton Street, Manchester M1 1HW
© Phill Gatenby & Andrew Waldon 2013

ISBN 978-1-909360-14-3

Back cover line-up from City's Matchday programme for the home game against Birmingham City, Saturday 28th December 1985. All 14 players would go on to win the FA Youth Cup later in the season.

Back row L-R: *Tony Book (coach), John Clarke, Andy Hinchcliffe, Steve Redmond, Steve Crompton, Paul Lake, David White, Ian Brightwell, Steve Macauley, Glyn Pardoe (coach)*

Front row L-R: *David Boyd, Andy Thackeray, John Bookbinder, Paul Moulden, Ian Scott, Steve Mills.*

Printed in Great Britain.

CONTENTS

ABOUT THE AUTHORS

PHILL GATENBY has been a season ticket holder at Manchester City since the age of seventeen (1980-81). His first venture into writing was sending regular letters from 1984 to the *Manchester Evening News* Postbag and Pink Postbag pages (all the published letters he has in a scrap book!) He then joined City's first fanzine 'Blue Print' from the 4th issue in 1988, until it folded. He started his own City fanzine, 'This Charming Fan', in 1993, with an obsession for using Smiths and Morrissey song titles to head up his articles. This lasted six issues until he realised standing outside the ground in all weathers selling the fanzine with his two year old daughter wasn't really an ideal scenario!

During this time he wrote a chapter in the first two editions of "Survival Of The Fattest", a compilation of fanzine editor's view of each season. Post 'This Charming Fan', he also wrote the scripts for the cartoon series that appeared in the fanzine 'City Til I Cry' entitled 'Dagenham Dan The Manyoo Fan'.

When the Platt Lane/Umbro stand opened, Phill found himself in the Family Stand with his daughters and on the opposite side of the aisle to Andrew Waldon and their friendship started from that point. Phill contributed to Andrew's first book "Maine Road Voices" in 2003.

Phill became secretary and treasurer for the Rochdale branch of City's Centenary Supporters Association from 1998-2002 and became the General Secretary of the CSA from 2002 - 2005. During this period, he also led a one man campaign to have a German style 'safe standing area' designed into the then un-built City of Manchester Stadium. He joined the Football Supporters' Federation and was elected as a National Council Member from 2002-2009 as well as an Executive Committee member from 2007-2009.

Phill's first book was 'Morrissey's Manchester' published in 2002 (reprinted in 2009) followed by 'Panic On The Streets' in 2007 (reprinted 2012) and 'The Manchester Musical History Tour', (2011) co-written with Craig Gill, The Inspiral Carpets drummer with whom 'Manchester Music Tours' was set up.

In September 2011, Phill packed his bags and left Blighty for a new life in Boston, Massachusetts - watching City's Championship winning season via live streams or The Banshee Bar in Dorchester, Boston. He has two daughters, Rohannah and Leah and two grandchildren, Phoebe and Lucas.

ANDREW WALDON is a veteran Manchester City supporter, who has seen his favourite club play at over 200 different grounds. He has been a supporter of the club for over 40 years and has seen many highs and lows during that time, but his support has never faltered.

A promising football career as a goalkeeper disappeared when Manchester Boys over looked him after trials and now he churns out the usual story of how his auspicious career was wrecked by a knee injury sustained in a five a side tournament.

Andrew is now happy to bestow upon others the virtues of supporting the Blue side of Manchester and has to thank his mother for introducing him to City as her role as a primary school teacher in the shadows of Maine Road allowed her complimentary tickets for matches.

He writes regularly, first submitting articles to the 'King of the Kippax' fanzine but later finalising a move on a Bosman transfer to rival fanzine' 'City Til I Cry' funnily enough in direct competition to Phill and his publication "This Charming Fan".

The creative writing talents of this honorary Mancunian (he moved north from Hemel Hempstead when he was six months old) have been recognised by many. For several seasons he had his own column in the official Manchester City match day programme, travelling the length and breadth of the country to provide match reports for the reserve pages. Those reports also appeared on the club's official website. As well as providing the basis for reports on Greater Manchester Radio and in the *Manchester Evening News*.

Andrew has also made literary contributions to several other publications including The Official City Handbook. The Official City Monthly Magazine, *Liverpool Echo* and *Liverpool Post*, *Newcastle Journal* plus several other North East newspaper publications and also for The Masonic Quarterly. For one season he even produced a four page programme for Manchester City's home reserve games.

This then allowed him time to spread his talents to writing and producing several books on his beloved team. He was responsible for all the statistical elements of the Tempus publication 'Images of Manchester City', as well as co writing 'Manchester City Classics'. He then flew solo with 'Maine Road Voices' and 'Waiting for the Whistle'.

Since taking early retirement and taking up a new career as a couch potato,

Andrew has taken on a number of other literary projects , most recently he has had published 'My Eyes Have Seen The Glory' and 'Manchester City in Europe' with more publications for release before the end of the year. Andrew also runs a website about the Reserve and Academy sides of City.... www. mcfcreservesandacademy.co.uk

Away from the roller coaster life of Manchester City, Andrew enjoys attending Beer Festivals to sample the delights of real ale, travel and music and not forgetting to be The Bank of England and a Taxi Driver to his two children, the future of Manchester City, Daniel & Jessica.

ACKNOWLEDGEMENTS

FIRSTLY A BIG THANK YOU to all of the Class of '86 for their amazing support during the writing of this book – David Boyd, Ian Brightwell, John Clarke, Steve Crompton, Andy Hinchcliffe, Paul Lake, Steve Macauley, Steve Mills, Paul Moulden, Steve Redmond, Ian Scott, Andy Thackeray, David White and to Susan and David Bookbinder for their total trust and enthusiasm that they gave us.

Hopefully all the emails, phone calls and text messages that we badgered you all with for over a six month period has produced a book that you are all proud of as much as we were putting it together.

Secondly to Paul Power for producing his excellent foreword.

To Gary James and Ian Cheeseman for their vital, initial support and for always being willing to answer any question put to them.

To Joy Setele for her regular trips to Manchester Library to research old copies of the *Manchester Evening News*.

To Darren Page for providing copies of team sheets and programmes from the FA Youth Cup run, visit his website http://manchestercityprogrammes. weebly.com

To Ashley Shaw and John Ireland for supporting the project.

To John Leigh and Rob Dunford for spending time going through old programmes for various information and proof reading.

To Fergus Beatty in trying to help track down John Clarke in Dublin! Jim & Linda Ferris for not only storing all of Phill's books in their garage, but for also sending a couple of books over to the States in the post that were needed for research, John Duffy and Mike Kelly for also helping out when memories were fading, Peter Brophy for his time and input and Ric Turner for allowing us to shamelessly plug the book on the Blue Moon forums and Philip Alcock @ MCIVTA for his plugs as well as Alistair Hay for his promotion of the book.

Finally, to The Undertones for supplying the book's title after a fantastic and ageless song.

BIBLIOGRAPHY

Gary James - Manchester The Greatest City (Polar Print Group Ltd 1997)

Paul Lake - I'm Not Really Here (Arrow 2011)

Jimmy Wagg - This Simple Game: The Footballing Life of Ken Barnes (Empire Publications 2005)

Craig Winstanley - Bleak & Blue (Sigma Leisure 1998)

Various Manchester City match day programmes and City Magazines

Various *Manchester Evening News* and *Pink Final* editions

INTERNET RESOURCES

www.11v11.com
www.bluemoon-mcfc.co.uk
www.footballpundette.blogspot.com
www.mcfc.co.uk
www.mcfcforum.com
www.mcfcstats.com
www.youtube.com

STATISTICS LEGEND

The combined appearances tables should be read as follows:
Appearances (Substitute appearances + Unused substitute appearances), Goals
Eg:

DAVID BOYD	21 (2 + 1), 2

David Boyd made 21 appearances, two as a substitute, once as an unused sub and scored two goals.

FOREWORD

BY PAUL POWER

MANCHESTER CITY CLUB CAPTAIN
1980 – 1986

IN 1976 I PLAYED in the League Cup semi-final second leg against Middlesbrough. In that game at Maine Road, ten home-grown players, albeit from different eras, featured in the game - Joe Corrigan, Colin Barrett, Willie Donachie, Mike Doyle, Kenny Clements, Alan Oakes, Ged Keegan, Peter Barnes, myself and Tommy Booth, who was on the bench. Only Joe Royle and Asa Hartford had not progressed via the club's youth system. Having lost 1-0 in the First leg at Ayresome Park, we beat Middlesbrough 4-0 on the night and went through to beat Newcastle United 2-1 in the final at Wembley, with eight of the twelve players in the squad having come through the ranks of the club.

Ten years later, I had great hopes that the same feat might be repeated when City's youth policy - under the guidance of Ken Barnes, Terry Farrell, Tony Book and Glyn Pardoe - developed quality individuals such as David White, Andy Hinchcliffe, Paul Lake, Steve Redmond and Ian Brightwell - who amazingly all came through at the same time.

The team won the Youth Cup in April 1986 and I attended the game that night; as club captain I was invited into the dressing room to be photographed with the players and the trophy. I was reluctant to do so because I didn't want to steal any limelight from the players and staff. It was an incredible achievement for all involved and it was their night. However I have often seen copies of the photo taken with the youth team and they provide proud memories of my involvement with the future of Manchester City. The nucleus of the successful youth team featured in the 10-1 thrashing of Huddersfield Town in 1987 and the unforgettable 5-1 destruction of Manchester United in 1989, with many others from that squad of players going on to have successful careers in professional football elsewhere.

I played against David White in many training games and when he was on form he proved a really difficult opponent as he was so quick, even aged seventeen!

Ironically, the success of the youth team and rapid development of the individuals involved had a hand in my departure from Maine Road in June 1986. I have no doubt that when Howard Kendall enquired about the possibility of me signing for Everton, City's manager Billy McNeill would have been at ease with the move because Andy Hinchcliffe was ready to progress to City's first team at the age of seventeen. That deal proved to be good business for the club as Andy went on to play regularly for the club and eventually for England.

And who knows what Paul Lake could have achieved if he hadn't received such a cruel injury?

Manchester City has always produced and developed good individual players – but rarely have we produced a team as good as the 1986 Youth Cup winning team.

INTRODUCTION

ARE TEENAGE DREAMS SO HARD TO BEAT?

1986

I F ONE YEAR IN MY (so far fifty years) life stands out above the rest it would be 1986. Aged twenty-three, it wasn't so much a case of sex and drugs and rock 'n' roll, more football, beer and rock 'n' roll - so please allow me to be a little self-indulgent in sharing with you some of those magic moments of that year in setting the scene for the rest of the book.

1986 was the final full year of my three and a half years on the dole - living in a bed-sit in Sale and signing on in Stretford every other week. It was the year of my first visit to the Glastonbury Festival - watching the likes of The Cure, Psychedelic Furs, Lloyd Cole & The Commotions, The Waterboys and Half Man Half Biscuit among others. Me, my mate Jim and his dog Casey, drove down in my Ford Escort Mk2 Estate, armed with one hundred litre cartons of orange and apple juice, bought for 33p each from Makro and sold at 75p each on the Friday morning. The profit paid for our £19 tickets (also bought on the way down from HMV in Bridgewater) and a little towards the petrol money.

The 1986 World Cup Finals in Mexico was held at the same time. Today's "Glasto" has live screenings of games - back then, it was a little different. A marquee was set aside for games but these had to be recorded firstly onto a VHS tape in the farm house and then played in the marquee straight afterwards. One quarter final game was France v Brazil and it went to extra time and then penalties. As the shootout reached its climax, the screen went blank. The tape had ended.... there were no mobile phones to call or text, no Twitter to tweet. The apology offered was accepted by the large crowd in the marquee, but we just wanted to know who had actually won - which the person responsible for recording didn't know! They had simply pressed 'record' and returned later to collect the tape and brought it to the tent for us to see the game. It was the following morning via the car radio that we found out that France had won 4-3.

On the final day, the Sunday, The Housemartins were on just after noon - but it was the same day England were to play Argentina in what became "The Hand Of God" game. Fearing a mass exodus after The Housemartins and long traffic queues, we missed the band to make an early getaway and got home in plenty of time to watch the very worst and then the very best of Maradona sending England home. I did get to see The Housemartins eventually, in the autumn, when they became the first band to play at the International 2, on Plymouth Grove in Longsight.

In between there was The Festival of the Tenth Summer, a Factory organised week-long festival celebrating the tenth anniversary of The Sex Pistols' 1976 Free Trade Hall gig and the impact it had on the city culturally. The climax of the week was a gig at GMEX featuring The Smiths, New Order, The Fall, Howard Devoto, Pete Shelley, OMD, Sandie Shaw, John Cale and more – all under one roof for £13.

The following day, at Salford University, The Smiths again took to the stage in what for me was my greatest ever gig. I would see The Smiths a third and final time that year in October at The Free Trade Hall – little did we know at the time that it would be their penultimate gig and that the greatest band of my generation would be no more within a matter of a few months.

I did a little bit of travelling too – I started volunteering at a local youth centre – Sale Annex – and being able to drive a minibus, this took me on an eighteen day youth exchange to Hamburg for £40 (the staff visit to the Holsten Pils brewery being the highlight!), a week in Denmark for £25 and a weekend in Belfast for £15. Me, Jim and Casey also went on a Lake District, Galloway & Dumfries five day trip in the Escort estate again, taking advantage of a warm summer and scenic routes. Signing on? Yes, it was a pain, but was never a problem – most of the trips didn't fall on the signing on week, except the visit to Hamburg. I informed the dole office I was camping in Cornwall and would call my parents every day to see if they had received a phone call about a suitable job that I wasn't looking for. Having supplied them with my parent's number, the UB40 office never called my parents once – and neither did I!

And then there was the football. Even to those of us on the dole (and there were many of us) football was affordable. There was even a turnstile for those of us presenting our UB40's and getting in cheaper. Looking at some of the gig tickets I still have from that period, on the ticket it states '£5.00 – UB40 £4.00' as a price.

For City, the 1985–86 season was a 'middle year'. Promoted back into the top flight in May 1985 – then known as the First Division – the club would be relegated once more into the Second Division in May 1987. This was manager Billy McNeill's third season at the club, having taken over in the summer of 1983, picking up the pieces of a club shattered after the first relegation in twenty years.

The club's first season back was one of consolidation. Finishing 15th (four points above the relegation zone) and having a trip to Wembley in the Full Members Cup Final against Chelsea. But there was one aspect of the club that was gaining more and more attention as the season went on - that of the youth team.

City had always been renowned (like clubs such as West Ham and their famed academy) for developing their own players. The hallowed late 60's team had Tommy Booth, Mike Doyle, Alan Oakes, Glyn Pardoe (who at fifteen and three hundred and fourteen days is still City's youngest-ever first team debutant) Harry Dowd - and the late Neil Young. The mid to late 70's team that won the League Cup in 1976 and were league runners-up the following year had Joe Corrigan, Kenny Clements, Paul Power, Peter Barnes, Gary Owen and Willie Donachie all coming through the ranks. The team that lost in the 1981 FA Cup final to Spurs contained Joe Corrigan, Ray Ranson, Tommy Caton, Nicky Reid, Dave Bennett, Tony Henry and was captained by Paul Power.

And in 1986, an exciting crop of kids were coming through the ranks and being talked up greatly. City had never won the FA Youth Cup. They had been close twice, losing two successive finals in 1979 (Millwall) and 1980 (Aston Villa). In 1986, they were hot favourites to win the cup. This book is the story of that team and the story of what became of the players involved as a team, individually and what they did after leaving City. Containing so many different emotions, covering so many scenarios, it tells the story of fourteen teenage lads. Two went on to play for England, three were heart-broken in being rejected by the club weeks after winning the Youth Cup, one would almost die on the pitch, before having his career cruelly taken away from him by serious injury and one, very sadly, succumbed to cancer aged just thirty-seven.

I was too young to remember the late 60's glory days under Joe Mercer and Malcolm Allison and only thirteen when the League Cup was won in 1976 – so supporters of my vintage had not seen City win any trophy with our own eyes. This was our opportunity - not only that, but the players in the team were of our age, many came from Manchester and we could relate to their taste in music and fashion. To my generation of City fans, the names Brightwell, Hinchcliffe, Lake, Moulden, Redmond and White are still spoken about proudly. And yet while the six above named players are - understandably - mentioned frequently, there were eight other lads fighting for the Blue cause too, each with their own tale to tell.

This book is their story.

PHILL GATENBY

MANCHESTER IN 1986

MANCHESTER - SEVEN YEARS into the Thatcher Government's eleven years - was a very different looking city. There were no apartment blocks all over the city centre. The Metrolink (or Light Rapid Transport system) was six years away and the buses were orange. Madchester was three years from its peak and the Hacienda was empty most nights. Canal Street was row upon row of empty warehouses, with the three or four gay pubs situated behind Chorlton Street bus station being a very unsafe and seedy place to be in or around.

Two iconic Manchester buildings had a very different life in 1986. After four years of renovation - the former Central Railway Station being empty since 1968 - GMEX was opened as a conference centre and gig venue and became the first building in Manchester's regeneration programme.

Yet for Withy Grove, on Shudehill, it was a different story. Having been the home of the Northern press (and indeed the national press during the Second World War when Fleet Street was bombed), the building was closed down in 1986 having been bought by Robert Maxwell for £1. He re-named the building 'Maxwell House' before subsequently closing it down. The building was left unused for over a decade and fell derelict until regenerated (after the IRA bomb in 1996), re-opening as The Printworks. There was no Northern Quarter, Castlefield or Deansgate Locks. Boddingtons Bitter was made at the Strangeways brewery and HMP Manchester was called HMP Strangeways.

Undoubtedly, at least on the surface, the city was poorer but culturally it seemed far richer than it does today. Manchester, via its burgeoning music scene, was just about to re-brand itself on the world's conscience. In just a few short years this rainy post-industrial wasteland would be plastered on the covers of style bibles the world over as international trend-setters flocked to witness the scene that exploded in the city.

Over a quarter of a century later the chief pre-occupation of most Mancunians hasn't changed. Yet from the vantage point of 2013 there's little doubt that the city's two football clubs have been transformed beyond recognition - this is the story of how life for the supporters of one of them was made that little bit more bearable.

MANCHESTER CITY

MAY 1983

MANCHESTER CITY are in the doldrums. The 1982-83 season had ended in disaster. City had never been in the bottom three of the First Division all season yet they had been in free fall over the final months. The club found themselves with one game to play against Luton Town – City fourth from bottom versus Luton third from bottom - in a winner-take-all game. City needed only to draw the game to retain their place in the top flight where they had proudly sat since 1966.

With four minutes remaining and the game drifting toward a goalless draw, the Luton Town substitute Raddy Antic wrote his name into football folklore by crashing home the winner. The final whistle witnessed the visiting manager, David Pleat, perform his famous skip across the turf followed by a quick retreat as hundreds of City fans invaded the pitch and attacked some of the Luton players as mounted police came to their rescue.

The aftermath of relegation saw manager John Benson (who had only taken over from the resigning John Bond in February) sacked and Glasgow Celtic legend Billy McNeill was installed in his place to lead the club into the 1983-84 campaign, bringing with him the long-serving Oldham Athletic manager Jimmy Frizzell as his assistant. Relegation hit the club hard financially too – the club was cash-strapped as it was, having invested heavily on million-pound players Steve Daley, Kevin Reeves and Trevor Francis over the previous years. The perennially under-fire chairman Peter Swales, had to undergo a cost-saving exercise in order to balance the books based on playing in the Second Division. The one positive spin off from this would be the progress of City's respected youth policy - with Ken Barnes and various scouts plucking the best of the crop from around the north west and beyond, developing them into future first team players under the guidance of Tony Book and Glyn Pardoe - both were former City players during the glory years of the Mercer/Allison era, with Book also a former City first team manager too.

The youth set up was as follows. There was the 'A' team in the Lancashire

League, playing the reserve teams of local clubs outside of the First Division – such as Tranmere Rovers, Stockport County, Crewe Alexandra and Rochdale. Then there were games against First Division sides' respective 'A' teams such as Manchester United, Everton and Liverpool. Non-League teams such as Southport, Barrow and Runcorn also pitted their reserves against the 'A' team in the Lancashire League.

The next step up would be the full reserves team, playing alongside experienced pros not in the First team or coming back from injury and in need of match practice.

Then there were two cup competitions exclusively for eligible players – the prestigious FA Youth Cup and the Lancashire County Youth Cup. To be eligible, a player had to be younger than eighteen years of age when the season started.

The seeds of the 1986 FA Youth Cup winning team were sown in the 'A' team for the 1983-84 season, beginning with a home game against UMIST and would continue over a staggering fifteen seasons...

1983-84

ROCK AND GOAL HIGH SCHOOL

THE LANCASHIRE LEAGUE 'A' TEAM would be the starting point for many young players, making their debuts as fifteen and sixteen year-old school kids or first or second year Youth Training Scheme (YTS) trainees. Often though, there would be appearances from regular first team players making a comeback after a lay-off through injury. This season, the young players would benefit from playing alongside Geoff Lomax, Duncan Davidson, Asa Hartford, Kevin Bond and Ronnie Hildersley, who had made just one first team appearance. John Beresford was another regular. Though he would never make a first team appearance for City, he went on to play almost four hundred league games for Barnsley, Portsmouth, Newcastle and Southampton.

29th October. David White, Ian Scott and Paul Moulden appear on the 'A' team sheet for the first time at home against UMIST (University of Manchester Institute for Science & Technology). All three were in their final year at school, Scott (in midfield) and Moulden (on the bench) had just turned sixteen, while White (on the wing) was fifteen years old – celebrating his sixteenth birthday the very next day.

Paul Moulden was one of two players on the bench – sitting alongside him was Darren Beckford; the pair would go on to form a prolific goal scoring partnership in the 'A' and reserve team.

That partnership started in this game as both of the subs played their part in a 4-0 win, with White and Scott marking their debuts with a goal each with Beckford and Jamie Hoyland adding the other two goals.

In the starting line-up was future first-team players Earl Barrett and the aforementioned Hoyland.

The 'A' team played all of their home games at the Platt Lane training ground, usually on Saturday mornings – although for this game, as one of the trio recalls, the three debutants had an unexpected surprise that morning.

David White: "I woke up to a massive frost and my dad drove me to Platt Lane assuming the game was off. Sure enough when we got there the pitch was unplayable but I could not believe it when Tony Book (Skip) told us we were going to play the game at Maine Road. I don't remember too much about the game but can remember my goal at the Platt Lane end, a typical run from the right and shot across the keeper into bottom left corner. It was a dream come true."

FA YOUTH CUP FIRST ROUND

1st November. City beat Oldham Athletic 3-1 at home. Ian Scott came off the bench. Jamie Hoyland (2) and Paul Simpson were the goal scorers.

FA YOUTH CUP SECOND ROUND

6th December. The next round saw City travel to Middlesbrough and come away with a 2-0 win thanks to goals from Darren Beckford and John Beresford. Scott and Moulden started the game and White was an unused sub.

17th December. Paul Moulden scores City's goal in a 1-1 draw away against Chorley Reserves in the 'A' league - but fractures his leg five minutes from time and is out for the rest of the season.

FA YOUTH CUP 3RD ROUND

4th January. Stephen Redmond makes his debut for City as all hopes of winning the FA Youth Cup came to an end at Barnsley, with a 3-1 defeat. Scott and Redmond started the game, with White coming off the bench. Beckford had scored City's goal - but once captain Ricky Adams had been sent off, the odds were stacked against a City win. Redmond was aged sixteen and in his final year at school.

11th February. Steve Redmond makes his 'A' team debut at home against Crewe Alexandra reserves in a 3-0 win. In the starting line were first team players Clive Wilson, Gordon Dalziel and Paul Simpson. David White came off the bench to score alongside Dalziel and Darren Beckford.

LANCASHIRE YOUTH CUP FIRST ROUND

23rd February. City dispatched Rochdale 4-0 at home with goals from Beckford (2), Simpson (penalty) and trialist Mike Conroy, who had been released from Coventry City. Ian Scott started the game.

LANCASHIRE YOUTH CUP SEMI-FINAL

5th March. Manchester United were the opponents and hosts in the semi-final - with City repeating the previous round score in winning 4-0. White and Scott started the game, Scott getting on the score sheet along with Beckford (2) and Simpson. In the United line up that day was a certain David Platt - soon to be given a free transfer by United to Crewe Alexandra - the beginning of a long and illustrious career taking in Aston Villa, Bari, Juventus, Sampdoria (playing alongside Roberto Mancini), Arsenal and player-manager at Nottingham Forest, collecting sixty-two England caps along the way to becoming City's assistant coach.

17th March. Steve Crompton made his debut as goalkeeper for the 'A' team in a 2-2 draw at home against Bolton Wanderers 'A'.

With seven of the 1986 Youth Cup winning squad making their debuts this season, this game against Bolton Wanderers contained the most in one game – with four in the side; Crompton, White, Redmond and Scott. Also in that team was Darren Beckford and former first team player Tommy Caton's younger brother, Paul.

When looking at the sides the 'A' team would play, the 'keeper was quite appreciative of the range of experience this brought into the teams development.

Steve Crompton: "We played against a proper mixture of teams. We played United, Liverpool, Everton A teams, and we also played against teams like Marine Reserves. I think the eclectic mix of opposition was a good test for us, because it certainly toughened us up as a team. It was one thing playing against United and their apprentices with their shorts rolled up so far up their backsides, and another playing against grown men, hardened by non-league football".

20th March. Just as they had made their 'A' team debuts together five months previously, both Ian Scott and David White became the first two of the Class of '86 to play for the reserves - Scott started the game and White came off the bench in a 2-0 (Wilson, Simpson) home win against Chesterfield.

The call up came as a complete surprise to White, who two hours before the kick-off, recalls he was playing in a school game!

David White: "This was all quite bizarre. I was playing in a house game on the school fields at about 4.30pm. I was also 'managing' the team as my house (Lincoln) only had one teacher keen enough on football to stay behind, so he was looking after a different age group on another pitch. Now my dad watched every game I played wherever it was when it came to City games and Salford Boys - but he had to draw the line at school games. Suddenly he appeared on the side-lines beckoning me. When there was a break in play, I ran over and he told me I was wanted at Maine Road for the reserves that night! I couldn't believe my ears and I had to sub myself there and then and leave pronto! The reserve games kicked off at 6.45pm, so we just about had enough time to get over to report by the 5.30pm deadline. I was sub and remember getting on later in the game, which was a huge honour."

LANCASHIRE YOUTH CUP FINAL

9th April. City faced Bolton Wanderers away in the final and came away with a victory and the trophy. The 3-0 win had White and Scott starting once more, along with Redmond coming off the bench. Indeed, Scott and Redmond were scorers alongside Beckford once more.

This was the third successive season that City had won the Lancashire Youth Cup and the sixth time in total that they had lifted the trophy.

14th April. Andy Thackeray aged sixteen and still at school, makes his debut for the 'A' team, featuring in the starting line up in a 3-0 away win against Bolton Wanderers 'A' team. He was the only Class of '86 player in the side, with goals from Beckford, Milligan and Hoyland.

21st April. David Boyd (the eldest player in the Youth Cup winning squad) was the final 'A' team debutant of the Class of '86 this season, starting in the home game against Rochdale reserves alongside White and Redmond. Boyd marked his debut with a goal in a 9-1 rout – with the other goals coming from Simpson (4), White (2), Redmond and Milligan.

PLAYER COMBINED APPEARANCES - 1983-84				
	'A' TEAM	LANCS/FA YOUTH CUP	RESERVES	TOTAL
DAVID BOYD	1, 1	-	-	1, 1
STEVE CROMPTON	2, 0	-	-	2, 0
PAUL MOULDEN	2 (1), 1	1, 0	-	3 (1), 1
STEVE REDMOND	4, 3	1 (1), 1	-	5 (1), 4
IAN SCOTT	10 (1), 1	5 (1), 2	1, 0	16 (2), 3
ANDY THACKERAY	1, 0	-	-	1, 0
DAVID WHITE	5 (4), 7	2 (1), 0	(1)	7 (6), 7

1. STEVE CROMPTON

Born: Partington, Manchester, 20th April 1968

S TEVE WAS AN ALL-ROUND SPORTSMAN, who excelled at many sports in his youth. He gained recognition for Cheshire in Athletics (Javelin) and for the county schoolboy cricket team. During his school days at Oughtrington High, Lymm he skippered their rugby team, but it was a sighting in a five aside tournament for Oughtrington Rovers that opened the doors for Steve to forge a career in football. He was offered trials by Manchester City, the outcome of which was the offer of schoolboy forms which he signed on his 14th birthday. It however was not an unopposed path for Steve's potential as both Manchester United and Liverpool appeared on the scene at one stage.

Steve explains how he arrived at City. "The first thing I remember was actually being invited to go for trial by City. I was spotted by Eric Mullender playing in a tournament in Flixton for Oughtrington Rovers. I went along to the ground in Cheadle, where City then trained, and was overawed at the facility! It had its own stand! The other thing was pulling on a City kit for the first time, and how scary it felt.

"We played a series of games during the trial, and I don't remember much about them, apart from this massive centre forward playing against me! He was tall, fast, black, and called Darren Beckford. I had never played against somebody as good as him and was star struck. I think he was playing for England schoolboys at the time, so that's a measure of how good he was.

"At the end of the trials, after we had changed, Ken Barnes spoke to me and my dad, and said how impressed he was and that they wanted to sign me on schoolboy forms. You can't imagine how great that felt. As a 13 year-old being told that - it felt like you'd made it! On my 14th birthday, Tony Book came to my school and I signed the forms in the headmaster's office. Strange really, because ours was a rugby playing school so it didn't go down so well.

"I then started playing for the City schoolboy team - Blue Star Pegasus - managed by Mike Grimsley. I think one of the reasons we were so successful, apart from having some great players, was because the majority of the team that won the youth cup played together in that schoolboy team for 2 or 3 years. It was amazing that so many local lads were so good. From my point of view, it was great to be in a team that won 10-0 every week, but I didn't have much to do. I was used to playing for Oughtrington Rovers where we were getting beat 10-0 every week. I think that's where I learnt the most in those days.

"As a schoolboy, we used to get invited to train with the club during school holidays. It was terrifying because it meant going to the stadium where all the apprentices and first team met and got changed. Walking into the away dressing room and seeing Jamie Hoyland, Paul Simpson, Darren Beckford, John Beresford, and Earl Barrett was quite scary as a fourteen year old kid.

"At the age of sixteen, the time came to learn if we were going to be offered an apprenticeship. I remember having the meeting with Tony Book and my dad, and being offered a one year YTS Apprenticeship. In some ways it was a disappointment, because I'd hoped for two years. But the chance to go and play professionally was just too great and I signed YTS forms. I'd dreamt all my life of being a professional footballer and now I had the opportunity to do it. I was paid £25 a week, and my mum and dad were paid money to cover my digs.

"The first few weeks of pre-season training were a real eye opener. The training was like nothing I'd ever done before. As a goalkeeper, I wasn't the fittest, and to go from almost nothing, to training with the whole City squad was tiring. That first pre-season, we trained at the University playing fields near the Princess Parkway/M60 junction. The fields were massive - literally hundreds of acres - the weather that summer was hot, and I remember running around those fields day after day, morning and afternoon, for about 8 weeks. As a YTS, we had to keep a diary of what we did, and I remember getting home in the afternoon, lying on my bed writing in the diary, and then falling asleep at about 8pm because I was so knackered."

Keen to make the grade at City, he joined the club on the government's Youth Training Scheme and his baptism of fire for the Blues came during the 1983-84 season in a Lancashire League fixture against Bolton Wanderers. Steve then became a regular member of City's 'A' team and was ever present between the sticks during the 1985-86 season winning success in the FA Youth Cup.

He was handed his reserve debut at home to Stoke City in August 1984 and was a regular for three seasons but realised, with three regular keepers ahead of him, his opportunities at first team level would be severely restricted. It's at this point we let Steve take up his own story...

"With regards to my move to Carlisle United, it came about because at the time City had 3 senior keepers – Alex Williams, Eric Nixon and Perry Suckling – so there wasn't room for a fourth, inexperienced keeper such as me! So the club released me. I was contacted by a few clubs and had a couple of trials, but I eventually got a call from Harry Gregg at Carlisle, who offered me the opportunity to play First team football. Given the fact that it was Harry Gregg (former United keeper and Busby Babe) it was an opportunity that I thought would be great for my career.

"The move to Carlisle was a bit of an eye opener because as a Fourth Division club, the set-up and facilities were so different to City, so it took a bit of getting used to. However, things started off well and I was playing in the First team. Then one day, we were playing Cardiff away and I got a terrible back-pass off our left-back (name escapes me) which resulted in me getting injured quite badly. As we had no reserve keeper in those days, I finished the game and had treatment over the weekend. Just to reiterate the differences, Harry Gregg was also the physio!

"We had a League Cup game against Oldham on the Tuesday night, at Brunton Park, and my leg still had a lump the size of a tennis ball sticking out from it. However, I was deemed fit enough to play, and subsequently had a nightmare! This, together with the fact that I was still clearly injured, forced the manager to draft in a loan keeper – Martin Taylor from Derby County – and I never played for the First team again. Harry Gregg was subsequently sacked, a new manager came in who brought a keeper called Mark Prudhoe with him, and at that point I asked to leave as Asa Hartford at Stockport County had been enquiring about me.

"I joined County towards the end of the season as a non-contract player, and played a few reserve team games. They had a First team keeper called Chris Marples who was really good. I got a couple of First team games at the end of the season and did well, but was only offered a 6 month contract for the following season."

After leaving Stockport, Steve did not join Mossley as some internet searches show, explaining, "It's strange but at the same time I was playing, there was another keeper called Steve Crompton who had played for Stockport. He was the one who went to Mossley!

"During the summer, I was contacted by Jim Kelman (Wycombe's manager) as they needed a keeper to go on tour to Malta with them. Their regular keeper was injured. He had been given my name by Dario Gradi. I went on tour with them, played a couple of games, and then got offered a 2 year contract by them on better money than Stockport were offering, and they gave me a job too. So overnight I doubled my salary, and as a twenty-something year old it felt like I had won the pools (they had no lottery back then!) So I joined Wycombe Wanderers, then of the Vauxhall Conference, and eventually ended up working for Advanced Industries which was owned by one of Wycombe's directors."

Steve later joined 'Komfort Workspace Limited' as sales director while continuing to play football for Harrow Borough, Gloucester City and Cirencester

Town. He was then offered a role at Witton Albion as the sports therapist when Nigel Gleghorn was the manager whilst playing football for Trafford and made appearances for City's Legends and Old Boys playing with Tony

1. STEVE CROMPTON 1983-84 to 1986-87	
RESERVES	43,0
'A' TEAM	95, 0
FA YOUTH CUP	13, 0
LANCS YOUTH CUP	4, 0

Book, Glyn Pardoe (both of whom he describes as absolute legends), Frank Carrodus and several others.

Steve has now not been in involved in football for a number of years and is currently the managing director of Interior Recruitment Consultants based in Birmingham.

1984-85

THE FROST ON THE TYNE

CITY'S FIRST TEAM had finished the previous season last in a four horse race, with the first three clubs – Sheffield Wednesday, Chelsea and Newcastle – gaining promotion at the expense of the Blues who just missed out on an immediate return to top flight football.

Confidence was high at the start of the new season that City would be promoted second time round. The club were also confident that the crop of youngsters coming through the ranks were also in for a successful season.

The 'A' team very quickly took shape as developing into the team that would eventually lift the FA Youth Cup at the end of the following season.

The first game started with four of the team on the pitch, with two others joining them from the bench.

25th August. Paul Lake made his first 'A' team appearance at home to Morecambe, coming off the bench. Lake was aged fifteen (turning sixteen two months later) and in his final year at school.

Also in the starting line-up were Crompton, Redmond, Boyd, Scott, and White with Thackeray coming on as a sub too.

Goals from Redmond (2), Scott (2), White and Lewis, secured a 6-2 win.

Having played in the first game of the season as a sub, Lake would have to wait until the final month of the season, in May, for his next appearance, making his full debut in a 5-0 away win against Bolton Wanderers 'A'.

28th August. Steve Crompton, Steve Redmond and Paul Moulden all made their reserve team debut at home to Stoke City. Crompton and Redmond start the game, with Moulden coming off the bench.

In the side were first teamers Ray Ranson, Geoff Lomax, Nicky Reid, Steve Kinsey, Jim Tolmie and Andy May. City won 4-0 with goals from Kinsey, Beckford, Reid and the debutant Moulden.

The goalkeeper – like all the Boy Blues – was thrilled at the opportunity to start playing with and against far more experienced and big named players.

Steve Crompton: "This was a brilliant experience because as well as playing alongside City's first team players, we played against some massive names at the time. One in particular that stands out for me was when I played against United reserves at Old Trafford. That alone was awesome for a lad from Partington, but Remi Moses was playing for United! It was strange to see my name on the same team sheet as stars like that."

By now, the elder members of the squad were turning seventeen – a landmark remembered fondly by two of the team.

Steve Crompton: "In the early days, I wasn't old enough to drive, so I used to get a lift into Manchester from my cousin who worked in town and at the end of the day I would walk down to the Parkway from the ground and catch a bus home. Eventually, the lads in the Youth Team started to turn seventeen and bought their own cars, but because my birthday wasn't until April, I was one of the last to get one. In those days the main cars they had was a Fiesta, a Beetle or a Golf, and I remember looking at the cars that some of the lads had with envy as I walked in the rain to catch my bus home! I eventually passed my test and got a Polo."

Ian Brightwell: "I didn't stay in digs as an apprentice. I remained at home with my Mum, Dad, older brother Gary and younger brother David in Congleton. I was just within range of Maine Road so that I didn't have to move. I wasn't old enough to drive so I used to ride my bike from home to Congleton station, put the bike on the guards van and take it off at Piccadilly station. I would then cycle from Piccadilly to Maine Road where we used to report, get changed and then train. I did this for about six months until I'd passed my driving test – and I've got to say it was character building and good fun. The lads thought it was hilarious and regularly took the piss and tried to hide my bike, let the tyres down etc. – but I became one step ahead of them and would hide it in the laundry room where the lovely Joyce Johnstone, the laundry lady, would keep it safe or Stan Gibson (The Grand Master Groundsman) would make sure it wasn't dismantled or hidden. The good old days, eh!"

6th –10th September. Paul Moulden makes his England Youth Team debut in the 'Trophy Yugoslavia' tournament. Moulden – and fellow City player John Beresford – appear in all three games against Austria 2-2 (6th), USSR 0-1 (8th) and Sweden 1-1 (10th)

22nd September. Ian Brightwell makes his 'A' team debut away against Everton 'A'. Aged sixteen, Brightwell had signed YTS forms for City in the summer. Starting alongside him was Crompton, Redmond, Scott, Moulden and White, whilst Thackeray was an unused sub.

Moulden was City's scorer in a 3-1 defeat.

Ian Brightwell: "I returned home and my Mum said Tony Book had phoned and I was to call him back. This was two days before the game and I was told I'd be playing centre half and was delighted and nervous at the same time, but couldn't wait to play my first 'A' team game. It was a strong league, not only in terms of ability but also physically. 'A' teams were usually made up of youth and reserve team players but you would also get seasoned first team players coming back from injury who were playing to get their fitness back. We played at Bellefield, Everton's famous training ground and the pitch was magnificent by the standards of the day. I can't remember the score, I just remember really enjoying the whole experience and wanting some more."

Brightwell soon gained a reputation for being a joker in the pack, as one team member testifies.

Steve Mills: "Ian Brightwell was a nutcase – always saying stupid things throughout games. During one 'A' team match I was on a post defending a corner and he was shouting and then screaming 'Millsey... Millsey... MILLSEY'. Eventually I said 'WHAT'?' Then he whispered, 'the spiders are coming'. You'll have to ask him what he meant!"

Ian Brightwell: "Ha ha!! Yes, I remember that! It was one of those stupid phrases that I'd heard on TV or a film (no idea what it was now though) and it stuck in my head. I remember we were winning the game and shouting at Millsey, but I really can't think why I said it at that exact moment. Very strange!"

Steve Mills: "A few matches later Ian asked me – after about seventy minutes – 'Millsey, is this the first half?' Thinking it was a wind up, I said 'f*** off', but then he asked me again, 'What half is this? What score is it?' Although he was always taking the mick, this time was a bit different. I called the ref over and it turned out he had a bang on his head and was concussed!'

6th October. Andrew Hinchcliffe makes his 'A' team debut away against Burnley 'A' in a 6-2 win (Beckford 3, Moulden 2, Parlane) Hinchcliffe, still aged fifteen, was in his final year at school. He was joined in the team by Crompton, Thackeray, Redmond, Scott, Moulden with White coming off the bench.

16th October. Paul Moulden plays for the England Youth Team at Maine Road against Iceland. Both Moulden and fellow City player John Beresford score in the 5-3 win.

Meanwhile, David Boyd makes his debut in the reserves away at Bradford City, starting along side Redmond and Scott. Darren Beckford scored the game's only goal in a 1-0 win.

31st October. Tottenham Hotspur are reported to have made a "name your price" offer to City for strikers Paul Moulden and Darren Beckford. In programme notes for that evening's League Cup game against West Ham

United, manager Billy McNeill discussed the topic, easing fears that the club could cash in. McNeill began talking about the opponent's famed academy and linked it to that week's offer from Spurs.

"It's a relief that my Board of Directors see the future this way too. The stories of an 'open cheque' offer from Tottenham Hotspur to buy our promising young strikers Darren Beckford and Paul Moulden might have been flattering and tempting, but I'm convinced it would do the club no good at all in the long term to even contemplate such approaches.

"The story was taken quite out of context… it wasn't quite as dramatic as the newspapers made it. Sure there was interest expressed - and I wouldn't blame any club being interested in these two teenagers because they've been showing amazing potential. So much so that they're knocking on the first team door.

"But let's not overlook that it is only potential we are talking about. Both lads are in the apprentice stage of their learning and they've a long way to go to achieve a reputation. My concern is such 'name your price' approaches could fill their heads with a lot of nonsense and take their feet off the ground. I know they are both stable, sensible boys… but it can happen to anyone when publicity of this nature runs riot.

"I was warned that the story would appear and called them both in for talks about the future and the speculation. I'm sure they listened intently and are not carried away with the rich publicity they've received. They both accepted my assurance that here at Maine Road they will get as good a grounding for a successful future in the game as they could do anywhere else in the game.

"I don't want either lad going out trying too hard to impress, to do things not

in their natural game. I'm concerned that even fans might now start to expect more from the boys than they are yet capable of providing. They don't deserve to have this responsibility thrust on their young shoulders at this stage - remember, Darren was only seventeen last May and Paul had his seventeenth birthday as recently as September.

"Let's give them a chance to breathe, to enjoy their game, and develop that explosive talent. I won't demand too much from them too soon and I hope the City fans won't be carried away with all this glamorous talk of open-cheque offers. Importantly, the lads have to stay level-headed and realise just how much they have got to do."

Paul Moulden: "Billy McNeill brought us into the office, he told us to read all the papers if we wanted to, but that the club wanted us and no way were we going to be sold. We weren't given any idea as to what the extent of the offer was and we both just got on with carrying on as we had been doing, we knew we were in the best hands possible at City under Tony and Glyn.

"We had known each other from the England School Boy trials some two years before. I attended even though I was a school year behind the rest of the lads. Darren was probably the best header of a ball that I ever played with. A combination of the all the work Tony and Glyn had done with us and our own hunger to score goals - well it just clicked from day one. It was a shame this never reached first team level. Why? Well I have a few theories!"

In 2000, City fan Peter Brophy helped to organise a weekend supporter's event at the Platt Lane training complex. On the Sunday Ken Barnes turned up to watch the five-a-side tournament and during the day Peter was able to have a long chat with Ken.

The conversation eventually turned to the 1986 Youth Cup winning team - including the Spurs offer for Paul Moulden and Darren Beckford - with Ken Barnes backing Billy McNeill's claim that "it wasn't as dramatic as the newspapers had made it".

Peter Brophy: "Ken said that the offer certainly hadn't been as big as the media had implied, suggesting that the City board had deliberately talked up the fee. As far as Ken could remember, the actual figure was probably somewhere around £250K to £300K guaranteed for the pair, which could have risen substantially depending on first team appearances, success and England caps. Alternatively, City were given the pick of a couple of Spurs squad players (still solid enough performers) to take in part-exchange."

Brophy adds his own theory into the equation "At the time, Swales was under immense pressure because City had been relegated in 1983 for the first time since the early '60's and had failed to come back at the first attempt. There was a lot of speculation in the press about the club's financial plight and I can well believe that Swales and his fellow directors would have been keen to portray the image that the club was financially sound enough to reject such a huge offer."

FA YOUTH CUP ROUND 2

City were one of the favourites to lift the trophy for the first time and got off to a blistering start.

9th November. City lined up with eight of the team that would lift the trophy the following season:

Crompton, Barrett, Thackeray, Redmond, Finlinson, Scott, White, Beresford, Beckford, Moulden, Boyd. Sub. Hinchcliffe.

Preston North End were hit for six as City romped to a 6-0 home win. Goals from Beckford (3), White (2) and Moulden, showed why expectations were high.

Although Beckford hit a hat-trick, the Man of the Match was Paul Moulden, hitting the post twice in the first half and scoring the goal of the night with a 30 yard screamer.

10th November. City's physio, Roy Bailey, supplies the team with tickets for U2, supported by The Waterboys, performing at the sold out Manchester Apollo. Music mad David Boyd and his then girlfriend, who had travelled down from Glasgow, made their own way to the Apollo and enjoyed what to this day still remains one of his favourite gigs of all time. However, one of the squad tells a different story of what happened that night to the rest of the lads.....

Andy Thackeray: "We all set off in a minibus, but we never went inside the Apollo. As soon as we got off the bus, a tout offered us £60 a ticket, which was just over two weeks wages to us!"

15th November. Andy Thackeray came off the bench to make his reserve team debut at home to Huddersfield Town in a 4-4 draw. He joined Redmond, Scott and Moulden in the team. The scorers were Eves (2), Moulden and Paul Simpson.

27th November. Paul Moulden scores again for the England Youth team, in the 2-1 defeat against Scotland at Fulham's Craven Cottage. Along with Beresford, future City goalkeeping coach Tim Flowers played too.

1st December. John Clarke gets on the team sheet for the first time in the 'A' team as an unused sub for the home game against Bury reserves that City won 5-3. (Beckford 4, O' Boyle). Crompton, Thackeray, Redmond, Scott and White were all starters in the game. Clarke would make his full debut on 13th March away at South Liverpool reserves. White and Scott bagged the goals in a 2-0 win.

FA YOUTH CUP ROUND 3

9th December. A trip into the unknown to the North East, saw City at non-league amateur side Billingham.

City: Crompton, Barrett, Thackeray, Redmond, Finlinson, Scott, White, Beresford, Beckford, Moulden, Boyd. Sub. Hinchcliffe.

This time City improved on their score against Preston North End, as hat tricks from both Beckford and White,

along with singles from Thackeray, Moulden, Scott and Beresford, sealed a 10-1 victory - to become City's record Youth team score.

It wasn't unusual for midweek away Youth Cup games outside the immediate Greater Manchester area to have very few City fans travelling to support the team and therefore it was mostly family members of the players who were there cheering them on.

Andy Thackeray: "The parents also developed into a close group, meeting en route to away games such as Billingham, Fulham etc. They would meet, have meals and drinks, before leaving in convoy to arrive in good time for the kick off and support their boys. I am sure this is one of the reasons why many of that group of players went on to represent City so well, and players like myself who played over six hundred professional games. We had the best possible start - support and encouragement from not only our families but also the City coaching staff too."

David Boyd: "Billingham! That was one hostile crowd who were behind a single railing, just out of reach of the playing surface!"

LANCASHIRE YOUTH CUP ROUND 1

15th December. A home game against Burnley resulted in a 2-1 win, with Beckford and White sharing the goals. This game, coming a week after the 10-1 thumping of Billingham, had the same line up once more.

FA YOUTH CUP ROUND 4

15th January. Nottingham Forest came to Maine Road and - like Preston North End and Billingham in the previous rounds - were similarly thrashed!

City: Crompton, Barrett, Thackeray, Redmond, Finlinson, Scott, White, Beresford, Beckford, Moulden, Boyd. Sub. Hinchcliffe.

Beckford's third consecutive hat-trick, along with goals from White (2), Redmond, Moulden and Scott sent Forest packing having been licked 8-0 in front of the shell shocked Forest boss Brian Clough.

FA YOUTH CUP QUARTER-FINAL

11th February. City faced a tough tie away at Newcastle United but remained confident of securing a victory.

City: Crompton, Barrett, Thackeray, Redmond, Finlinson, Scott, White, Beresford, Beckford, Moulden, Boyd. Sub. Hinchcliffe.

Despite dominating the game, the Blues came home nursing a 2-1 defeat.

On a frozen pitch, City just couldn't repeat their scoring exploits of previous rounds, despite outplaying Newcastle during the game. Moulden hit a post and had one cleared off the line in the first half, while Boyd missed an open goal. Even the prolific Beckford couldn't find a way through. Paul Gascoigne opened the scoring for the Geordies in the 16th minute, with Ian Scott equalising for City. However, Joe Allen hit the winner for the home team, to send City disappointingly out of the competition they had been heavily touted to win.

The players have bitter recollections of that night in Newcastle - and in particular towards referee George Courtney, who hailed from nearby Spennymoor, County Durham.

David Boyd: "The game should not have been played - we all had to wear our astro trainers and the pitch was like an ice rink. There was a hand ball in the box to control it before they scored. We all complained to the ref, who more or less told us to shut up and stop being a bunch of moaning Mancs - I let him know I was from Glasgow! We were all gutted after the game and were sitting in silence in the dressing room, only to hear Billy McNeill coming down the tunnel calling the ref all sorts, we were told that he had to be physically restrained!"

Steve Redmond: "Courtney was so biased it was unbelievable. I went up to him on more than one occasion to try and have a word, but he kept blanking me. Some of the decisions were so blatant, we just couldn't believe he got away with it."

David White: "The pitch was terrible and I am sure we would have battered them on a decent pitch at Maine Road. I know they were given a dodgy free kick by Courtney, which they scored from and it just was not to be."

Paul Moulden: "Newcastle away - Courtney cheated us out of a result and it was on a pitch that should not have been played on."

Steve Crompton: "We firmly believed that we could have won the cup in my first year. We got to the Quarter-Final and had been drawn away to Newcastle United. When we got to St James' Park, the pitch was virtually frozen. We thought that there was no way the game could be played because the conditions were so bad. Yet the referee, George Courtney, declared the game on, so on we went.

"On any other day - and with any other ref, we would have beaten Newcastle, even with a certain Paul Gascoigne in their side. But Courtney was a controversial ref at the best of times and he clearly had an affinity for Newcastle United. This, combined with the conditions, saw us get beat on the night - and Newcastle went on to win the Cup that year. For us first year apprentices, this was hard enough to take, but at least we would have another opportunity the following year. However, for the Second year lads it was obviously a major blow at the time. The bus journey back home that night was pretty quiet."

Indeed, for leading goal scorer Beckford, along with Barrett, Beresford and Finlinson, it was their final chance in the Youth Cup as they would be ineligible to play the following season.

David Boyd: "We were gutted at being knocked out but with retaining most of the same team and the addition of Lakey, Ian Brightwell and Steve Mills, we knew it was going to take a very good team to beat us the following year."

25th February. Moulden (and Beresford) appear in England Youth Team's 1-0 defeat at Tolka Park in Dublin against the Republic of Ireland.

3rd - 8th April. Paul Moulden was in the south of France appearing for the England Youth Team in the Cannes Tournament, playing in all four games: USSR 2-1 (3rd), Italy 2-2, (5th), Holland 1-3 (7th), Scotland 1-0 (8th)

4th - 9th April. City entered a side into the annual International Youth Tournament at Entente Sportive Waquehal, on the outskirts of Lille, northern France.

The squad of sixteen included John Bookbinder, Ian Brightwell, John Clarke, Steve Crompton, Andy Hinchcliffe, Paul Lake, Steve Macauley, Steve Mills, Steve Redmond and Andy Thackeray.

After playing the Belgian side SK Beveren (1-0, Steve Redmond penalty), there was a 0-0 draw against Stoke City, followed by two games against French opposition - the hosts Lille (2-0 - George O'Boyle and John Bookbinder) and Nancy (0-1). City then faced Stoke City again in the third place play off final. A Paul Lake goal had the game ending 1-1, with City winning on penalties to claim 3rd place, whilst AC Milan won the overall tournament.

LANCASHIRE YOUTH CUP SEMI-FINAL

18th April. A repeat of the previous season's semi-final had the boy blues crossing the city to play Manchester United again. Once more, City had the edge over their neighbours, winning 3-1 with goals from Scott, Beckford and White. The only change in the regular youth team starting line-up was Boyd dropping onto the bench and Lewis taking his place.

27th April. An unlikely pair of substitutes appear on the team sheet for the 'A' team's home game against Crewe Alexandra reserves. With the first team having a couple of injuries, Jamie Hoyland and Steve Redmond had travelled to Portsmouth with the rest of the seniors. Whilst the 'A' team were at Platt Lane, at the same time, City also fielded a side of schoolboys and 'A' team players in a behind closed doors game at Maine Road against England U15's.

There was also another 'A' team game the following day too, away at Alsager College - so in an effort to make up the numbers, Tony Book (aged 51) and Glyn Pardoe (aged 38) named themselves as subs! According to Book, there was a lot of ribbing from relatives of the players on the side-lines, but they had only agreed to play if needed through injury - both remained off the pitch, which City won 3-0, with Hinchcliffe grabbing one of the goals.

Boyd, Brightwell, Crompton, Hinchcliffe and Moulden played against Crewe, with Clarke, Lake and Mills lining up at Maine Road against the England schoolboys, which ended 1-1.

2nd May. Ian Brightwell would make his debut appearance in the reserve team at home to Newcastle United in a 1-1 draw (own goal), playing alongside Scott, White, Moulden and Redmond, with Thackeray on the bench. Brightwell would play in the next game too - the penultimate reserve game of the season, at Liverpool which also ended 1-1 (Beresford, penalty)

Ian Brightwell: "I was asked to play centre forward for my reserve team debut and I should have scored about four goals but my finishing was crap and I didn't even get one! I ended up playing in every outfield position for the first team but only once as a centre forward - no surprise really as I was hardly a prolific goal scorer! I'm sure Paul Gascoigne was playing for Newcastle that day, but at that stage no one knew how brilliant he was destined to be. It was a great experience to play at Maine Road for the first time on one of the biggest pitches of its time. I was selected to play for the reserves again at Anfield the week after, playing against the likes of Jan Molby and Craig Johnston. Again, to play at Anfield for City (even if it was only the reserves at that stage) was a dream come true."

6th May. Steve Redmond, aged seventeen, becomes the first of the Class of '86 to be named on the First Team's team sheet – as he was a shock inclusion (as an unused sub) in the penultimate game of the season away at Notts County. City's first team were heading for promotion back into the First Division at the second attempt, but were stuttering across the finish line, not helped by a growing list of injuries, hence Redmond's elevation to the First team squad.

The game was memorable for all the wrong reasons. A crowd of just under 18,000 (two thirds of which were City fans) witnessed County racing into a 3-0 half time lead, including one goal from future City player Justin Fashanu.

At half time, a section of frustrated City fans caused the second half to be delayed by forty-five minutes (Billy McNeill made a pitchside appeal to fans to calm down) as they tried to pull the fencing down and get onto the pitch. Such was the presence of City fans throughout the ground, it was Notts County fans who had to move from the Main Stand into the section behind one of the goals to escape further trouble.

The second half commenced and despite a Paul Simpson brace, the Blues lost 3-2. There was one final game left to play for – and a home win against Charlton Athletic would eventually see the Blues clinch the second promotion spot.

16th May. Steve Mills makes his 'A' team debut at home to Liverpool 'A' in the final months of being a schoolboy. In the team that day was Crompton, Thackeray, Brightwell, Scott, White, Moulden and Boyd.

Brightwell was City's scorer in a 1-1 draw.

This was the penultimate game of the season and Mills also played in the final game against Crewe Alexandra reserves.

Once out of school and having signed YTS forms, those players living outside of the Greater Manchester area were accommodated in homes that City had approved as suitable for hosting the young Blues – at a rate of £65 per week per player. Any thoughts that this may involve luxurious and palatial surroundings soon evaporated.

Steve Mills: "I moved to Manchester in time for my first pre-season. I stayed with Steve Macauley at a right dump in Heaton Mersey in digs arranged by the club. The place was filthy, we were sharing a room in bunk beds and the landlady wasn't exactly Michelin rated. We both lasted about a month. I'm not sure where Steve went, but I went to Denton where my friendship with Paul Lake strengthened. We would travel in together – catching the No 204 bus, changing at Belle Vue for the No 53."

Steve Macauley: "It was a s★★★hole! I stayed there a bit longer than Steve; it was two doors from John Clarke, Lindsay Curry and George O' Boyle. I think the last straw for Steve Mills was seeing the son of the landlady come home from school wearing one of his coats! I eventually moved to Burnage and stayed with a distant relative. It was next door to Perry Suckling and close to David Boyd."

Six of the squad were from Greater Manchester and remained living at home, as did Ian Brightwell in Congleton. Five of the lodgers were from no more than fifty miles away - and whilst living in digs, they could easily return home at weekends to Liverpool, Blackpool, Derby, Huddersfield and Sheffield respectively. However, for Irishman John Clarke and Scot David Boyd, it was a different situation.

John Clarke: "My digs were fine, clean and comfortable - but it was difficult at weekends because many of the lads would go home and with my home being in Dublin, I obviously couldn't do the same. The lads were very supportive though and for a lot of weekends I would go with Millsey to Sheffield or to Steve Mac's in Blackpool - or go out in Manchester with others. George O' Boyle (from Belfast) lived in the same digs as me, so we would go out for a pint, although other times I was on my own and I couldn't wait for the weekend to be over so I could get back to training and the craic with the lads and hear the stories of what they had got up to at the weekend.

"I then moved from Heaton Mersey and lived with Andy Hinchcliffe and his family and I will always be grateful for their hospitality and we had some great fun playing head tennis in Andy's hall way - maybe his mum wasn't that impressed with us but we loved it!

"For a while we went to college every Monday with some lads from other clubs from around the Manchester area, mainly Manchester United players and I found out the Irish players at United went home every six weeks - all paid for by the club - so home sickness wasn't an issue for them, which really made a lot of sense. At City I got two paid flights a year, which had me pining for my home - City were quite a penny pinching club at that time!"

David Boyd: "For my first year at City I was in digs with Steve Redmond in Burnage - a few doors down from Paul Simpson and Jamie Hoyland. Reddo went home every weekend and eventually moved out (to live back at home!) the year after and John Bookbinder moved in. Our digs seemed to be worse than all the others. Virtually every night we had to go out to the local shop or chippy as we were still starving after our evening meal. We didn't feel part of the family at all and got the impression they really just needed the money. During my first year, one of my old team mates from Glasgow (Gary Docherty) was also at City - his parents had bought him a car so we used to head home fairly frequently on Saturdays after 'A' team games (we both had girlfriends back home!) when the first team were away. We used to travel back down to Manchester at 5am on Monday's and head straight to college. The following year he was no longer at City, so like John Clarke, I didn't really enjoy our Sunday's off too much. In hindsight, I should have said more to the club at the time. However, I do recall asking to go home at Christmas but being told to be back on New Year's Eve as we had an away 'A' team game against Chester City reserves on New Year's Day 1985. Hogmanay was a huge deal in Scotland back then where people went to parties for two or three days in a row. I got back to my digs around 10pm on the 31st December to find everyone in bed!

The next day we all had a bit of stinker in the first half and got a bollocking from Tony Book. For some reason (maybe the fact I had asked to go home?) he singled me out, yelling "F★★k off back to Scotland if you want!" (For the record the game ended 2-2 with Moulden and Beckford scoring for City)

I had been away from home every weekend from the age of thirteen, so I was used to being away, however, the situation regarding the state of the digs and lack of attention from the club on checking on things didn't help matters. I suppose Clarkey, myself and George should maybe have done more on our own – but then again we were only seventeen or eighteen. Or maybe we could have arranged more things with the local lads like Lakey etc. Hindsight is a wonderful thing!"

LANCASHIRE YOUTH CUP FINAL

WIGAN ATHLETIC V MANCHESTER CITY

City: Steve Crompton, Andy Thackeray, Colin Finlinson, Earl Barrett, Ian Brightwell, Ian Scott, David White, Paul Moulden, John Beresford, Darren Beckford, David Boyd.

21st May. Wigan Athletic played host to the final on a Friday evening as a small crowd assembled in the seats high up in the main stand in the ramshackle Springfield Park. Wigan Athletic had only been in the Football League since 1978 and were now in the Third division. City were expected to win comfortably but went behind in the 24th minute. Wave after wave of City attacks proved fruitless until finally – with nine minutes remaining – White crossed for Boyd to smash the ball home.

The game went into extra time where City moved up a gear (or Wigan were simply out of gas!) as Moulden, Scott and Boyd put the game beyond the hosts, before Moulden added his second and City's final goal in a 5-1 win as City won the Cup for the fourth year running.

David Boyd: "For my equaliser, I can still recall the ball coming across the box and it was almost as though things happened in slow motion - I should have hit it earlier and could hear everyone on the bench screaming at me to do so, but for some reason I waited, and then took a touch before slotting it home."

Ian Brightwell: "It was a really tough game for the first ninety minutes until we edged ahead and dominated the game in extra time. Tony and Glyn were going ballistic until it looked like we'd sewn the game up because their standards were so high. They never accepted less than 100% and these values were instilled into all of us and they wouldn't stand for anything less. They were winners, along with the Grand Master Ken Barnes and they wanted us to have that mentality too. They gave us a great grounding."

PLAYER COMBINED APPEARANCES - 1984-85				
	'A' TEAM	LANCS/FA YOUTH CUP	RESERVES	TOTAL
DAVID BOYD	21 (2 + 1), 2	6, 2	2 (1 + 1), 1	29 (3 + 2), 5
IAN BRIGHTWELL	9, 2	1, 0	2, 0	12, 2
JOHN CLARKE	5 (+4), 0	-	-	5 (+4), 0
STEVE CROMPTON	34, 0	7, 0	1, 0	42, 0
ANDY HINCHCLIFFE	5, 0	(7), 0	-	5 (7), 0
PAUL LAKE	3 (1), 0	-	-	3 (1), 0
STEVE MILLS	2, 0	-	-	2, 0
PAUL MOULDEN[†]	23 (1), 16	7, 4	20 (3), 6	50 (4), 26
STEVE REDMOND	24 (+1), 10	6, 1	24 (2), 3	54 (2), 14
IAN SCOTT	19 (3), 10	7, 4	17 (2 + 7), 1	43 (5 + 7), 15
ANDY THACKERAY	20 (4 + 3), 2	7, 0	9 (4 + 1), 0	36 (8 + 4), 2
DAVID WHITE	19 (2 + 1), 9	7, 9	10 (1 + 1), 2	36 (3 + 2), 20

[†] *includes 10, 0 for England Youth*

2. STEVE MILLS

Born: Sheffield, 13th October 1968

STEVE GIVES US THE BACKGROUND to his junior days and his journey to his current life in South Africa. "I lived in Sheffield until the age of about 10 but then we moved just outside town to a place called Grindleford. I attended Hope Valley College and played football for Sheffield schoolboys and Yorkshire County youth. During that time I managed to get into the England Schoolboys team (Under 15). I missed the first two games but made the team for the next five games against Switzerland away, two against the old West Germany, one against Wales and the highlight, beating the Netherlands at Wembley. I was lucky enough to return to the Berlin Olympic Stadium for the 2006 World Cup final. I was there with my best mate John Beresford (remember him from City?) and our two sons. Bez mentioned that I'd played at the stadium and my son's reaction was along the lines of, 'Yeah, right'...

"I played in Sheffield on Sundays for a team Greenhill & Lowedges between the ages of 10 and 12. Scouts would be at quite a few games (both school and Sunday league). I don't remember who originally invited me to City but I do recall another guy from Aston Villa and both Sheffield clubs being interested. I ended up playing for an unofficial City nursery team (called Midas) that included Whitey, Reddo, Lakey, Scotty, Steve Crompton and Andy Hinchcliffe. Quite a Sunday League team! So, by the time we won the youth cup the bulk of us had played together for a number of years.

"It was always football for me at school; I had no interest in other sports. I had signed schoolboy forms for City at 14 in Ken Barnes' office (no idea what for – all it did was tie you to a club and not allow other clubs to approach you). I remember the Headmaster pulling me into his office prior to leaving school and trying to persuade me to stay on and do 'A' levels, university, etc. No chance. I was a teenager, I knew everything and I was to be a footballer of course. Little did I know!"

Steve made his Lancashire League debut against Liverpool on May 16th 1985 and his Reserve debut followed at Leeds United on March 11, 1986. Steve recalls the reserve team game that had a significant impact on his career.

"The reserve match against Manchester United was a turning point in my life. I was playing right back. Early on I ruptured my anterior cruciate ligament in my right knee and I never played for City again and was released at the end of my YTS contract.

"So, three years and four operations later I eventually got back playing, but nothing like I had been. I spent two years at Sheffield Wednesday in rehab with Alan Smith the then England physio. Then Howard Wilkinson left for Leeds and Big Ron (Atkinson) arrived. He immediately got rid of the dead wood. Trials at Mansfield and then Lincoln came to nothing so I dropped into non-league, playing at Eastwood Town, Shepshed Charterhouse and Leek Town briefly before a stint at Accrington Stanley (yeah, I know, who are they?)

"My old man was working in South Africa and I decided to go over and have a look in 1992. I started playing for a club called Wits who played in the Professional Soccer League. We played against the "giants" of South African football like the Kaiser Chiefs and Orlando Pirates where there were often crowds of 40 or 50,000! We played in Soweto against the Pirates the day after Chris Hani had been shot - the country was on the brink of civil war! A full house of 40-odd thousand and a volatile crowd - believe me, it was a good match to lose. Thankfully we managed a 4-0 defeat.

"I then moved to Pretoria City and in the same league for a season. That was my last season, I'm guessing around 1994-ish. My knee had finally given in. The football in South Africa was part time so I had to get a proper job. For a spell I was in the IT industry then found myself in the print business. I started my business around 1996 when my son Brad was born. I finally had the kick up the backside I needed in life. We've grown steadily over the years and I now employ about thirty-five people. I have no passion for the industry but it pays the bills.

"Living in South Africa you can't help but be converted from football to rugby. I must admit, I fell out of love with football years ago. My passion now is watching Brad play rugby. He captains the local U16 team and made his debut last year (giving away two years) for the U18's. He plays scrum-half or fly-half and kicks most conversions and penalties - clearly his kicking ability is from his mother's side. I admire the honesty and commitment in rugby - there are no players throwing themselves to the ground feigning injury or waving imaginary yellow cards around.

Steve now lives in the town of Harbeespoort Dam situated in the North West Province of South Africa, about an hour's drive north of Johannesburg where his company HMV Litho is based.

2. STEVE MILLS 1984-85 to 1986-87	
RESERVES	13 (1), 0
'A' TEAM	46 (1), 0
FA YOUTH CUP	12, 0
LANCS YOUTH CUP	2, 0

1985-86

OUR BRAVE NEW WORLD

THE FIRST TEAM HAD RETURNED to the top tier after a two year absence following a dramatic end to the season – needing to beat Charlton Athletic on the final day of the season at Maine Road, a patched up side won 5-1 on a sun soaked day in front of 48,000 delirious fans.

Once more, expectations were high with regards to the much lauded youngsters playing underneath the first team – rapidly gaining experience and also developing a close bond as a team unit – and it wouldn't be long before the calls to promote some of them to the first team were becoming strong – with two of the young Blues forcing their way into the First XI over the coming months.

It would be easier to list "the outsiders" – those players not involved in the Youth Cup – than to keep naming those that were involved, such was their dominance throughout the season in the 'A' team.

The reserve team also became a familiar place for the Boy Blues. Six of the fourteen team squad had made their debuts for the reserves during the previous season – Crompton, Redmond, Moulden, Boyd, Thackeray and Brightwell. Scott and White had made their debuts two seasons ago. This season Hinchcliffe, Lake, Mills, Macauley, Clarke and Bookbinder would also take the next step up the football ladder.

17th August. The first 'A' team game of the season, at home to Southport had only John Beresford and Darren Beckford in the line up outside of the eleven, who in just eight month's time would be crowned the cream of the country's youth players. The two players not in the starting line-up were Boyd (unused sub) and Redmond.

City won 4-1, with Beckford (2), Hinchcliffe and Scott starting the season off with a win.

23rd August. Andy Hinchcliffe and Paul Lake make their reserve team debuts in the first game of the season – alongside Redmond, White and Scott, who came off the bench to replace White, in a 1-3 defeat at Hull City. The strong City team line up also contained Eric Nixon, Earl Barrett, Andy May, Graham

Baker, Jim Tolmie, Darren Beckford and former Scottish international Gordon Smith.

Hinchcliffe's performance drew rare public praise from Tony Book, commenting in the following City match programme. "I don't like getting carried away by any performances from a player because the game knocks down predictions and reputations as fast as it threatens to build them up. But from young Hinchcliffe I saw the most impressive debut from a young lad at that level that I have ever seen. It was almost a complete performance. At defending, his chasing, getting forward, the crosses, he did everything that you would want from that position. His display was a credit to him and he is capable of staying sensible and building from the little platform he has made for himself".

24th August. John Bookbinder makes his first appearance on the 'A' team sheet, being an unused sub away against Burnley 'A' in a 4-0 win. The first team player Jim Melrose scored a brace, backed up by goals from Beckford and Scott.

Bookbinder would be an unused sub three times before making his debut away at Tranmere Rovers on 2nd November.

24th - 26th August. Paul Moulden and John Beresford travel to Baku, Azerbaijan, for the World Youth Cup. Moulden came off the bench in both games as England drew 2-2 against Paraguay (24th) and lost to China 2-0 (26th)

7th September. The 6-1 'A' team home win against Marine reserves had only Earl Barrett and Darren Beckford as 'the outsiders', with Brightwell and Thackeray on the side-lines. Once again, Beckford grabbed the headlines with four goals, with Moulden and Lake chipping in with the other two. Beckford had scored seven goals in the first four games, one of which he was a used substitute.

As a result of his prolific goal scoring rate, he was loaned out to 3rd Division Bury for three months - scoring five goals in twelve appearances.

11th September. Paul Moulden plays for the England Youth Team in a 5-0 win away against Iceland.

Paul Moulden: "I was lucky to play in many different countries and represent club and country. For a lad from Bolton to be in Iceland on his 18th birthday and all in the name of football – scoring goals which was the icing on the cake – well I couldn't believe my luck."

LANCASHIRE YOUTH CUP - FIRST ROUND

City had won the Lancashire Youth Cup for the previous four years and set out for a fifth consecutive victory.

17th October. The first time all season that the classic line up that would win the FA Youth Cup would start together – and an away tie against Oldham Athletic resulted in the Latics being soundly thrashed 12-0 (Lake 3, Boyd 2, Scott 2, Moulden 2, White 2 and Thackeray).

Match report from a City programme

City team: Crompton, Mills, Hinchcliffe, Brightwell, Redmond, Thackeray (Clarke), White (Bookbinder) Moulden, Lake, Scott, Boyd.

The young Blues have been record breaking again! The remarkable romp at Oldham last week in the Lancashire Youth Cup second round tie produced a record score for a City youth team - and it's under 12 months ago that the milestone was set.

Eight of the youth team that hammered Billingham to a 10-1 defeat in the FA Youth Cup in December last year - which was a history making score - were again in action in the rout of Oldham.

But the feature of this stunning success was the even spread of scoring glory, proving that the blend and balance in the youth ranks is looking good and effective in every area.

The two wingers scored a pair each, David White, a torment to Oldham down the right flank, scored his couple in the 26th and 63rd minutes. While his winger partner, David Boyd, proved just as deadly and netted his pair in the 15th and 60th minutes.

The two inside forwards (remember the days of those fetch-and-carry experts?) were also on target. Paul Moulden scored in the 53rd and 70th minutes and his midfield partner Ian Scott pounced in the 18th and 77th mins.

The centre forward was also among the glory - and had the extra goal bonus you'd expect from the main striker. Paul Lake's hat-trick was exploded in the 36th, 42nd and 57th mins, fine examples of finishing.

And supporting all this scoring effort from midfield was a 35th min goal from Andy Thackeray.

It was an excellent start for the City youngsters on the trail of the club's fifth successive Lancashire Youth Cup triumph. It augurs well for the FA Youth Cup campaign ahead.

The Blues were vastly superior, though it must be recognised that Latics did have an inexperienced side with several schoolboy recruits and also had the misery of losing 15 year old Adams in the 15th minute with a double fracture of the leg.

City star DAVID WHITE

One of the team recalls the game with a plausible theory behind the sizable win.

Steve Mills:"The thing that sticks out the most was their centre half breaking his leg badly in a tackle with Steve Redmond early in the match. It was one of those bones through the skin breaks. Awful. Maybe they didn't fancy it much after that, which may have contributed to the result."

One very impressed onlooker that Thursday night – and probably more qualified to comment than anyone else – was Ian Niven, a City director and Director of the Youth Development Programme. Since 1966, Niven had missed very few youth team games. In a City programme in early 1986, Niven described the game against Oldham Athletic as his best ever youth team performance.

"It was 12-0 at Oldham, in the Lancashire FA Youth Cup, which people may think was too one-sided to be of interest. But on that night in Oldham, I saw deluxe football, all that I consider youth football to be about. Our lads were incredible, great stuff to watch. It is why I believe we could win the FA Youth Cup this season."

Niven went on to compare the current crop of young players with those of the past. "This is the best squad. I would class the squad of 1967-68 as the closest in quality – from that squad we had players like Tony Towers and Derek Jeffries, who made the first team at an early age."

For the record, prior to this record breaking 12-0 victory, the previous highest score by City in a Youth Cup competition was the aforementioned 10-1 win at Billingham the previous season – which equalled the highest score by a City youth team in all competitive games when City beat Bolton Wanderers 10-1 on 13th August 1969 in the Lancashire League 'B' Division. Before that, the highest Cup score had remained in place for thirty-two years, when City beat Yorkshire Amateurs at home 8-0 in the FA Youth Cup on 29th October 1953, the inaugural season of the competition.

19th October. Steve Macauley is on the 'A' team sheet for the first time, as an unused sub at home to Crewe Alexandra. Aged sixteen and the youngest of the Class of 86, Macauley had signed YTS forms during the summer after leaving school. The starting line-up contained all but one of the Cup winning team, Jamie Hoyland in place of Andy Thackeray.

White and Scott secured a 2-1 win.

Two weeks later, Macauley would make his debut away at Tranmere Rovers reserves, announcing his first start in style, with a goal in a 2-1 win, with John Bookbinder (another full debutant) the other scorer.

Macauley was the last of the FA Youth Cup squad of fourteen to make an appearance on the team sheet for the 'A' team.

2nd November. The game against Tranmere Rovers away was also memorable (apart from Macauley and Bookbinders' first goals) for a novelty appearance by Steve Redmond - in goal! City's first choice keeper, Alex Williams, was playing a rare game for the 'A' team as he came back from an injury, but had to be taken off during the game. According to the City programme report of the game, Steve Mills came on to replace Williams on the pitch, but it was Redmond who donned the 'keeper's shirt and gloves for the remainder of the game.

"Honestly, I don't remember that at all", Redmond admits, jokingly adding "if we won 2-1 then I bet it was 2-0 when I went in goal, but I just don't recall me going in goal for the 'A' team."

Two seasons later, he would definitely remember putting on the keeper's shirt and gloves for the first team...

4th November. Paul Moulden became the first of the Class of '86 to take the field in City's first team, coming off the bench in the 108th minute against Sunderland in the Full Members Cup Northern Semi Final at Maine Road. After a drab 0-0, City won 4-3 on penalties, with Mark Lillis, Nicky Reid, Andy May and Paul Power converting for City, with Paul Simpson shooting his kick wide. Power's winning penalty sparked a mini pitch invasion amongst the sparse 6,642 crowd that resulted in the club having to install extra fencing around the ground at a cost of £50,000!

Moulden's place on the bench was a complete surprise to the player. "I hadn't a clue the boss was even thinking of me. We'd finished training on the Monday and the boss asked me to join the senior squad for a team meeting. There were fourteen of us in the meeting and only thirteen in the squad, so I just thought he wanted a word with me about something else when his main meeting was over. Then he named the two subs and I was one of them!"

With an FA Youth Cup game away against Tranmere Rovers the following evening, Moulden wasn't sure he'd get on the pitch, but with Gordon Davies feeling the effects from an injury picked up in the previous game, he came on with twelve minutes of extra time remaining and was satisfied with his performance. "I wasn't on the pitch for long, but I was pleased with the five or six touches I had. I was quite surprised to find you get so much time on the ball - it's all helter skelter and instant challenges in the Lancashire League".

THE FA YOUTH CUP

The road to winning the FA Youth Cup for the first time in club history started on the Wirral in November and ended in triumph in Moss Side the following April with twenty-six goals for and just five against.

The starting line-up for each of the nine games was exactly the same -

Steve Crompton, Steve Mills, Andy Hinchcliffe, Ian Brightwell, Steve Redmond, Andy Thackeray, David White, Paul Moulden, Paul Lake, Ian Scott, David Boyd. Three different substitutes were named on the bench over the course of the competition – John Clarke (6 times), Steve Macauley (2) and John Bookbinder (1) in a competition where only one sub per game was permitted.

All match reports come courtesy of City's match day programme.

5TH NOVEMBER - FA YOUTH CUP FIRST ROUND
TRANMERE ROVERS 1 MANCHESTER CITY 7

City: Crompton, Mills, Hinchcliffe, Brightwell, Redmond, Thackeray, White, Moulden, Lake, Scott (Clarke), Boyd. Scorers – White (2), Redmond, Scott, Boyd, Moulden, Lake

WHITE LIGHTNING!

The young Blues roared off on the FA Youth Cup trail again through a sparkling 7-goal success at Tranmere with one of the many highlights being the inspirational way that David White celebrated his acceptance of full time pro' terms the previous day following his 18th birthday.

F.A. YOUTH CUP at Prenton Park on Tuesday,
5th November, 1985 – k.o. 7.30 p.m.

TRANMERE ROVERS	v	MANCHESTER CITY
1. D. GRIERSON		1. S. COMPTON.
2. J. CONWAY		2. S. MILLS
3. S. WRIGHT		3. A. HINCHCLIFFE
4. S. VICKERS		4. I. BRIGHTWELL
5. S. GARNETT		5. S. REDMOND
6. M. CUTTS		6. A. THACKERAY
7. D. O'BRIEN.		7. D. WHITE
8. I. TARPEY		8. P. MAULDREN
9. J. SIMPSON		9. P. LAKE
10. P. LEADBETTER		10. I. SCOTT
11. J. FLANAGAN.		11. D. BOYD
12. J. BERRY		12. J. CLARK

White scored twice, laid on two more and generally waltzed his way at will down the wing to the constant consternation of the home team's defence. It was the 6th minute opening goal from White which probably deserves the tag as best-of-the-match, too - he scored it on the angle just outside the 6 yard area after Ian Scott crossed to the far post for him to control and then hit it home.

The swirly wind made conditions difficult but once City got the ball tamed and played the game to feet it was clear the way the story would unfold.

It was 2-0 in the 23rd minute when Steve Redmond headed in a corner from David Boyd.

And then Scott followed up 9 minutes later when he rounded off a move from White and Paul Moulden. Scott unfortunately failed to complete the game because of a knee injury which had at first threatened his place in the side.

By the interval it was 4-0, White getting the next in the 35th minute courtesy of Moulden's work. The threat from White completely unhinged Tranmere and the leggy youngster could have easily ended with a bigger personal haul and certainly proved the

provider on many other occasions.

It was 5-0 from Boyd in the 54th minute, the set up coming from the deadly combination of White and Moulden. Two minutes later, Moulden - fresh from his first team debut the previous night - got his just rewards as that-man-again White laid it on.

Tranmere's retort came from Flanagan in the 75th minute, but they rarely had a serious look-in and in defence City had a fine performance from Steve Mills to ensure they were mostly secure.

Another accurate cross from White completed the story, this time Paul Lake converting the opportunity. That goal came 3 minutes from time and was the 19th scored in two cup games by the young Blues this season.

It augurs well for the future as the youngsters now storm onto the next rounds of the Lancashire FA Youth Cup and the FA Youth Cup.

City Star: DAVID WHITE

The Star man gives an insight into the managerial support the young blues were receiving at the time.

David White: "I remember my second goal at Tranmere which I absolutely hammered and Billy McNeill telling me that if the net had not been there it would still be travelling now! The first team manager saying anything positive about you was an incredible boost. I can recall McNeill coming to most, if not every youth team game, and whilst his presence put on extra pressure it was great when you did well. He had no issues with coming in at half time to give out a bollocking or two and Skip would have no issue with it either. But McNeill was also more than happy to come down and congratulate you when you had done well."

Despite the Boy Blues being favourites to lift the trophy and scoring for fun, life wasn't all a bed of roses for the YTS trainees - on £26.50 per week. Here is a snapshot of typical day for the young trainees.

Steve Crompton: "We got into a normal routine of training in the morning and having the afternoon off. We'd get to Maine Road at 9am, do all our duties - laying out the kit, cleaning boots etc. - train at Platt Lane, go back to the ground to do all the cleaning, before Skip (Tony Book) gave us the nod that we could go. We used to work in teams when we did our jobs, and I honestly can't remember who was in my team, but our job was to do all the training kit for the reserves and apprentices. So we laid it out in the morning, and would then clear it all up after training and take it to the ladies in the laundry room. I also recall that Andy Thackeray was the best floor mopper I have ever seen! Never has a floor been cleaned so quickly and so efficiently before, and probably never will again."

Youth team boss Tony Book was a strict disciplinarian whose style often would not have been out of place on a drill field rather than a football field – an approach he made no apology for. When interviewed in a City programme, Book spelt out his expectations.

"First thing we do is try and build up a relationship both with the lad and his parents. We have to earn their trust. Then, as apprentices, a proper professional attitude has to be installed in them. We are strict on discipline – I can be very hard on them if necessary – and it is vital within the first few months to make sure they have the correct approach both on and off the pitch. The lessons they learn in those very early stages should stay with them for the rest of their lives."

In his autobiography, Paul Lake recounts tales of being made to suffer collectively if one of the chores hadn't been completed satisfactorily or someone had been slacking in their duties – twelve laps of the Maine Road pitch became an all too common practice! Many professional players in their later years will insist that this kind of hard line approach was 'the making of them', whilst there will always be those players who disagree.

One such player in the squad was John Bookbinder. Bookbinder's Manchester born father, David Bookbinder was a well-known politician being the Leader of Derbyshire County Council form 1981 – 92. Often labelled by the media as one of the "Looney Left" along with Derek Hatton at Liverpool council and Bernie Grant at Brent council, Bookbinder senior spent a good deal of the 80's battling against the Thatcher government (she described him as her least favourite councillor!) Indeed, John's father had negotiated a separate employment deal with City in comparison to the other trainees, in which City paid John's £26.50 per week as a gesture that the club demonstrated a 'commitment', as his father disagreed with the way companies used YTS trainees as a free or cheap source of labour.

Clearly this political upbringing rubbed off on John (ironically a left winger on the pitch!) and he would frequently be at odds with the unquestioning boot camp ethos and would challenge the authority of Book and Co on more than one occasion – as well as refusing several requests to "get yer haircut lad".

Bookbinder's hair was his pride and joy and he would only have it cut it when he wanted it cut.

Steve Mills: "John had quite wispy hair and would spend hours treating it with conditioners and then blow drying it. Once he'd finished this work of art, one of us would sneak up and stick a dollop of shampoo on his head so he had to start the process off again."

Paul Lake: "That maybe true, it may not have been it was always shampoo or conditioner put in his hair sometimes as well, but that was only because he was so meticulous with his hair!"

John's sister, the broadcaster Susan Bookbinder, recalls further evidence of her brother's vanity: "Apparently John would fluff his hair up before he took a corner or a free kick, so I'm not surprised it wound Tony Book up so much!"

Bookbinder was referred to as 'an argumentative c★★t' and 'like father like son' by those charged with managing him. Yet, according to his sister, far from being affected by the comments, he positively revelled in winding them up! However, it wasn't just the management that could see how Bookbinder's demeanour differed from other players, as Susan testifies:

"I remember Paul Lake telling my Mum that John was actually better than him, but that he should watch his attitude as he was always arguing with Tony Book and it wasn't going down well." Lake would further describe how John would argue about everything from the team formation to the mops used in the changing rooms!

28TH NOVEMBER. FA YOUTH CUP SECOND ROUND
MANCHESTER CITY 7 BLACKBURN ROVERS 1
(ATTENDANCE 858)

City: Crompton, Mills, Hinchcliffe, Brightwell, Redmond, Thackeray, White, Moulden, Lake, Scott, Boyd. Sub. Clarke Scorers – Moulden (3), Lake, Scott, Thackeray, own goal

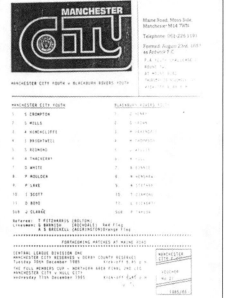

GOAL BLITZ CONTINUES...

Youth is definitely having its fling at Maine Road…this easy passage to the next stage of the FA Youth Cup swept the boy Blues scoring blitz to 26 goals from 3 cup ties this season. So the City youngsters look in shape to reach the final of the competition for the third time in club history.

And maybe, just maybe, reward City with their first ever triumph in this prestigious FA Youth Cup. In the 1980 Final the young Blues of that season were beaten 2-3 in a two-legged final against Aston Villa: the following year (1981) there was a crushing 1-7 aggregate defeat against West Ham United.*

But this season's youth team has got up a fair head of steam already and there was never any question of losing from the moment Paul Lake struck in opportunist

style to open the scoring in the 10th minute. That was the signal for one-way traffic to the Blackburn goal and but for gallant goalkeeping by John Henry the City score may well have rolled into double figures.

The Blues ran rampant. The score was 3-0 at half time with Andy Thackeray, having a masterful time in midfield, smacking in a firm 20 yarder in the 32nd minute. It was the best goal of the night. And Paul Moulden started on his notable hat-trick - the second such scoring feat he's accomplished in Youth Cup games this season.

But while Moulden got the hat-trick - his other goals were scored in the 51st and 83rd minutes - there were heroes in every department of the side. David White once again ran riot on the flank and his pace and deadly crosses piled up the chances. Lake artfully put Moulden into scoring positions on a couple of occasions and apart from Thackeray's impressive form there was a skilful contribution from Ian Scott, who scored in the 77th minute.

Blackburn did hit the target…twice. The first was an own goal from Jim Willis in the 46th minute, a remarkable effort, and then Lee Bickerton headed a reply for Rovers just before the flood-gates opened on their hard-pressed keeper.

By the finish Rovers were exhausted with the run-around they'd had and so they became the second Youth team to be slammed 7-1 by City in the FA Youth Cup… it was the identical margin which disposed of Tranmere in the first round, an away tie.

This is the second time the Blues have had a very convincing start in this competition. Back in 1976-77 they stormed through Blackpool by 5-1, South Liverpool by 8-1 and Shrewsbury Town by 7-1, all home games in the opening three rounds. And last season when many of the current squad were on duty too, the Blues were in even more devastating form…they blasted Preston by 6-0 in a home tie, slaughtered Billingham 10-1 in an away match and then thrashed Nottingham Forest 8-0 at home. But in 1984-85 warranted dreams of success were ended in the fourth round at Newcastle 1-2 - and Newcastle went on to win the cup!

This season's City team looks nicely blended with nine of the players having had more than one season of operating together as a team. And the fire-power looks just as ferocious with goals being promised from every area of the team.

City Star ANDY THACKERAY

*The City programme incorrectly stated that City lost the 1981 final on an aggregate score of 1-7 to West Ham. City were beaten finalists in 1978-79 season, losing 2-0 on aggregate to Millwall and then again in 1979-80 as stated, losing 2-3 on aggregate to Aston Villa. The following season City reached the semi-final and missed out on a third consecutive final, losing to eventual winners West Ham 1-7, who beat Tottenham Hotspur 2-1 in the final.

28th December. The Youth Team squad appear on the front cover of the programme for the First team game against Birmingham City, wishing everyone a happy new year. Amazingly - for the purpose of this book - there are fourteen players (alongside Tony Book and Glyn Pardoe) captured on the picture, taken five months before the Youth Cup final - the exact fourteen players who featured throughout the Youth Cup run.

1st January. Paul Moulden makes his full first team debut in a 1-0 win away at Aston Villa, replacing Gordon Davies and lining up alongside Eric Nixon, Nicky Reid, Paul Power, Kenny Clements, Mick McCarthy, David Phillips, goal scorer Mark Lillis, Andy May, Neil McNab and Paul Simpson, with Jim Melrose on the bench in front of a paltry 14,215 New Year's Day crowd at Villa Park.

From the *Manchester Evening News* match report: "Moulden made an impressive debut as a replacement for the injured Gordon Davies. Billy McNeill said young Paul was up against two highly experienced defenders on an extremely tricky pitch but he did very well. A highly commendable New Year's Day debut."

The following game Moulden would come off the bench away at Walsall in a very snowy FA Cup tie that really shouldn't have been played. City won 3-1 with goals from Simpson (2) and the returning Davies against a Walsall team with former million pound man Steve Daley in the line up! Then in the next game, at home to Southampton, Moulden was an unused sub. His final appearance for the first team this season would be as a substitute in the 0-1 home defeat to Watford on 15th March.

7TH JANUARY. FA YOUTH CUP 3RD ROUND BLACKPOOL 0 MANCHESTER CITY 1 (ATTENDANCE 322)

City: Crompton, Mills, Hinchcliffe, Brightwell, Redmond, Thackeray, White, Moulden, Lake, Scott, Boyd. Sub. Clarke Scorer - Scott

This was never an easy passage. On a wicked winter's night, spectator weather exclusively for proud parents or football nuts, the young Blues slid into the next round through a well worked Ian Scott goal in the 35th minute.

After successive 7-1 successes, in the Cup's early rounds, this was a tie with no room for airs and graces and certainly not a platform to parade skills. It was a skidpan surface carpeted by

continual snowfall, bitterly cold... truly, a credit to both sets of youngsters that they tackled the task with spirit, some with more appetite and application than others, of course.

If the object of these games is to get them played so there's no fixture pile-up and nobody gets inconvenienced, then the referee responsible for passing the conditions as playable cannot be faulted. But if the Youth Cup is supposed to have an objective, to mean something - and since it's about the future of football, I hope it does - then the decision to start it was an utter nonsense. This is a proud and prestigious competition and at Bloomfield Road on this night the whole object of youth football was devalued by the decision to play.

(And please don't be long-in-the-tooth and say that senior footballers have to play in all types of weather: the job at this stage is to develop footballers, not breed Arctic explorers!)

The players did their best to cope. Blackpool made a very sprightly start with Craig Bell forcing Steve Crompton to save at the foot of his near post after a corner. Crompton's edgiest moment in the first half came (25th) when a high ball punted in by Mark Bradshaw had the keeper clutching snowflakes.

A bad back pass by Steve Mills (37th) needed prompt attention by the diving Crompton and everyone in the City defence was wrong-footed and holding their breath when a long range shot deflected from Ian Brightwell and just skimmed wide of a post.

But overall City were strong in defence, marshalled with fine leadership from skipper Steve Redmond, always in charge and City's outstanding player on the night.

Referee Breen disallowed an 8th minute "goal" from David Boyd when this improving youngster smashed a low cross-shot into the far corner. It seemed an absurd judgment since the City player penalised for offside was nowhere near the incident and interfered with nothing.

Best of the other early efforts were a glancing header from David White (15th) and a 20-yarder from Boyd, both zipping quite close past the target. Paul Moulden's 33rd minute shot, snapped up from White's clever free kick, was capably covered by schoolboy 'keeper Richard Powell.

Most moves were ragged with balls punted rather than played forward. Busy Andy Thackeray made an exception with one of the best passes of the half, a penetrating through ball to White dashing down the right but the flank man couldn't finish it with a suitable cross. The other outstanding pass paved the way for the winner... Paul Lake made it, a diagonal ball to his right which White and Moulden weaved with the latter doing well to keep his feet and set up Scott. The midfielder's 12-yard shot was deflected on its way in.

White would have done better to try a cross rather than shoot when Moulden and Lake combined (39th) and pre-interval Lake shot on the turn and was denied by the home 'keeper. Redmond made a scoring bid with a fine header from a free kick and the interval came with White just wide from Moulden.

The tussle between Moulden and his 'shadow' Ian Boyle, who man-marked him throughout, provided plenty of spills and a 50th minute booking for the Blackpool man. White always trying to get involved, Moulden did not have his own way - though tactically he showed naivety his general attitude will always win him admirers.

Blackpool might have been level with a back header from Steven Hornby after a corner (47th) with 'keeper Crompton badly caught out, but there were covering defenders on the line.

City had another effort ruled out (59th) when Boyd dropped in a difficult ball which had the Blackpool 'keeper struggling under heavy challenges which were judged illegal, and correctly so.

Andy Hinchcliffe made a sensible contribution at left back, preferring this time to get the ball forward rather than himself, as he did his work cleanly and effectively. Not that Blackpool's No 7, Carl Lancashire, was allowing anyone a free run on that flank - this 16 year old looked useful.

Boyd's perseverance won him a shot, just wide, from Moulden and Ian Brightwell was over-the-top from a follow-up corner.

In the last minute City should have made it 2-0. Moulden was on a dash into the box when brought down by Martin Clark, who had been shoulder-to-shoulder trying to stop the striker. But White's penalty was splendidly saved by Powell…and that was virtually the signal for the final whistle.

Always looking the better side, but far from easy, Blues. Really, it should not have started. This, my dear referee, is not what the Youth Cup should be all about.

City Star STEVE REDMOND

The official attendance was 322 and it is a compliment to City's support that at least 100 were fans who had braved the elements and travelled from Manchester. And it was also gratifying to see club chairman Peter Swales and five colleagues from the Board of Directors also forsake their firesides and a James Bond movie on TV to take an interest in the City youngsters.

For the scorer of the game's only goal, the game has stayed fresh in his mind.

Ian Scott: "Blackpool was memorable for three things. 1. It snowed throughout the entire game and it was freezing cold. 2. I scored the only goal of the game which proved to be the winner. 3. The next morning Fred Eyre mentioned me on the radio, regarding the goal and the game and I think that was the first time I had ever been mentioned on the radio. That was a good feeling and one I obviously wanted to repeat!"

Ian Brightwell: "I particularly remember the game against Blackpool at Bloomfield Road. It was a freezing cold night and when we left Manchester it started to snow. And snow.... and snow... and snow! By kick off there was two – three inches of the white stuff on the pitch and the game shouldn't have been played. It even continued to snow throughout the game as we played with an orange ball. The game was a lottery but Scotty scored for us and we won 1-0, though it was a close run thing. A few years later I was talking to Sam Ellis about the game when he was City's assistant manager alongside Peter Reid. At the time of the game he was manager at Blackpool and he said he was desperate for the game to be played because he knew the horrendous conditions were Blackpool's only hope of a result that night!"

27th January. Steve Macauley is an unused sub in the reserves 2-2 draw at Leicester City (Jim Tolmie with a brace). The City team includes Northern Ireland captain Sammy McIlroy, Jim Tolmie and Jim Melrose, fellow youth team players Crompton, Thackeray and Hinchcliffe as well as Clive Wilson, Jamie Hoyland, Earl Barrett, John Beresford and Darren Beckford.

It would be 26th March when Macauley would make his full reserve team debut, against Barnsley away.

30TH JANUARY. FA YOUTH CUP 4TH ROUND MANCHESTER CITY 4 LEICESTER CITY 1 (ATTENDANCE 1,298)

Team: Crompton, Mills, Hinchcliffe, Brightwell, Redmond, Thackeray, White, Moulden, Lake, Scott, Boyd. Sub. Clarke Scorers - Moulden (2), Redmond, Thackeray

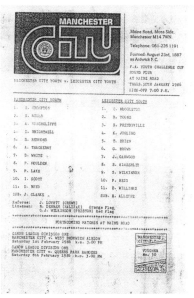

Reward for a never-in-danger victory which puts City in the last 8 of the Cup was quite unexpected when the boy Blues trooped into the dressing room at full time. Hustled into their track-suits they were promptly dispatched out into the freezing night air again to spend a further 15 minutes in a desolate stadium stamping down divots kicked up during the tie against Leicester.

The key to the juniors going on 'jankers' could well have been the muttering from youth coach Tony Book, accompanying his squad in their floodlit penance. "I'm disappointed, we didn't pass the ball around. We should have done so much better."

It's a measure of the high standard which City's youngsters have set that the performance was not being judged anywhere as near as pleasurable as the result. A stern verdict in sub-zero conditions, though the second half was a huge anti-climax. It did little to chase the cold from the 1,298 hardy souls who were prepared to perish for the privilege of watching the youth team unveil their quality and unleash undoubted power (15 goals from the opening 3 rounds of this competition!)

The Blues started with a fizz that promised everything. In the opening 7 minutes there were, truly, 5 distinct chances for home goals. Ripping Leicester open down the right flank, Paul Moulden slashed the ball across the goal face - it went begging - then David White aimed in a similar cross at which Moulden just failed to connect. David Boyd's shot from a free kick (3rd) was deflected over the bar; 'keeper Carl Muggleton caught well before Boyd pounced after Andy Hinchcliffe had barged his way down the left and crossed; Boyd pulled a drive wide; and Paul Lake, with the best of these opportunities, blasted over the top after the visitors right back Andy Ling had made a hash of trying to cut out a through ball from his opposite number Steve Mills.

So everyone settled back for a blitz. But this tornado start was quick in blowing itself out. Leicester, neat and nimble though rarely reaching a destination with their approach work, did provide problems down their left flank. Left winger Darren Williams, possibly their best player, exposed City several times and all the Leicester threats materialised from this area where Mills was having his difficulties.

After a brief burst of Leicester activity, during which Steve Crompton saved alertly at the foot of a post (12th) and Andy Thackeray had gone close from a difficult angle at the other end, the Blues went ahead.

Paul Moulden, a class apart from everyone else on the night, scored it (18th) after Lake stroked the ball out to White and the leggy winger had crossed. Moulden virtually lifted his shot into the spot he'd picked.

Missing with a cheeky chip (20th) Moulden scored his next (30th) after Boyd played the ball in and defender Tony Brien bungled in trying to clear. As sharp as a razor Moulden was on the chance on the edge of the 6 yard box - and it was 2-0.

Moulden gave his plucky marker Brien a torrid time. Ability to blend the ball into attacking moves, aided by confident control, and the gift to twist and turn an opponent into a tizzy, showed why he's already first team material.

On the other hand, Boyd probably cannot believe the type of night he had. A bundle of opportunities were lost as he pulled, mishit, mistimed or swiped at the ball. One of his best (32nd) was from a Moulden cross which White teed up, but with all the time to control and conquer he blazed over. At least he was on target later in the match, though his shot was tame (78th) into the 'keeper's hands from a Moulden push-back.

Down the other flank White often looked like a lad in doubt about how much explosive ability he possesses. When he realises it consistently most defenders will quake

- when he did hit his stride, and his crosses there was menace. One lung-bursting dash (35th) from inside his own half had the crowd tingling with excitement... the winger cut inside but Moulden couldn't control the final delivered pass. Similarly, he set up Lake (50th) with a penetrating pass and it needed a one-handed save by Muggleton to push the resultant low shot wide.

At 3-0 City were home and dry and the game began to drift cheerlessly after Steve Redmond scored it (46th). It came from Ian Scott's left wing corner hitting the point of the upright and bouncing out to Redmond who crashed a low shot into the net from near the edge of the penalty area. Skipper Redmond, who always looked capable of coping in defence, revealed the extent of his powerful presence more in the first half than the second.

Leicester cut the arrears (57th) after centre forward Steve Wilkinson skipped through the home defence too easily for words after tight inter-play with the lively Williams on the left corner of City's area. There was a fleeting minor tremble for the Blues - Jason Garwood beat Hinchcliffe in a dash but Paul Reid headed over the bar. All short-lived hope for Leicester. Within 3 minutes of that flurry the Blues had netted again (60th) with Scott and White the architects and a Thackeray 20-yarder looking to be held by the leaping 'keeper - but disappearing out of his hands into the corner of the net.

The game was fast petering out, though Crompton had one of his rare exertions in saving cleanly from Shaun Kimberley after Scott had slipped up and lost possession in midfield (76th).

Not the Blues at their best, apart from the opening bombardment (which few teams could have maintained!). But a youth team that had the look and even feel of true quality and possibly the best that's been seen at City for many seasons.

The divot-stamping was a valuable job. It helped ensure City's heated pitch would be in table smooth condition for the league game 48 hours later.

Here, the after match exercise is confirmed - and the reason behind it explored.

"We thought the result against Leicester was superb," explains David White, "but we were brought back down to earth by Skip who after meagre praise told us to put our flats (trainers) on and get back out on the pitch where we promptly spent a long time repairing the divots on the pitch as the first team had a game a couple of days later. Skip was excellent at this. Over these two years we lost maybe a handful of games but our feet were kept very firmly on the ground."

8th February. Steve Redmond makes his first team debut in a 2-0 home win against Queens Park Rangers. Partnering Mick McCarthy in defence, covering for the injured Kenny Clements, it was a solid debut for Redmond, as goals from Simpson and Davies sealed the win. Redmond was awarded City's Man Of The Match and the papers were full of praise for the debutant.

Manchester Evening News match report: "It was the display of Redmond that really caught the eye as he made his league debut. That was as impressive as any I have seen by a City Player in more than 20 years."

Sunday Mirror: "He showed all the enthusiasm we'd expect from a teenager, but there were signs of maturity and a big future, too, as he marched carefully through the game."

Sunday People: "Showed courage and skill beyond the call"

Sunday Express: "Can look back on pride on his debut"

Daily Express: "Showed composure beyond his years"

Daily Telegraph: "Thoroughly satisfactory debut"

Daily Star: "Looked a first rate prospect"

The Guardian: "He tackled sharply, used the ball well and above all seemed to have plenty of time"

8TH MARCH. FA YOUTH CUP QUARTER-FINAL
FULHAM 0 MANCHESTER CITY 3
(ATTENDANCE 195)

City: Crompton, Mills, Hinchcliffe, Brightwell, Redmond, Thackeray, White, Moulden, Lake, Scott, Boyd. Sub. Clarke Scorers – Lake, Redmond (2)

In less than 60 seconds the City youngsters had flattened a reputation. Fulham's proud defensive record in the FA Youth Cup, having never conceded a goal in their three earlier ties, was sent crashing when a 25-yarder from striker Paul Lake zipped City into a first minute lead.

There couldn't have been a better start or confidence booster against a team known for having a useful goalkeeper and two towering central defenders who have conceded little in the past.

The chance came after a drop-ball decision by the referee after an infringement mid-way in the Fulham half. It broke loose to Lake, who struck it true to catch the home 'keeper on the hop.

It was a measure of City's control of the tie that Fulham didn't manage a corner in the whole of the match. And they only had one shot...even that was off target, struck in the 60th minute by Justin Skinner as a belated response when the Blues had established a three-goal margin. By comparison, the Blues had twelve corners and an abundance of attacks.

The first half was a tale of City's territorial advantage, carved out for them by the midfield mastery of Ian Scott and Andy Thackeray, but little in the way of penetration. There were a series of corners which threatened the Fulham goal, but the home pivots dealt firmly with possible danger.

The menace that had been provided so often in the earlier rounds by lightning winger David White and crafty striker Paul Moulden (8 goals between them from the previous 4 Cup matches) was markedly subdued.

It was left to skipper Steve Redmond to notch the second goal, scoring it in the 31st minute as he connected with a left flank corner from Ian Scott to head in a comfortable chance.

Playing a 4-2-4 system, City looked good for more goals as the game wore on. Sure enough, they collected their third very quickly after the break (47th) and once again it was the bold Redmond who showed the way. He advanced for another Scott corner kick, this one taken from the right, and as the ball skimmed over the heads of the home defenders the City captain headed home. Clearly Redmond was untroubled by a knock he'd taken earlier in the match.

Then came a flurry of attacks in which in which Fulham's fifteen and a half year old 'keeper Trevor Jones showed good ability in keeping out the Blues.

⋆ 66th minute David Boyd broke down the left and finished his run with a right-foot shot which the keeper held.

⋆ 67th minute Ian Scott received an excellent pass from Moulden but was thwarted when Jones dived at the midfielder's feet to smother the chance.

⋆ 70th minute Paul Lake brought Jones to yet another save

⋆ 72nd minute Moulden was looking good for goal on a very exciting run which was terminated when he was brought down on the edge of the penalty box.

Cheered on by two coach-load of City fans who had decided to support the youngsters at Craven Cottage, though the first team were not far away playing at Chelsea, the bonny young Blues were full value for a semi-final place... the first of this season's quarter final ties to be decided.

They've now cracked 22 goals in the FA Youth Cup's five rounds to date and the prestige prize which has eluded the club for so long now really does look within the grasp.

City Star STEVE REDMOND

Foot note: As the report said, City's First team were playing team were playing 1.4 miles away at Stamford Bridge on the same day, losing 1-0 watched by a crowd of just 17,573. The Fulham Youth Cup game (originally due to be played three days before but postponed because of a waterlogged pitch) kicked off at noon allowing the two coach load of Blues to watch both games.

Steve Crompton: "I do remember going down to Craven Cottage to play Fulham, firstly because of the changing rooms being in that corner in the 'Cottage', but also because it was the first time we had ventured down south to play a team. All our games, both 'A' team and reserves, were Northern and

Midlands based, and we never got to play any of the London clubs, so we didn't really know what to expect from Fulham, unlike Tranmere and Blackburn - but as usual, the lads in front of me did their job and we ended up winning 3-0."

11th March. Steve Mills makes his reserve team debut in a 2-2 draw away at Leeds United (Moulden and Darren Beckford on the score sheet). Fellow youth teamers Crompton, Hinchcliffe Moulden and White (used sub), lined up with Jamie Hoyland, Nigel Johnson, Graham Baker, Darren Beckford and the Scottish duo of Jim Tolmie and Jim Melrose. The effects of his reserve team debut lasted beyond the player's ninety minutes as the player explains. "My reserve debut came as a surprise. I got into the ground as usual in the morning, to be told to go straight back home and come back later – 'you're playing in the reserves tonight'. I don't remember anything about the game except their strong centre forward, Lyndon Symonds, raking his studs down my calf towards the end of the match. I remember Skip going mad at the ref after the game, ripping my torn sock down and making me hobble in front of him, showing off my lovely memento from my first game – six stud marks down my calf! I couldn't walk the next day!"

22nd March. Steve Redmond appears in his first Manchester derby. Playing alongside Kenny Clements, due to Mick McCarthy being suspended. City come from 2-0 down to draw 2-2 with United player Arthur Albiston becoming an instant 'City Legend' with his own goal equalising for the Blues! The youth team captain explains, "I'm in the changing room thinking 'I'm up against Mark Hughes, Peter Barnes, Peter Davenport' and I'm crapping myself... but once the game started, that just goes out of your mind and you get on with the game - and then straight after the game we are on the coach and driving down to London and spent the night in a hotel."

23rd March. The following day City played in the final of the Full Members Cup at Wembley Stadium. Seven of the youth team squad would play on the hallowed turf that afternoon. Before the game against Chelsea commenced, there was a City v Chelsea schoolboy's penalty shoot-out, followed by a City v Chelsea 'apprentices' five a side game.

The apprentice's team was John Bookbinder, Ian Brightwell, John Clarke, Steve Crompton, Steve Macauley and David White. The game was played across the width of the pitch and City won 2-1 with goals from Brightwell and Bookbinder.

Steve Macauley: "We travelled there and back the same day in a minibus"

Ian Brightwell: "This was the only time I played at Wembley and I managed to score our first goal as we won 2-1. Later in my career, I played twice at the Millennium Stadium (in play-off games for Walsall and Stoke City) whilst Wembley was being rebuilt, but I would have loved to have played in a full match at Wembley. We then watched the first team almost pulling off a miracle by clawing back from 5-1 down to lose 5-4. Both Chelsea and City had played the day before - imagine that happening today? No chance!"

Steve Redmond again lined up for City in the main game of the day, this time partnering Mick McCarthy, free from suspension, as Clements went off injured the previous day and was unfit to play.

Steve Redmond: "It was a totally weird game; we went 1-0 up and then 5-1 down. In the last few minutes we just went crazy and Mark Lillis scored twice and there was an own goal and we are 5-4 down. Chelsea seemed to have just ran out of energy - we had both played twenty-four hours earlier - had there been a few minutes more we would have scored again, I believe that!

This game - as with Ian Brightwell - would be Redmond's only appearance on the pitch below the Twin Towers, as he reflects on a missed opportunity. "I always thought I'd return after that, I mean I was only eighteen, so I'd have plenty of chances. Then when I was at Oldham Athletic, we reached the semi-final of the FA Cup against Manchester United in 1994 and they played it at Wembley. I was one booking away from a ban - and got booked the week before the game. I begged the ref not to book me but he wasn't interested, so I had to sit that out. It was the game where Neil Pointon scored in extra time for us, but Mark Hughes equalised in the last minute and we then had a replay at Maine Road. My suspension was up, so I thought I'd have another chance to get to Wembley and also beat United at Maine Road at the same time! But that never went as planned either as Joe Royle - and fair play to him - took me to one side and said it was only fair to stick with the side that played so well in the first game. I was on the bench at Maine Road and by the time I was brought on, we were 4-1 down."

25th March. Steve Redmond makes his England Youth Team debut, coming off the bench in a 4-1 win over Scotland in Aberdeen. Also in the side are Tony Daley and Neil Ruddock.

26th March. John Clarke makes his reserve team debut away at Barnsley, where Darren Beckford scored the game's only goal. Nine of the cup winning squad were on the field - joining Clarke was Crompton, Macauley (his full debut), Brightwell, White, Moulden, Scott, Lake and Boyd on the bench. John Beresford and Graham Baker joined Beckford on the team sheet.

John Clarke: "My first reserve game was against Barnsley and I was playing right full back and in those days it was number one to eleven so when we were warming up, I was trying to see the number eleven so I could see who I was up against. When I spotted my opponent my heart sank – he was a tall black lad and under the floodlights his muscle bound legs looked huge so I decided that the first chance I got, I was going to let him know who I was. After about five minutes the ball was played out to the winger and as he took control of the ball, I slid in from about ten yards away to win the ball and clatter the man as he went several feet into the air and landed with a thump! Tony Book jumped out of the dugout and roared "That's fucking genius son, fucking genius", which boosted my confidence no end and it went on for the rest of the game."

However, one incident involving John Clarke had Tony Book reacting in a different manner towards the young player. "In my early days at the club, Skip walked into the dressing room while I was doing an impersonation of him – the lads were in stitches laughing and he just stared at me. It was horrible for me and although he never mentioned it – there was no bollocking – he was obviously annoyed and made sure I paid the ultimate price by spending a lot of time sitting very close to him on the bench. Maybe that's why I became very good at taking him off! It was only a bit of fun although he obviously didn't look at it that way and I felt it had a huge part in stopping my progress as a player."

Steve Macauley recalls, "There were many impersonations of 'Skip' but John's was by far the best! It was never done in front of him, but we all regularly mocked his accent when he was out of sight (as brave as we all were!)" Clarke wasn't the only player to impersonate the West Country accented Book and get caught; Jason Beckford also felt the wrath of the coach – only to discover the joke was on him!

Ian Scott: "I remember us all setting up Jason Beckford, who was one of the younger ones at the time. Jason used to do a great impersonation of Skip, so we got him in the changing rooms to do a grand performance for us all, Jason was in full flow when Skip burst in – we had tipped him off and told him what we were doing and he was more than happy to catch Jason out! We wound Jason up for weeks on that one."

29th – 31st March. Andy Hinchcliffe and Steve Mills make their debuts for the England Youth Team in the Cannes Festival. The pair played in all three games played over three days: (29th) Brazil 0-0, (30th) Hungary 2-0, (31st) France 1-2.

Steve Mills: "I'd managed to get into the England Youth team with Andy Hinchcliffe alongside Matt Le Tissier, Vinny Samways, the Holdsworth twins and Carl Bradshaw. We travelled to Cannes for a tournament and somehow beat Hungary and drew with Brazil on our way to losing to France in the final. I was a bit embarrassed that I'd made the team and Lakey missed out. We all knew how good he was."

31st March. The youth team travelled to the Isle of Man, beating an IOM Youth XI 2-0 (Hoyland, Moulden). After the game, Tony Book allowed the lads to relax a little, with one player over stepping the boundary just a little bit too much!

Steve Crompton: "'We stayed in a Bed & Breakfast and in the evening, Skip had said that we could have a drink, but we weren't allowed shorts or pints. So I, in my wisdom, decided to drink both, got really pissed and went to my room where I hung out of my bedroom window shouting across the courtyard to the other lads. Unfortunately Skip heard me, gave me a bollocking from his bedroom window and told me to see him in the morning for another bollocking. Ian Brightwell took great pleasure in getting me the phone number for Alcoholics Anonymous!"

Ian Brightwell: "This was a mid-season break where Tony and Glyn had said their famous last words 'Enjoy yourselves but be sensible!' Crommo was pissed as a rat and received a rocket off Skip. The same night, I think it was me, Millsey, Reddo and John Beresford were sneaking around the corridors and generally pissing about which we thought was hilarious until we turned a corner to be met by Glyn, laughing his head off, telling us we were all to be fined. We turned to run back to our rooms, only to be met by Skip who had blocked the way through. He was laughing even louder, informing us that our fines had just been doubled! We thought we were being clever, but they were always two steps ahead of us. When I meet up with the pair of them today, this episode still comes up in discussions."

6th April. Four of the youth team members – Brightwell, Moulden, Redmond and White – travel up to Tayside to play in a testimonial game for Bobby Glennie against Dundee, alongside Darren Beckford and the more senior players in Eric Nixon, David Phillips, Paul Power, Graham Baker, Gordon Davies, Neil McNab, and Clive Wilson. Only Nixon amongst the senior players had not played the previous day at home to Arsenal – Steve Redmond was also in the starting line-up. Beckford and Davies scored the goals for City in a 2-2 draw.

Billy McNeill, in the following home game programme notes, had praise for the two lads yet to make the first team.

"David White did enough to indicate the extent of his potential. His pace on the flank set up the first goal and there were other flashes of his speed which got him away from the opposition and he delivered some good balls into the attacking area. Ian Brightwell (three days away from his eighteenth birthday) competed well, good signs from a youngster coming into this level for the first time. He produced some nice football – it was a confident display."

Joining City in the FA Youth Cup semi-finals would be the three other triumphant Quarter-Finalists: Arsenal, Coventry City and Manchester United. Talk of an all Manchester final had whet the appetite amongst fans of both clubs for a number of weeks. The two clubs had met previously on two occasions in the FA Youth Cup semi-finals, with both clubs winning one tie each. In 1963-64★, United ran out winners with an 8-4 aggregate score (4-1 at Old Trafford & 4-3 at Maine Road), whilst in 1979-80 City won the second leg at Maine Road 3-1, which was also the aggregate score.

★The semi-final tie in 1963-64 was the subject of a book by Colin Schindler, with the annoying title *George Best and 21 Others* in which, like this book, Schindler traced the careers of those players on the pitch back in the day.

As it turned out City were drawn with Arsenal with the first leg at Highbury on the 16th April, returning to Maine Road for the Second leg six days later. United would travel to Coventry City for their first leg tie. Arsenal's journey to the semi-final saw them victorious against Plymouth Argyle 5-0, Luton Town 2-0, in a replay after a goalless draw, Wimbledon 1-0, and Millwall 4-1, after a 1-1 draw in the quarter final.

Joint top scorer with five goals was Paul Merson and also in the team was Michael Thomas – who three years later would score the dramatic injury time winning goal at Anfield in the final game of the season to land The Gunners the First Division Championship on goal difference at the expense of Liverpool.

Arsenal keeper Nicky Hammond went on to play for Swindon Town and Reading. In 2000, the then Reading boss Alan Pardew offered him the role of Youth Academy Director and in 2003 he became the Berkshire club's first Director of Football – a post he still holds to date. Also in the team was Roger Stanislaus, who failed to earn a full time contract in 1987 and then spent three years at Brentford and five seasons at Bury, before joining Leyton Orient – however in February 1996 he received a one-year ban from football as punishment for taking cocaine in a much publicised incident. His contract was terminated immediately and a year later, on completing his suspension, Stanislaus signed for Peterborough United.

Steve Redmond: "Out of the other three clubs in the semi-final, it was Arsenal we feared the most, we knew it would be us or them that lifted the trophy – so if we were to win the cup, we would have to be at our best."

16TH APRIL. FA YOUTH CUP SEMI-FINAL FIRST LEG.
ARSENAL 1 MANCHESTER CITY 0
(ATTENDANCE 487)

City: Crompton, Mills, Hinchcliffe, Brightwell, Redmond, Thackeray, White, Moulden, Lake, Scott, Boyd (Clarke).

There might well have been a 60th minute equaliser from Andy Thackeray with the best chance of the match; there could have been a penalty award for the Blues in the 75th minute when EIRE youth international defender Pat Dolan was suspected of handling; and it was a close shave for Arsenal when Paul Moulden broke away threateningly in the last minute only to be thwarted by a timely tackle. But the fact is that City's youth team suffered their first set back of the season's competition and now have to roll up their sleeves and make up lost ground when the teams come face-to-face in the second leg at Maine Road next Tuesday night (kick off 7.30pm)

THE AGGREGATE WINNERS WILL HAVE A TWO-LEGGED FINAL WITH MANCHESTER UNITED

Arsenal, having scored 13 goals from their 6 games in the Cup to reach the semi (two of their games forced to replays), scored their winner in the 52nd minute with a brilliant individualistic effort from Paul Birch. A slip up by City sub John Clarke in midfield gave Birch the chance to pounce and the young Gunner made a brilliant 40-yard run past 2 defenders and right into City's penalty area before unloading a scoring shot into the net.

It was a signal for a very adventurous second half after both teams had earlier found themselves bogged down in the Highbury mud - the pitch was very heavy and the conditions were not suited to City's footballing style.

Yet the Blues were the first to cause a scare. In the 27th minute a neat combination between Ian Brightwell, David White and Ian Scott left the midfielder with an opening...but Scott hit his shot wide.

No pattern emerged before the break. Patches of excitement came to the large contingent of City fans at the tie when David White stretched his legs - and the Arsenal defence - with several sorties down the flank where his pace menaced the

home team. But there was little end product with 'keeper Nicky Hammond not being forced into a save.

City were handicapped with a 13th minute injury to David Boyd, suffering a strain as he over reached for a ball. The left flank forward struggled through the rest of the half, the condition plainly deteriorating, and was replaced at the break. The change did unbalance the Blues, though they were equal to most home attacks.

The best performances came from the full backs where Steve Mills and Andy Hinchcliffe were the City heroes - Hinchcliffe in particular had an immense game throughout. There were also bright spells from White and Scott in the first period - they faded out after the break.

Thackeray's opportunity to level the score on the hour was wasted when the youngster lost his composure after gathering the ball outside the area and looking in a favourable position.

Arsenal also had an exceptional full back showing with Mike Thomas being very effective. Youth cap Dolan, inside forward Greg Allen and scorer Birch also showed fine potential.

Arsenal's record proves they give little away. Four times they've kept clean sheets from their six matches and they've won one and drawn two of their away matches in the tournament. It's an intimidating record which City will have to deal with next week.

Your support would be a great bonus to the young Blues. Try and get along next Tuesday night. Admission is exclusively to the Main Stand with admission prices of 150p for adults and 100p for juniors. It's a match that should be worth seeing…and the prize of a Final against the Old Trafford Reds is a very enticing prospect.

Steve Mills: "For me, the toughest challenge was the two legged semi against Arsenal. We lost the first match and I remember a ball knocked into the channel to their centre forward. At first I thought, no danger, Reddo will sort that out. Well the Arsenal lad kept Reddo at bay with pace, touch and power and then smashed the ball into the bottom corner. I thought 'fucking hell, he's a bit handy'. You see, no one got away from Reddo. Anyway, after the game I was expecting a bollocking and all we got was, 'It's only half time lads – let's get them at our place'.

Steve Crompton: "In the semi-final we were drawn against Arsenal. Again, another strong London team, and probably favourites to win it. The First leg was away at Highbury, and there are two things that stick with me from that day. The first was how small the pitch was. We were used to playing at Maine Road, which was one of the biggest playing surfaces in the league, and it felt like at times, if I kicked it hard enough, I could probably trouble their keeper, Nicky Hammond. The second thing was that the pitch had a massive crown in the middle, which meant that when the ball was in the opposition penalty box, I couldn't see it!

"From memory, the game was probably our hardest match we had played. Michael Thomas played for them, who eventually went on to have a great career with Arsenal and Liverpool. We lost the game 1-0 to a Paul Birch goal, which he hit incredibly hard from just outside the box low into my bottom right hand corner. I don't think there was much I could have done with it."

There were encouraging words and praise for the Boy Blues from the first team manager, when writing his programme notes a few days before the second leg game.

"It's only the half way stage for our youngsters but they've got a hill to climb. They are going to have to lift a major performance from their many talents to pin down this Arsenal side. But if the young Blues produce their best, which they have done on so many occasions already this season, then I feel it is well within their compass to clinch an aggregate success for the second leg. People who have been involved with City for a long time do assure me that this line up is the best yet fielded in the competition down the thirty-three years it's been operating. So I do not despair at the task next week. And nor should the youngsters themselves."

22ND APRIL. SEMI FINAL SECOND LEG
MANCHESTER CITY 2 ARSENAL 1 - AET
(ATTENDANCE 5,056)
AGGREGATE SCORE 2-2 - CITY WIN 5 - 4 ON PENALTIES

City: Crompton, Mills, Hinchcliffe, Brightwell, Redmond, Thackeray (Macauley), White, Moulden, Lake, Scott, Boyd. Scorer – Moulden (2)

It took simply 6 minutes for City to stay in pursuit of a dream. The really hard work, wearing on youthful legs, had been packed into 210 minutes of totally committed action which had covered the first leg (Arsenal won 1-0) and took the second leg (City won 2-1) to an extra time deadlock after extra time.

At 9.54pm the true, but very exciting, test of nerve took place as both teams squared up for a penalty shoot-out. By this time City looked the more exhausted side and Arsenal must have been feeling that their flurry of activity in the last period of extra time - four threatening assaults on City's goal - deserved to pinch the verdict. City deserved better.

★*Steve Crompton faced the first of the 10 penalties. Greg Allen blasted it straight through him, head high and accurate, Arsenal 1-0.*

★*Nicky Hammond took his turn. Paul Lake made no mistake rattling his shot wide to the 'keeper's left with Hammond going the wrong way. It was 1-1.*

★*Fleetingly Crompton seemed to be the night's hero as he dived to his left to block Paul Merson's spot-shot. But fussy referee Phillips, the one irritant to an excellent night of youth football, ordered a retake. He judged the City 'keeper moved. Merson breathed again - and scored. Arsenal 2-1*

★*Hammond had no chance as Paul Moulden made it 2-2.*

★*Crompton got his hand to the penalty slammed to his left by Mike Thomas - but it wasn't enough to halt the ball. Arsenal 3-2*

★*Hammond picked the next one out of the net, firmly slammed in by skipper Steve Redmond. It was 3-3.*

★*By this time, Crompton was employing the famous Bruce Grobbelaar shimmying tactics (remember the Liverpool 'keeper's entertaining but distracting antics in similar shoot-out circumstances!) which referee Phillips wagged his finger at. But Lawrie Osborne went for power and not accuracy and his penalty sailed over the bar. Still 3-3.*

★*The responsive crowd were at fever pitch as Hammond watched Andy Hinchcliffe's spot shot zip past him. Now 4-3 to City.*

★*Crompton could do little with Roger Stanislaus' effort. It was 4-4.*

★*But while heartbroken Osborne was being consoled on the far touch-line - with comforting words from Redmond to show the spirit of the occasion - up stepped Ian Scott with great composure to slot in the final penalty. It was 5-4 to City. It was exactly 10pm.*

The shoot-out will be long remembered. But the 120 minutes of action will not be forgotten either. It featured many thrilling moments, not least of all the two excellent striker's goals from Paul Moulden. They were both classics.

The game lit up quickly in the 4th minute with a David White dash that finished with a cross that slashed menacingly across the goal face. After Crompton had dashed out to collect a dangerous pass poked through by Allen (7th) there was some Moulden dazzle in beating two players and laying on a shot for Paul Lake, the strike lacking strength.

Arsenal were handicapped with the loss Adrian Pennington, injured trying to cut out a City right wing raid, and they introduced Paul Birch (10th).

Sleight-of-foot from Moulden got Boyd in on the bye-line which before whipping the ball across the Arsenal goal, though an angled pass might have had better effect.

The visitors carried their threat through the lightning-fast right winger Paul Smith, who often left City's defenders for dead and in the 15th minute got past a mistimed tackle from Andy Hinchcliffe to set up Merson. Alert Ian Brightwell blocked the shot. And 5 minutes later Crompton comfortably gathered a high cross from Smith.

Boyd had a shot (23rd) when three Arsenal players got in a tangle, but the winger couldn't quite reach a smart diagonal ball from Moulden following a probing pass from Scott (24th). City pounded away but Redmond's header from a White free kick was inconsequential (28th).

After a Boyd snap shot was stopped and cleared (30th), Steve Mills had to step in quickly to stop Birch on a break. Arsenal striker Merson was a handful and in the 36th minute he timed a run onto Smith's fine cross only to be denied by Crompton tipping over, the best save of the night and made at point blank.

City needed a goal badly and Moulden almost set it up on the right side with a high ball which Boyd headed on target and which Hammond got away as he fell backwards. Then it was Lake to Moulden, a cute back heel to White and a terrific cross in - but no-one there to connect. White was being double marked and drifting out of the game.

There was a 44th minute black mark for Allen, booked for a foul on Boyd, before City scored from the free kick. Scott flashed in the ball from the left and Moulden breasted down and shot, all in the same action, to watch the ball loop high into the net - right on the stroke of half-time.

City resumed meaning business. Moulden had a threatening shot through the goal face after a fortunate 'nutmeg' from White, and then Birch cleared a Moulden cross (51st).

The 56th minute was a desperate one for City. Merson shot across the penalty box after Smith had caused further trouble with a pacey burst and waiting at the far post was Osbourne, who side footed home for 2-1 (aggregate). City had been sloppy.

Redmond headed into the 'keeper's hands from a corner (58th) before a significant City substitute. On went Steve Macauley to partner Steve Redmond in defence, subdued Andy Thackeray was withdrawn - and Brightwell went into attack with great effect. The combination of the very determined Brightwell, inputting every ounce of energy and no small measure of skill, and Moulden hitting a purple patch, finally put Arsenal on the rack. City were back in front in the 63rd minute following a Boyd corner. Redmond headed it forward and Moulden turned and hooked a shot in the same motion, a brilliant opportunist goal from 8 yards.

Taking a relief from his exposed defensive work, Hinchcliffe had a surging 67th minute run from which Boyd won a corner. By now Redmond's power was evident, the young first teamer gaining in strength and stature as time wore on.

Scott got his timing just right (77th) after Moulden had teed him up following a *full-flight run down the right, but the shot just whipped low outside the post. Arsenal were getting submerged despite an Allen free kick being deflected wide (82nd) and 5 minutes from time, Moulden and Brightwell combined in a move of pin-ball pace which ended with Scott brought down. The 'keeper saved the free kick.*

Extra time loomed as Crompton saved a fierce ground shot from Thomas (89th) and Moulden tried a back header (90th) from a corner.

By now City were running out of puff and looking by the far fresher team the Gunners took up the running. Osbourne shot by the post (101st) and Crompton saved from Birch (107th) after the whippet Smith had linked with Merson. City's keeper had to hold a firm high shot from Paul Turner (108th) and then turned over another attempt by Turner (111th) that looked bound for the top corner.

Brightwell spent the whole period trying to ease the pain from legs seized with cramp, a sight which summed up the effort that the Blues had put into their game.

The annoyingly fussy referee Phillips finally blew time to set up a stirring penalty finish. And the crowd rose, quite rightly, to enthusiastically applaud a quality night of youth football.

Star Men: Paul Moulden (City)...... Paul Merson (Arsenal)

After the initial ninety minutes, there were fears that City had actually been knocked out of the competition, as Steve Crompton recalls, "The second leg was about a week later at Maine Road. We were under added pressure because United had already won their semi-final. Again, it was a really tough game, and for once, I think I had a blinder that night, making a number of saves during the game. We won the game 2-1, which meant it was 2-2 on aggregate after 90 minutes and I honestly believed that we had been knocked out on away goals. Fortunately, this wasn't the case, and after a further period of extra time with no more goals, it was time for penalties.

"I actually fancied myself with the penalties, as I wasn't bad at guessing the right way and I do recall on one of their penalties, I gave it the Grobbelaar wobbly legs routine that he had used during the European Cup Final not long before. I thought it had worked – as Lawrence Osbourne blasted it over the cross bar. However, years later we both played at Wycombe Wanderers and he told me that he had no idea that I'd even done the wobbly legs thing! Anyway, we won the game on penalties and my last memory of that night was walking off down the tunnel with Billy McNeill's arm around my shoulders!"

The coolest player on the pitch was the player taking the last spot kick, who under immense pressure scored the winning penalty, Ian Scott. "I volunteered to take the last penalty for us and as it happened it went to the final penalty and I had to score to win the game. It seemed like a long walk to the penalty box but I had total confidence that I would score. I remember putting the ball to the keeper's left and running off to celebrate in front of the Main Stand and with the other players. It was a great feeling knowing we had made it to the final."

"We never consciously practiced penalties in training," recalls captain Steve Redmond, "but what we all used to do after training was stay back and we'd take penalties against Steve Crompton and also shots from outside the area from different angles. We did that most days. I always knew where my penalties were going - to my left hand side every time. I never changed that. Against Arsenal, I stepped up and knew exactly where it was going. All five of us scored that night, so our extra practice must have paid off."

Andy Hinchcliffe recalls that, "Both games against Arsenal were incredibly tight and we just had the extra bit of luck needed to squeeze through. Throughout my career taking penalties never really worried me too much. I remember clearly picking my side to aim for and stuck with it!!"

For one of the lads, it was touch and go as to whether he would be in the line-up. "In the first leg, Michael Thomas had 'done me' near the half way line," remembers David Boyd. "I tried to carry on, but only lasted until half time. I honestly thought I was going to miss the second leg as it was so close, but I managed to make it. Arsenal were a great team and this was the best game I've ever played in. In extra time, I recall loads of players dropping to the ground with cramp. At one point, I made an attempt to get past Michael Thomas - but nothing happened, my legs had gone!"

Ian Brightwell: "The semi-final against Arsenal was a tough game - in my opinion the only team that might have beaten us that season was Arsenal. We went into the second leg at Maine Road needing to win - it was a warm night and the game was very tight and tense. We were up against a top side that was out to do us. In the second half, Tony and Glyn took a chance and brought on Steve Macauley and moved me from centre half to centre forward to get more men forward as we were behind on aggregate - five minutes later we were level! By extra time, we were all shattered and I remember getting cramp in both legs in the second period of extra time but still trying to run! It must have been hilarious to anyone watching but I was desperate not to let the team down. The match went to penalties in which our boys all scored and I think it was Scotty who wrapped it up for us. It was an amazing night and we knew we had been in a game."

"I found the Arsenal games very tough as I was in direct opposition to Michael Thomas," recalls David White, "who even then was playing in Arsenal's first team. He was my toughest opponent to date by far and was so strong. We were lucky to get through. I had missed a penalty in an earlier round (at Blackpool), so I did not fancy taking one in a semi-final!"

Manager Tony Book was full of praise for the Boy Blues. In an interview in a City programme he said: "The home leg against Arsenal is the hardest youth match we've had. They were a lot better than I had given them credit for – I'd say Arsenal is the best opposition we have faced all season at this level. Although I didn't feel we played particularly well at Highbury in the first match, when I assess the Arsenal performance at Maine Road, I must admit that I didn't give the City lads the credit they deserve in holding them to 1-0 in London."

23rd April. John Bookbinder became the final squad member to make the reserve team, coming off the bench to replace John Clarke, in a 2-0 home loss to Huddersfield Town. The game was played the evening after the Youth Cup Semi-final Second leg against Arsenal – and a day before the First leg of the final! Therefore it was hardly surprising that only Clarke and Bookbinder from the squad played against Huddersfield – both of whom would have had a mutual disappointment in being the two players to be missing out. In the absence of the regular reserves, the pair lined up alongside experienced first teamers such as Eric Nixon, Jamie Hoyland, Steve Kinsey, David Phillips and Clive Wilson.

24th April. Just two days after the Boy Blues beat Arsenal via energy sapping extra time and penalties, they had to travel the short distance across the city to face local rivals United at Old Trafford.

UNITED'S ROAD TO THE FINAL AND PLAYER PROFILES

Second Round: Burnley 0 - United 2

Third Round: Chesterfield 0 - United 6

Fourth Round: Notts County 0 - United 3

Quarter-Final: United 3 - Sheffield United 0

Semi-Final First leg: Coventry City 0 - United 2

Semi-Final Second leg: United 1 - Coventry 1

From United's team that played in the final, four would go on to play for the first team and five others would have a career with other clubs.

Gary Walsh – fifty appearances for the Reds and one hundred and seventy-four in spells with Middlesbrough, Bradford City and Wigan Athletic.

Tony Gill – ten appearances for the Reds before a serious leg injury ended his professional career.

Lee Martin – seventy-three appearances for United and scoring the winning goal in the 1990 FA Cup Final replay against Crystal Palace. He played a further nineteen games for Glasgow Celtic.

David Wilson - four appearances for the Reds before a couple of loan games with Lincoln City, Charlton Athletic and Bristol Rovers, then playing in over two hundred and fifty games for various clubs in Finland.

Aiden Murphy - one hundred and thirteen appearances for Crewe Alexandra

Mark Todd - seventy appearances for Wolverhampton Wanderers and sixty-four with Rotherham United

Paul Harvey - moved back to his native Scotland and played for ten Scottish league sides over the following twenty years.

Karl Goddard - seventy-two appearances for Bradford City

Dennis Cronin - played briefly for both Stockport County and Crewe Alexandra before moving to non-league Northwich Victoria

A crowd of 7,602 watched the game; the crowd pretty much split 50/50. Whilst United's faithful occupied the Main Stand, City's more vocal support occupied the seats above what was the away fans terrace under K Stand.

United's players had enjoyed the luxury of reaching the final on 11th April – a whole thirteen days before the first leg final game, compared to City's forty-eight hour turn around from second leg semi-final, to first leg final games, yet self-belief in the City camp was high, as Ian Scott describes.

"We had every confidence of winning the game because in those days we beat United all the time in the reserves and youth team games. We were not big headed but we just felt we had enough if we played to our true potential. We were not fazed by the stadium because we had played there and won many times."

24TH APRIL. FA YOUTH CUP FINAL, FIRST LEG. MANCHESTER UNITED 1 MANCHESTER CITY 1 (ATTENDANCE 7,602)

City: Crompton, Mills, Hinchcliffe, Brightwell, Redmond, Thackeray, White, Moulden, Lake, Scott, Boyd. Sub. Macauley

United: Walsh, Gill, Martin, Scott, Gardner, Bottomley, Murphy, Todd, Cronin, Wilson (Hopley), Harvey. Scorer - Lake (penalty)

The evidence of the first leg is that City look the better team. But for the splendid goalkeeping of Gary Walsh, a fine prospect for the Reds, the odds could easily have been tilted a little further in the Blues direction for tonight's return.

Fears that the first leg would arrive too quickly for City after an exhausting extra time decider against Arsenal only 48 hours earlier proved to be unfounded. Long time among the hot favourites to win the Cup, the buoyant Blues were swift into action and a telling cross from David Boyd in the first minute deserved a better finish from David White, so often a menace but on this night less than his best.

But it was United who got to grips with the early stages and through the midfield influences of Jon Bottomley were ruling the exchanges. Steve Crompton was tested to the extreme by a David Wilson effort (10th) and the 'keeper was extended by the home team's Ian Scott (30th) as United seemed the likeliest scorers.

Apart from a Paul Lake attempt (20th) which gave the first indications of Walsh's goalkeeping talents, the Blues were slowly finding their feet. It was through good work between Andy Hinchcliffe and Boyd operating the left flank, and the non-stop input of Lake, that City began to emerge from their difficulties.

Paul Moulden shot wide (35th) and brought Walsh to a spectacular diving save (40th) with an edge-of-the-box shot which looked like breaking the deadlock.

There weren't many complaints, apart from the biased, at the 0-0 look at half time, though United had started the livelier. Hinchcliffe made a thrilling run down the left flank after the restart and smacked the ball across for Moulden, who looked like having a sitter at his mercy since he only faced 'keeper Walsh. But the City striker hurried his effort and shot past the post.

United were ahead in the 49th minute when the smart Bottomley converted a good opportunist goal with his left foot. Ten minutes later there might have been desperate problems for the Blues when Crompton threw out a careless ball to Steve Mills, which was pounced on by Harvey. 2-0 seemed on the cards - until Crompton redeemed his boob by saving at the expense of a corner.

The crowd warmed to the commitment and passion of the players. It was just a pity that in the 69th minute it got a little over-boiled and United's Murphy and City's Andy Thackeray were ordered off by the referee following a skirmish resulting from a heavy tackle by Murphy.

United were now back peddling, introducing sub Tony Hopley, and City were good bets to equalise. Except that time was running out and the Blues cause wasn't helped when Lake missed a gilt edged opportunity from a White pass (75th). Moulden brought more brilliance from Walsh (78th) until justice was done with 8 minutes to go. United's Scott was judged, quite rightly, to have handled in his area and the Blues were given a penalty.

Even at this stage Walsh almost thwarted the moment. Lake slammed his spot kick well, but Walsh dived to his right and blocked it. Fortunately for City, Lake was quickly following up and smashed home the rebound.

City showed none of the weariness which attacked tired legs in extra time against Arsenal two days earlier. They were full of vigour and good ideas with the defence in solid form and Ian Brightwell especially cutting an imposing figure. He was top of the City hits while the attacking pair also produced good work.

It was in midfield where City were below par, often taking second best to Bottomley's endeavours for United. Both goalkeepers were alert to the problems, though Walsh was the name on all the lips at the end of another excellent 'derby' between the clubs. His heroics are an indication of the superiority which City finally exerted and it would have been reasonable had City built up a worthwhile lead for the second meeting tonight.

Star Man: Ian Brightwell (City)........Gary Walsh (United)

Steve Redmond: "We should have won that first leg by two or three goals, it was only an excellent performance by Gary Walsh that really kept United in the game – but we were very confident of finishing the job in the second leg."

David White: "I had a nightmare in the first game at Old Trafford. I felt physically tired and mentally drained. It was only two days after we'd beaten Arsenal after extra time and I just couldn't do a thing right."

Ian Brightwell: "We went to Old Trafford in the first leg and the pitch was dreadful. I knew if we got a result there then we'd be able to beat them at Maine Road, especially as we knew they weren't as good as Arsenal."

Once more, manager Tony Book was complimentary in his review of the game that appeared in the Second leg match programme. "I think we all had the fear that the first test in the final against United would come too quickly after one hundred and twenty minutes and the penalty climax of the tie against Arsenal forty-eight hours earlier. I thought our team might be tired and could be caught because of it. But it didn't happen that way – we were as strong as they were in the final twenty minutes, a great tribute to character in this City side."

Book's counterpart at United, Eric Harrison, admitted to Book after the match that at halftime, he had urged his players to maintain the same pace as the first half, in belief that the City boys would not be able to sustain the energy levels required to keep up with the Reds. Book clearly acknowledged the toll that the end of season had taken on his boys. "The number of games we've had packed together in a short space of time has applied the pressure and been quite exhausting. In the space of nine days our lads played two testing semi-finals against Arsenal, the last one going to an extra half-hour. There's also been the first leg of the final, a Lancashire League match at Southport and for some of the youngsters there has been a commitment in the reserves – and Steve Redmond has played two first team matches. It has not been easy. Too much too quickly."

27th April. John Bookbinder starts his first full reserve game in a 3-0 defeat at Nottingham Forest. The second leg of the Youth Cup Final was just two days away and interestingly all three of the 'subs' in the squad - Bookbinder, John Clarke and Steve Macauley - were in the starting line-up for the one and only time together, alongside a trialist with the name David Cameron! Having played in the Second Leg of the semi-final and an unused sub during the First leg Final at Old Trafford, Macauley must have been the favourite to wear the No 12 shirt again in two days' time – however, a freak incident put paid to any hopes he had of making the bench, as the unlucky centre half recalls the moment that put him out of the final. "I played against Nottingham Forest in between the two legs, I think it was on the Sunday, and unfortunately clashed heads with Garry Birtles – the black eye is there to see on the celebration photos! It completely closed for a few days and yes, I was very disappointed to miss out as a result. However, I personally didn't feel like there was any competition between the two John's and myself as they were both playing in different positions to me, the changes made were always tactical."

29th April. City once again fielded an unchanged side - as they had done for all of their previous eight FA Cup games on the road to the reaching the second leg of the final - with only the substitute changing. This time, the unavailable black-eyed Steve Macauley, unused during the first leg, was swapped for John Bookbinder.

John Clarke: "I was upset about being left out of FA Youth Cup final squad, as a player the main thing is to be in the first eleven and in those days it wasn't like today with rotation of players or three subs, it was mainly the same eleven and if you weren't in the first eleven it was difficult to break into it and even harder when you didn't see eye to eye with the manager."

United made one change, the impressive Jon Bottomley being replaced by Karl Goddard. The attendance of 18,158 for a Tuesday evening was a decent turn out when considering the size of the crowds that the first team was attracting at the time (ignoring the frequent accusations that the attendance figures were being fiddled by the club at the time!). The final three home games of the season, all Saturday games, attracted the following comparative crowds: 5th April, Arsenal 19,590 - 19th April, Nottingham Forest 19,715 - 3rd May, Luton Town 20,361 – although it must be mentioned that there was also a sizeable support to cheer on the visitors.

In fact, it is fair to say the size of the crowd caught City by surprise. Previous FA Youth Cup games had all fans housed in the Main Stand, but for the final, the Main Stand and the vast Kippax Terrace was being used for City fans, with the corner section reserved for away fans in the Kippax and the Platt Lane stand being opened for the estimated 2,000 United fans. It was clear outside the ground just before kick-off - especially seeing the queues outside the Main Stand - that the seated stand would have too many fans trying to access it than it could possibly hold. Indeed, as the game kicked off, fans were being marshalled around the outside of the playing surface from the Main Stand and into the hastily opened North Stand. It would be well into the first half when the stream of Blues transferring from one stand into the other came to an end, as the North Stand filled up throughout that time.

It was a busy time for Steve Redmond, juggling first team duties with skippering the youth team. Redmond had to endure playing seven games in seventeen days, including one with thirty minutes extra time and penalties! Having played at Ipswich for the first team on the 12th April and then the First leg of the Youth Cup semi-final away at Arsenal on the 16th, he was also involved three days later in the first team home game with Nottingham Forest. Then came a ridiculous three games in five days as the second leg of the Youth Cup at home to Arsenal (including extra time and penalties) on the 22nd was immediately followed by the First leg of the Youth Cup Final at Old Trafford on the 24th and the League game away at Newcastle United on the 26th. Three days later, the second leg of the Youth Cup Final was held on the 29th at Maine Road.

The Blues also had to rearrange a first team fixture away at West Ham before the season ended. The game was rescheduled for 28th April, a Monday night and the night before the second leg of the Final. Thankfully, Redmond was rested from duty for the game, which City lost 1-0. It ended his run of eight consecutive first team games, which started by partnering Kenny Clements in the 2-2 draw at Old Trafford and then lining up alongside Mick McCarthy the following day in the Full Members Cup Final defeat against Chelsea at Wembley. Including England Youth games, Redmond played in sixty-one games throughout the season but as the player himself recalls, "'To be honest, it was great - you think I'd be knackered but the excitement of it all just carried me through - I'm aged eighteen and playing in the first team at Maine Road, Old Trafford and Wembley and in Youth Cup Semi-Finals and Finals. I wasn't complaining. I had no idea I'd played in sixty-one games until you mentioned it - can you imagine that happening today with a player?"

The heavy schedule on all of the young bodies had clearly been recognised by the management, much to the delight of the squad. "During the time between the first and second legs, Tony Book and Glyn Pardoe took the squad to a hotel in Manchester and we had a sauna and a Jacuzzi," recalls Ian Scott, "now we did start to feel like we had made it! This was a real treat in them days, we really felt like royalty."

JUNIOR BLUES NEWS

We have the lyrics ... can you supply the music? Mrs. Pat Carter, (JB parent) of 3 Woodlinn Walk, Harpurhey sent the following to the Junior Blues Office and we think it would be great if someone could come up with music to make it into a song ...

GOING BANANAS by Pat Carter

1. We have a mascot
   That no-one else has got
   You make not think it's brilliant
   You may not think it's hot

CHORUS:
   We've all gone bananas
   Bananas are the best
   So everybody get one
   And join in with the rest

2. We're very proud of our mascot
   Because of what it's done
   It's put the pleasure back in football
   And brought back all the fun
   Repeat Chorus

3. So we're waving our bananas
   Backwards, to and fro,
   Singing and swinging
   Happy as we go.
   Repeat Chorus

4. This craze has hit Maine Road
   Like a bolt from the Blue
   So come on down to the Ground
   There's one waiting there just for you
   Repeat Chorus

(Please contact Mrs. Carter direct)

Banana trees at the recent J.B. Panto—Paul Moulden and Nigel Gleghorn are joined by Junior Blue Chris Heywood.
(Pic: Manchester Evening News).

The January JB meeting is TOMORROW at the City Social Club, 10.15 a.m. Admission is free for members with current season's membership cards, 50p for non-members and parents.

Lucky pantomime programme numbers again are **14, 58, 116,** and **183,** so if you hold any of these programmes, bring them along to tomorrow's meeting and collect your prize.

For details of how to join the Junior Blues, please send s.a.e. to Mrs. Jessie Ward, at the Junior Blues office at Maine Road.

Sponsored by **HYDE GROUP LTD.** the complete *PRECISION ENGINEERED* package *DRIVEN by PROJECT MANAGEMENT*

29TH APRIL. FA YOUTH CUP FINAL, SECOND LEG
MANCHESTER CITY 2 MANCHESTER UNITED 0
(ATTENDANCE 18,158)
AGGREGATE SCORE CITY 3 UNITED 1

City: Crompton, Mills, Hinchcliffe, Brightwell, Redmond (captain), Thackeray, White, Moulden, Lake, Scott, Boyd. Sub Bookbinder.

United: Walsh, Gill, Martin, Scott, Gardner (captain), Harvey, Murphy, Todd, Cronin, Wilson (Hopley), Goddard.

Scorers – Boyd, Moulden

FINALLY MADE IT!

After waiting 33 years for the privilege of parading the FA Youth Cup prize, another 84 minutes of patience shouldn't have mattered a great deal at Maine Road last Tuesday night. But it did. Because Manchester United, fluent at football but puny on power, wouldn't easily let go of their chance to be winners (it would have been the 7th time in the reds history) in this second and deciding leg of the Final after a 1-1 meeting 5 days earlier.

As early as the second minute the bonny Blues staked their claim to win this prestige competition for the very first time in club history. Moulden, who has a devastating routine of twists and tight turns, corkscrewed the United defence deep inside the penalty area on the right hand side. His hither and thither jink opened the space and his cross looped over the goalmouth where David Boyd rose to it with a firm header which was well-directed and just about one of the few things that threatened all night to beat the superb goalkeeping of Gary Walsh.

It was a thrilling send off for City, hot favourites for the occasion. But they had to survive another 84 minutes, some of it edge-of-the-seat stuff, before securing the second goal that made them sure of the success for which they have worked so hard to achieve since the Cup campaign was launched last November.

Appropriately, it was a classic finish. Moulden, the one City attacker always in the picture, played a deadly through ball to White bursting through the middle. The winger struck his shot fiercely, the defiant Walsh responded with more excellence as he blocked the ball - but Moulden's nimble mind had kept ticking over and the striker was streaking onto the loose ball and swiftly steered it low in to the net from 6 yards out. For the first time there was no way back for United. And they knew it.

They were two glorious goals, taking the Cup tally to 27 from 9 games. Yet thousands of fans missed City's jubilation at the flying start. For 20 minutes into the match a huge queue of fans snaked out of the packed Main Stand to take seats in the North Stand, used as an overflow - but a constant flow of people being shepherded along the touch-line must have been an unsettling sight for youngsters trying hard to calm early edginess.

The response to this Final had been staggering, 18,158 watched the match, gate receipts approached £28,000, and while the tie never acclaimed the classic standard of the first leg it had plenty of 'oohs' and 'aaahs' for an enthusiastic audience.

In a nut-shell, City looked the likelier winners because they had strength to go with their style. Moulden always looked a good leader of the line, especially in wider positions; Thackeray, later to pay a cruel price for being sent off in the first leg, provided substance in midfield; and rising head and shoulders above all the young performers was Brightwell at the heart of City's defence, a cavalier in action, a just-18 year old playing with the innocence of youth and displaying a certainty of mind and a sure-footedness in everything he did.

It summed up the kind of presence he imposed in the 40th minute when he made one rampaging run of 40 yards which split United asunder. And Brightwell capped it with a blistering 25 yarder which the very wonderful Walsh tipped over the top.

City found left winger Goddard a perplexing customer, prodding in passes and chipping in crosses which often unhinged the Blues. United's football was of better quality but the power didn't compare.

There were see-saw moments. Brightwell cleared a menacing Goddard cross (6th), Scott blocked a distance shot from the winger (13th) while at the other end Boyd headed over from a Mills cross (10th), White just failed to convert a spidery leg with Moulden's left flank cross (14th) and 'keeper Walsh got his arm to a Boyd attempt following a White cross from a quick free kick.

There were four serious occasions when City might have lost the lead. A bad goal-kick from Crompton(18th) had Hinchcliffe grappling desperately to stop Wilson breaking clear and City's full back was booked for spinning his opponent round... Cronin passed up a penalty area gift (30th) after being chipped in by Goddard, the striker slicing wide of the post... Mills whipped the ball off City's line (37th) after a deadly Wilson shot from a Cronin corner... and Mills again performed heroics in heading off his line from a Wilson attempt after Murphy had headed on from a corner.

Meanwhile, Walsh was putting up the shutters in United's goal. He got his arm to an effort from Boyd to deflect it wide (17th)...two minutes from the interval he blocked White's bid when Moulden's piercing pass got the winger through...the 'keeper spread himself to great effect as Boyd homed in following Lake's very cute back heel in the box (53rd)...and there were eye-catching snatch saves from dangerous crosses from Moulden (65th) and Hinchcliffe (72nd) at full stretch. Additionally, White pushed off Martin to take control of a Moulden pass and rasped a shot which hit the side-netting and Scott's drive was stopped at the foot of the near-post by Walsh (72nd).

White, always capable of skipping the quite fantastic, found it difficult to maintain involvement while Boyd on the other flank was not firing effectively enough either, as United's full backs showed their passion.

Redmond led his lads into a period of supremacy as the second half wore on, though there was still a juddering shot from Goddard (80th) which rocked Crompton a few feet back on his heels. As he has been throughout the tournament, Crompton was safe and sound as proved by his record of only six goals conceded in the 9 ties.

It was not vintage young Blues, but it was good enough, it was worthy enough, to win the trophy which City started chasing back in 1953-54. United had made it a stiff test.

As Redmond led his team to receive the trophy, cheered by ecstatic City fans, they were scenes to remember. But it was also a sad sight to see Thackeray refused the honour of collecting a medal, punishment for his dismissal from the first leg.

Thackeray was consoled by members of the City staff but they were painful minutes, a stricture too severe to be imposed on any player who had battled his heart out for the cause, leaving a scar that may never be completely healed on a player so young. FA discipline at its barmiest, one might think. City will apply for the midfielder to receive a medal without ceremony at a later occasion.

Thackeray was first to be handed the trophy as the players assembled for their well-earned lap of honour. Hand-shakes all round - and special memories for one man, youth and reserve team coach, Tony Book, who had skippered City to same triumphs at the height of their post-war eminence in the late sixties. This Youth Cup achievement ended 10 years of silverware famine (minor competitions apart) despite some close calls.

For Book, his coaching colleague Glyn Pardoe, youth team aide John Collins - the kind of back-room worker no club should be without - and even dressing room caretaker Jimmy Rouse, this was time for champagne, cheers and tears. Along with members of the scouting staff, led by chief scout Ken Barnes, City were back amongst the celebrations.

The players certainly enjoyed the lap of honour, heading out from the players tunnel and turning right, taking the applause from the Main Standers' and heading towards Platt Lane – where the remaining United fans were goaded by the City players, (who were moving quickly to avoid a couple of thrown objects!) shaking the trophy in their direction. Then came the Kippax's turn to congratulate the team. The long, slow walk down the length of the pitch seemed to go on forever as the players lapped up the applause they so richly deserved, with the Kippax choir in full voice honouring the Boy Blues and their fantastic achievement, singing songs normally reserved for the first team. After the team had reached the end of the Kippax terrace, the fans patiently waiting in the North Stand finally got their turn to acknowledge the players performance and victory, before the final leg of the lap of honour took in the other half of the Main Stand before reaching the tunnel. Before heading down the tunnel, the team took one more turn and faced the Kippax triumphantly before heading back into the changing room, where the celebrations continued.

Ian Scott: "The thing I remember most about the night was the fact that the stadium was packed. I believe that there were around 18,000 fans in and after twenty minutes the stewards were still moving fans around the stadium by marching them around the track next to the pitch. I don't think anybody had imagined that the game would catch the imagination as it did. It was the greatest feeling to have won the FA Youth Cup with a group of lads that you had been with since fifteen years old and worked with and played with every day for the past two years. We all felt very proud and privileged at being part of such a fantastic achievement. It was a great time for us all. We shared a special moment in time that can never be taken away and will live with us forever."

David Boyd: "The game had only just kicked off and fans were streaming down the track as the ball went out wide, then the cross came in and as I stooped to head the ball home, momentum took me towards the touchline with all the crowd stopping in their tracks to celebrate. My dad had brought a bus load down from Scotland and they had only just got to their seats in the Main Stand as I scored!"

Andy Thackeray: "When the final whistle blew, after the initial hugging each other and shaking hands with United's players, we went over to the Main Stand where we would receive the trophy. I was stopped by an FA official and prevented from going up into the stand to collect a tankard with the lads. I had no idea this was going to happen until the FA official approached me, nothing was said beforehand. I just had to stand there and watch my team mates go up without me, I was devastated. I never did get a Youth Cup winners tankard! City later appealed on my behalf, but the FA were adamant that the decision would not be reversed. So instead, City bought me an inscribed watch, a nice touch – but it was never the same, although I still proudly have the watch today!"

Steve Redmond: "I couldn't wait to get up into the stand and receive the trophy. We had to go down the tunnel and up some stairs that brought us out into the director's box. I looked around at the fans in the ground cheering us all on. It was said there was 18,000 there, which was a joke as there was obviously more there that night. I was first in line and collected the trophy - an amazing experience and fantastic feeling as I turned and lifted the trophy aloft as the crowd let out an almighty cheer. The rest of the team collected their tankards and off we set on the lap of honour."

Paul Moulden: "Mine - and I hope the rest of the lad's - biggest disappointment was not beating United by more goals in the final. On paper we were worth four or five goals better than them but Walshy played a stormer in both games for them and managed to keep us at bay. For this and the previous season, the thing we had most was that as a group of lads we were winners. Really all we needed was a bit of luck and we could have won it two years on the run. The teams we played must have wondered what had come to town and I had the best job of all - scoring goals in front of a lot of very good team mates."

Steve Mills: "The biggest thing we had to overcome was their keeper Gary Walsh who was brilliant in the first leg. The second leg was a blur. I'm sure we played some great football but I don't remember much of it. The crowd were fantastic – you'll know the attendance, I don't. I recall doing a high-five in front of the Kippax with Ian Brightwell after the game and immediately regretting it when cramp struck."

David White: "The finals were a lot easier than the semis against Arsenal and we thoroughly deserved our win. In hindsight I think we were best team the year before and Arsenal were that year."

Andy Hinchcliffe: "Arsenal were the only side who really gave us a problem during that Cup run so once we got past them we knew United wouldn't be able to contain us. The huge crowd at Maine Road for the second leg spurred us on."

Steve Crompton: "The second leg was unbelievable. Maine Road was almost full on 3 sides – about 18,000 we were told, but it felt like more. I remember us scoring early in the game. United's goalkeeper was Gary Walsh and he had an absolute blinder in both legs. We battered them in both games and I think we deserved to win the final. The feeling going up to get the cup was brilliant, and we celebrated in the changing room afterwards with Skip, Glyn, and Paul Power. Afterwards a few of the lads went out for a few drinks with our girlfriends to celebrate and come down from the high."

Ian Brightwell "The second leg was incredible. The "official" attendance was 18,000 but I'm sure Bernard Halford had used his Abacus to calculate the number - either that or the turnstile counters must have been switched off because I swear there was way more fans than that! The atmosphere was electric, something I hadn't experienced before and the City fans went berserk when Boydy scored after a few minutes. We were comfortable for the rest of the game and I even had a couple of surging runs forward from centre half only to be denied by the United keeper Gary Walsh. Paul Moulden finished the game off for us and we had won the FA Youth Cup for City for the first time. I was then - and still am - proud of that achievement.

Paul Lake: "The post-match dressing room was awash with cheers and tears as we celebrated our win, the lads singing tunelessly and bouncing up and down with our arms around each other's shoulders. But what pleased me most that night was the look of sheer delight on Skip's face. I was so chuffed for him, Ken and Glyn, as their commitment and dedication had finally paid off."

In Paul Lake's autobiography, he detailed the winning bonuses the team members received each round, on their way to lifting the trophy, totalling £56:

First Round £2 win £1 draw
Second Round £2 win £1 draw
Third Round £3 win £1.50 draw
Fourth Round £4 win £2 draw
Quarter-Final £5 win £2.50 draw
Semi Final £15 win
Final £25 win

30TH APRIL - *THE MANCHESTER EVENING NEWS*

OUR BRAVE NEW WORLD - PETER SWALES

Chairman Peter Swales forecast a brave new world for Manchester City today, in wake of the club's FA Youth Cup Triumph.

"We have a bright future no doubt about it" said Swales who watched the Boy Blues beat United last night to lift the cup for the first time.

Swales said: "The lads were magnificent and with all respect to the United lads who took defeat so well, there has been no-one side in the tournament which has looked like beating us. We have the best youngsters in the country and if they develop as hoped our loyal fans can look forward to much better things."

This success has ended several traumatic years and is the reward for the new path we took after all the big spending. We decided to concentrate on rearing our own stars. It was a difficult task because it required great patience, but now we can reap the benefits.

HEROIC

More than 18,000 watched City beat United 2-0 in the second leg of the final at Maine Road with goals from David Boyd and Paul Moulden. The First leg was a draw at Old Trafford. It could have been more but for a heroic display from United goalkeeper Gary Walsh.

Moulden, Andy Hinchcliffe, and Steve Redmond leave soon for the England Youth tour of China. Two other City players who have progressed through the juniors, Andy May and Paul Simpson, have won England Under-21 recognition this season.

Swales added: "The potential is there and everyone at the club is excited about what the future might hold. We have some of the best young players this club has ever had."

Manager Billy McNeill said: "It was a marvellous night for Manchester football in general because it showed that both clubs have great youth potential, I'm absolutely delighted that the youth policy we have established in recent years has borne fruit. And tribute must be paid to Tony Book and Glyn Pardoe who have been dedicated to bringing these youngsters on."

First May. Just two days after the second leg of the Youth Cup Final, amazingly seven of the twelve on duty in the final are in the reserves side that (not surprisingly) lost 3-0 away at Derby County. Mills, Brightwell, White, Lake, Scott and Boyd started, with Bookbinder once more on the bench, coming on to replace Lake. The other two squad members – Macauley (now without the black eye) and Clarke were also in the starting line-up and the game was also notable as being the one and only time where both Paul Lake and his elder brother Mike (who appeared six times throughout the season on trial) played alongside each other for City. Eric Nixon and Jamie Hoyland were the other two players in the team.

5th – 13th May. Andy Hinchcliffe, Steve Redmond and Paul Moulden travel to China with the England Youth Team to play in the International Youth Tournament.

Hinchcliffe and Moulden played in the first, third and fourth games, with Redmond playing in all four. (5th) China 1-0, (7th) Thailand 1-2, (11th) France 1-1 (Moulden), (13th) Brazil 1-2. Future Blue Carl Bradshaw was also on the tour.

Steve Redmond: "That trip was surreal; I'd never seen so many bikes in my life! We had plenty of time to ourselves; it wasn't just training and playing. We went to the Great Wall and also to Tiananmen Square. Everywhere we went we had to wear England tracksuits, so obviously we had to behave ourselves!"

Interestingly, all three City players did make the trip - with City's manager Billy McNeill revealing in programme notes a few weeks before that the FA may have to do without their services.

"It's unfortunate that the way the season has panned out, there may be the need to disappoint the England Youth selectors when they tidy up their plans for an end of season tour to China. In all probability, we will have commitments in the FA Youth Cup, the Lancashire FA Youth Cup as well as a backlog of Junior team fixtures. It may not be practical to release England candidates like Steve Redmond, Andy Hinchcliffe as well as Paul Moulden for the far flung tour.

"I would love to co-operate with the selectors but I also have to look at City's priorities too and I can anticipate a tug-of-war developing for the services of this trio who have been in England's Youth planning this season."

LANCASHIRE YOUTH CUP

The fixture congestion had ended the youth team's chances of lifting another trophy. Having beaten Oldham Athletic in the record breaking 12-0 first round victory back in October, a semi-final and final proved to be impossible to fit in.

However, still keen for the competition to be completed, the Lancashire FA decided to hold the semi-final and final in August - deemed as being in the following season, so the majority of the FA Youth Cup winning side were ineligible to play. As a result, a more youthful looking City side took to the field away at Blackpool on 13th August, losing their grip on the trophy that had been held for the past four seasons, being defeated 3-1 with Jason Beckford grabbing the consolation goal.

LANCASHIRE 'A' LEAGUE CHAMPIONS

15th May. The Lancashire 'A' League would conclude in a victorious and abrupt fashion! City were crowned Champions for the first and only time after a 2-0 home win against Burnley 'A' (Beckford and White supplying the goals).

Eight of the Cup squad were on the team sheet - Crompton, Mills, Macauley, Scott, White and Brightwell, with Thackeray and Clarke unused subs.

As a result, the remaining three games - at home to Liverpool 'A' and home and away games against Manchester United 'A' - were not played as they were deemed unnecessary! All three games were 'awarded' a 1-1 draw to complete the league table.

The FA Youth Cup run and bad weather in the winter had meant a number of games were postponed and to catch up, City had to play a ridiculous six games in thirteen days - on May 3rd (South Liverpool reserves away), 7th (Alsager College away), 9th (Crewe Alexandra reserves away), 11th (Barrow reserves away), 13th (Morecambe reserves away) and 15th (Burnley 'A' home)

The season's statistics were very impressive. From the thirty-three games played, City won all but one - a 'shock' 4-1 home defeat by South Liverpool reserves being the only blot on the record.

There were two 9-0 wins (one taking revenge on South Liverpool reserves

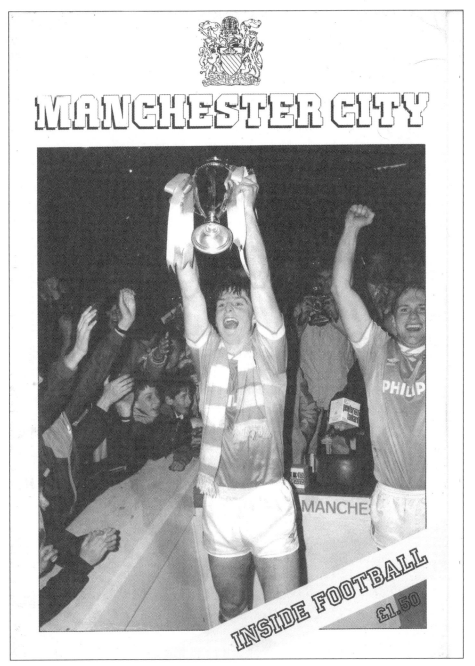

for their earlier win!) and an 8-1, 8-2, 6-1 and a 6-2 win, with the majority of the other games almost averaging four goals a game.

However, the final two 'A' team games would present a different statistic for three of the youth team Boy Blues. David Boyd and John Bookbinder (coming on as sub) appeared in the penultimate game at Morecambe, with Andy Thackeray remaining on the bench in the final game against Burnley. This would be the last time their names would appear on a City team sheet and the last time they would pull on the sky blue shirt of Manchester City. From the high of a Youth Cup Final triumph - the culmination of two years hard work - to the heart-breaking reality and despair of the rejection of a professional contract in just over two weeks.

David Boyd: "I had a one on one with Billy McNeill. I knew it was coming but it still didn't really soften the blow. No matter how well I played or how many goals I scored in the second half of my second year, I never got a look in, especially in the reserves. Even when we had lots of injuries virtually everyone got a chance before me. I think the three of us were told within a day or two of each other. I stayed around for about a week or so though John Bookbinder left the digs to go home a bit quicker than I did. There was no farewell drink (that I recall) or any big drama about leaving. It seemed just like one of those yearly occurrences as the previous year we'd seen team mates leave in the same manner too, such as Colin Finlinson and fellow Glaswegian Gary Docherty."

Andy Thackeray: "Unfortunately, I was released after we had won the Youth Cup. I was told in strange circumstances by the manager Billy McNeill and Jimmy Frizzell. I was on boot room duty, cleaning the first team players boots, when I was told to go to the sauna to see the manager. So in I go, me in full training gear, the manager with just a towel around his middle. Ten minutes later after the uncomfortable conversation, I was back in the boot room, gutted and sweating like a pig. It was very surreal."

Susan Bookbinder: "John, understandably, was devastated - but in true Bookbinder fashion, he had to have the last word! When informed of his release, he told Billy McNeill 'I am going out there to prove you wrong' and walked out the door".

The first break up of the squad was also a difficult time for the players remaining at Maine Road.

Steve Redmond: "We all heard Peter Swales saying 'we are the future etc.' and two weeks later three are out the door. Looking back I can understand why now, but at the time it left a bad taste in the mouth. They weren't just our team mates, they were our friends."

David White: "The biggest disappointment was losing my best mate Andy Thackeray immediately on the back of the Youth Cup. A few of us went off to Ibiza and I remember a very emotional night when it hit home to us that after the holiday Andy was going to have to go home and find a new club. The following years when others were released were less stressful, simply because of the passage of time and new players and team mates had come in."

Andy Thackeray: "The memories of that group of team mates go on and on and the friendships - even now as middle aged men - are on-going, even though we may not see each other as often as we should."

Clearly the remaining teenage Youth Cup winners had impressed manager Billy McNeill and a handful were included on end of season tours to Nigeria and Canada and the US.

David White: "I came on as sub during the first team tour of America. We were playing Hollywood Kickers. Within two minutes Ian Brightwell passed me the ball and determined to make an impression I passed the ball down one side of the left back and ran down the inside. I was a mile quicker than him and it looked an easy enough job to catch up with the ball and cross to Mark Lillis to claim an assist. My legs gave way and I went arse over tit and my right thigh had a horrendous graze on it. As I got up I noticed I had tripped on a length of Astroturf which had been laid over the pitch like a carpet. I couldn't believe my eyes when I peeled it back to reveal what seemed like a massive sand pit! The long jump pit was only on the pitch covered by Astroturf! Just what you need as a flying winger trying to impress."

That summer, as White mentioned, a handful of the lads went on holiday to Ibiza where the chance to unwind, relax and enjoy themselves after the exhausting but successful season had ended.

"The Ibiza trip was great," remembers Steve Mills. "I used to get stick for my gear from all the lads. A guy in Rotherham market used to make baggy suits for forty-five quid. Kind of Miami Vice, with a South Yorkshire twist. So I'd get out my new suit – sleeves rolled up, vest and espadrilles on and would be ready for a night out in San Antonio. Reddo and all the others would be verbally abusing my gear all night. Anyway, I met a couple of girls who asked me to go to Ibiza Town with them the night after. So, the next evening off I go with them, dumping the lads very quickly in case they cocked up my chances. I think we went to Ku and Space. I got back to San Antonio late morning and can't afford any more taxis so set off walking back to our apartments. I notice two figures in the distance staggering home. I'm walking a bit more quickly than them so I'm catching them up. As I get closer I'm thinking, wow, those guys look cool, great gear they've got on. Eventually I get close enough to recognise who it was – Reddo and Brighty proudly wearing my gear!"

Steve Redmond: "Guilty as charged!"

PLAYER COMBINED APPEARANCES - 1985-86

	FIRST TEAM	RESERVES	'A' TEAM	YOUTH CUP	TOTAL
JOHN BOOKBINDER	-	1 (2), 0	9 (5 + 4), 3	(1 + 1), 0	10 (8 +5), 3
DAVID BOYD	-	1 (1 + 1), 0	24 (2 + 3), 8	10, 4	35 (3 + 4), 12
IAN BRIGHTWELL	-	5 (+1), 0	26, 6	10, 0	41 (+1), 6
JOHN CLARKE	-	4, 0	9 (8 + 7), 0	3 (+4), 0	16 (8 +11), 0
STEVE CROMPTON	-	14, 0	32, 0	10, 0	56, 0
ANDY HINCHCLIFFE	-	24, 1	20, 1	10, 0	54, 2
PAUL LAKE	-	8 (2), 0	21 (1), 15	10, 7	39 (3), 22
STEVE MACAULEY	-	3 (+1), 0	13 (6 + 2), 1	(1 +1), 0	16 (7 + 4), 1
STEVE MILLS	-	3, 0	28 (1), 0	10, 0	41 (1), 0
PAUL MOULDEN*	1 (3 +2), 0	15 (1), 9	11 (1), 7	10, 11	37 (5 +2), 27
STEVE REDMOND†	10, 0	21, 1	14 (1), 3	10, 4	55 (1), 8
IAN SCOTT	-	5 (3 +4), 1	24 (+1), 11	10, 5	39 (3 + 5), 17
ANDY THACKERAY	-	8 (+1), 0	20 (2 + 1), 3	10, 3	38 (2 + 1), 6
DAVID WHITE	-	12 (5 + 3), 5	28, 23	10, 4	50 (5 + 3), 32

* plus 6, 0 for England Youth

† plus 4 (1), 0 for England Youth

3. ANDY HINCHCLIFFE

Born: Brooklands, Manchester, 7th February 1969

ANDY COMES FROM A FOOTBALLING FAMILY and his older brothers Alan and Richard gave him his first lessons as a kid, but all Andy can remember is being put in goal.

Spotted as a left winger with Manchester Boys Under-12's, Andy was selected whilst attending Sandilands Junior School. An athletic and energetic youngster he took little persuading to add another game to his weekly diary and began turning out with the Blue Star junior team, who were a well-known nursery side for would be City signings. He then graduated to the rugby playing school William Hulme and said "I missed my football at school, but the Blue Star games were regular".

Whilst playing for Blue Star he came to the attention of Leeds United and prior to City's offer there were overtures from Nottingham Forest but as Andy explains "No, it was always going to be City. As a lad at primary school I was a Manchester United fan, though I seldom went to the games, always preferring to play. The connection with Blue Star however changed my loyalties very quickly".

Although recruited to City's junior staff as an apprentice professional in the summer of 1985 (July 1st), he had already made his City debut in the Lancashire League at Burnley on October 6th, 1984 and signed professional terms on 13th February 1986. His impact was virtually immediate in the reserve league making his debut on August 23rd, 1985 away at Hull City and he was ever present in the 1986 FA Youth Cup winning side, which in his own words "was one of the highlights of my career".

There was talk of him being promoted to the first team at 17 but a back injury put him out for the best part of eight months and he had to wear a steel ribbed corset- "It was not the most comfortable of things and it stopped me from bending or twisting and kept my spine straight, but it did the trick," he comments. The injury kept Andy out of the spotlight and after impressing new boss Mel Machin, in the pre-season campaign of 1987-88, he came into the first team for the opening game of the season against Plymouth and became a regular at the tender age of 18. It was also during this season that he became the first City player to score in four different domestic competitions – the league and three cup competitions.

Having already won England youth honours, Andy graduated to

3. ANDY HINCLIFFE 1984-85 to 1989-90	
FIRST TEAM	134 (5), 11
RESERVES	49 (1), 0
'A' TEAM	35 (1), 1
FA YOUTH CUP	15 (3), 0
LANCS YOUTH CUP	3, 0

the under-21 team; however in July 1990 the then manager Howard Kendall transferred him from City to Everton in exchange for £200,000 and Neil Pointon. This was a move that many Manchester City supporters were severely critical of, they saw a promising prospect, a defender with a rich flair for going forward who could double as a midfielder leave in return for a journeyman.

That potential was rewarded by Glenn Hoddle, the England manager and Andy went on to win seven full England caps. After injury problems he was sold by Everton to Sheffield Wednesday but was forced to retire from playing football in March 2002, following surgery on his left knee.

Since retiring from the game Andy has been very active in the media, hosting the 'Talking Football' show on Manchester Radio station Key 103, saying. "Yes it was fantastic; I did a bit of work for GMR and then went to Key 103. I loved speaking to the fans because I'm a fan myself, just like them. In fact they were all very nice to me and not enough people came on to challenge my opinion".

He wrote a column for the official Manchester City website and became an ambassador for 'Football Aid' an organisation that aims to bring alive football dreams and ensure that you have a fantastic experience supporting those in need. He is currently a pundit for Sky.

1986-87

TOO MUCH TOO YOUNG

UNLIKE THE PLAYERS in the first team squad who were given the summer off, the younger players were not given the same luxury and spent the summer doing jobs all over the stadium as required. One such day in particular proved to be quite memorable.

Ian Scott: "Both Queen and Status Quo played a gig at Maine Road. After our duties, we spent the day looking around the changing rooms that had been turned green by Queen's road crew. They had three piece suites in there, lamps, you name it but all in green and the lights had a green shade on them. As the time got nearer to the gates opening we decided we would get the best view in the house, so out we went to the front of the stage and sat down on the pitch to await the arrival of the bands. Steve Redmond was there, but I can't remember who else was with us. All of a sudden the gates were opened and what seemed like about 20,000 people came charging towards us across the pitch from the far end of the stadium – all hell bent on being at the front. Well, we looked at each other and someone shouted 'fuck this!' – and we all got up sharpish and ran for our lives before we got trampled!"

With both the Youth Cup and Lancashire 'A' title in the trophy cabinet for the first time, and two of the squad having broken into the first team, now was the time for more of the players to progress to the next step up the ladder, in securing a regular place in the reserves and to start knocking on the door of the first team. The first target set would be the Central League title, which City had only won once back in 1977-78. The second target of aiming for the first team, would come sooner than expected.

23rd August. Ian Brightwell is a surprise name on the team sheet for the opening game of the season at home to Wimbledon. There were three debutants in Brightwell, 'keeper Perry Suckling and striker Trevor Christie. Steve Redmond joined Brightwell in the line-up as well as Andy May, Clive Wilson, Kenny Clements, Mick McCarthy, Gordon Davies, Neil McNab and Graham Baker, with Paul Simpson on the bench. A Baker brace and a debut goal from Christie gave City a 3-1 winning start to the campaign in front of 20,756 fans at Maine Road. This was Wimbledon's first game in the First Division, having only entered the Football League nine years before.

Billy McNeill had informed Brightwell the previous Monday that he would be starting the game – and he received his first booking on his debut after sending John Fashanu flying when caught off balance. But as the player recalls, "I was surprised by Fashanu's reaction. He got up straight away and tried to stop me from getting booked. He said 'leave him alone ref, he's a young lad, it's his first game'."

After a rough and tumble start against Wimbledon, Brightwell had to pinch himself that it wasn't a dream over the next two games. "We played Liverpool at Anfield, they had won the double the season before and Kenny Dalglish was player manager. They had Jan Molby, Alan Hansen, Mark Lawrenson and Ian Rush up front. They had an amazing team. Then Tottenham away and I was told to mark Glenn Hoddle – a world class footballer. It couldn't get any easier."

26th August. The reserves get off to a flying start with 5-2 home win against Leeds United with Jason Beckford (2), Steve Kinsey (2) and David White on the score sheet. Joining White in the side was Ian Scott, Steve Mills and Andy Hinchcliffe, along with Eric Nixon, the Beckford brothers, and Earl Barrett.

The following three games would see two more wins and one defeat, with Moulden grabbing two goals and Scott one, as the Blues made a decent start in the Central League campaign.

However, seven games into the season the manager Billy McNeill walked out on City to join Aston Villa, citing lack of funds from the board in his frustrations to be able to take City to the next level. The opening day win against Wimbledon had been the only success of the season, followed by four draws and two defeats. McNeill's last two games were both goalless draws – away at Oxford United and at home to Queens Park Rangers. Yet McNeill's resignation was inadvertently good news for the Class of '86. McNeill had appeared to be hesitant to unleash the young Blues into the first team – a theory David White offers a different perspective on.

"In those days there was only one sub so only thirteen players travelled to an away game. I had gone on the end of season tour to the USA and then the pre-season tour to Switzerland, but to be honest, other young players had done better than me. I tended to be in the squad for the first dozen games of the season but wasn't getting on the bench. I think we had bought Robert Hopkins from Birmingham who was playing on the right."

Paul Moulden: "As kids you do what you're told and that's that. All I and the others wanted was to play in the first team. Billy gave me that opportunity and I will always be grateful to him for that. I had then and will always have a great respect for him.

McNeill's assistant, Jimmy Frizzell, was promoted to manager and he was willing to take a chance with the kids, starting with his first game, away at Southend United in the Second round First leg League Cup game - a game where two subs were permitted!

23rd September. David White makes his debut at Roots Hall in City's third successive 0-0 draw, against Southend United in the League Cup Second Round First Leg. White (along with Moulden) came off the bench during the game (replacing the injured Brightwell). Steve Redmond was in the starting line-up.

The long journey to Essex began in a bizarre fashion - and one proud parent almost missed his son's debut!

David White: "Billy McNeill actually said his 'goodbyes' on the coach from the Fingland's depot - opposite Platt Lane on Wilmslow Road - to Bucklow Hill, where the Cheshire lads got on the bus and where Billy Mac got off! Jimmy Frizzell put me on the bench and I got on the pitch later on. My Dad had been undecided as to whether he would go all that way to the game, not knowing if I would be on the team sheet or not - but his good mate Fred Eyre told him he would never forgive himself if I made the bench - never mind the pitch - and he wasn't there. Thanks to those wise words, my Dad was there to see my debut."

24th September. A 5-2 reserves home win over Sheffield Wednesday (White 2, Moulden, D Beckford (pen), Davies) contained eight of the Youth Cup squad in the starting line-up: Crompton, Hinchcliffe, Macauley, Lake, White and Moulden (the latter two had also played the previous night at Southend), Scott and Clarke. For the majority of Central League games, there was an average of six of the Class of '86 in each game.

4th October. Having come off the bench in the previous two games (at Southend United in the League Cup and at Luton Town in a 1-0 defeat in the League) David White makes his full debut in the 2-1 home defeat against Leicester City, alongside Redmond and Moulden, Brightwell was an unused sub.

The *Manchester Evening News* match report: "...in the likes of Paul Moulden, David White, Steve Redmond, and Paul Simpson there is a solid foundation being established at Maine Road. Together with the jinking Simpson, White helped create City's goal heading clear at the near post following a Leicester corner."

David White, in an interview in a City programme just after his full debut, described his elevation to the first team as 'a dream come true'. "I knew my mum and dad and friends were there and obviously willing me to do well. I was quite pleased with my performance - you have to play to your strengths so I concentrated on using my pace rather than close ball control."

He also recalled his two substitute appearances. "At Luton I didn't really have time to get into the match (coming on with seven minutes remaining) but I was on for an hour or so at Southend because of an injury to Ian Brightwell and I really enjoyed it." Many a young player may have got carried away with themselves in similar circumstances - but White clearly had his feet on the ground. In a matter of weeks, he would be sitting his 'A' Level exams, as he explained. "At the moment, most of my spare time is taken up with studying. No great fun - but hopefully it will prove worthwhile in the future."

Despite a 2-1, second leg win over Southend United a fortnight after the First leg, Frizzell's start in the hot seat at Maine Road had a record of no wins, two draws and five defeats in his opening seven games, including exiting the League Cup away at Arsenal in the 3rd round. Frizzell took action, selling the summer signing Trevor Christie (ten games and three goals) and Robert Hopkins (who McNeill had only signed in early September and was out of the door inside six weeks having played seven games and scoring one goal.) In came experience. The much travelled striker Imre Varadi in a player exchange plus cash deal with Hopkins and journeyman midfielder Tony Grealish joining from West Bromwich Albion. A third signing was made with John Gidman crossing the city to join the Blues from Manchester United. Indeed, Grealish and Gidman made their debuts against the Reds in a 1-1 home draw on 26th October.

15th October. Paul Moulden scores four times for the reserves in an 8-1 win at home to Blackburn Rovers reserves, the other scorers were Gordon Davies (2), John Clarke and Steve Coward.

Yet the reserves were not having it all their own way. There followed a period of three defeats and a draw - including a 5-0 defeat at Goodison Park that included Crompton, Mills, Brightwell, Lake, Scott and Clarke. The substitute that night was sixteen year old Chris Coleman, who had signed for City in the summer fresh from school. Coleman had made one full reserve game appearance a month before the Everton game and was on the bench a total of four times, he also made twelve 'A' team appearances before leaving City due to homesickness - signing for his hometown club Swansea City. Coleman would eventually transfer to Crystal Palace, Blackburn and Fulham, whilst winning thirty-two International caps for Wales - the team he now manages following the death of Gary Speed.

Steve Crompton recalls Coleman's departure. "He had come up from Swansea, and seemed to be doing OK and enjoying himself. But then one day he just disappeared and we never saw him again. He got given the nickname 'Lord Lucan'! Obviously he did reappear and the rest is history."

Paul Lake: "I reckon the majority of City's youngsters benefited from Skip's autocratic approach, but it didn't suit everyone. Chris Coleman was a prime example. He didn't cope well with Skip's ruthlessness and took many of his criticisms to heart."

At times, Tony Book's style even raised the eyebrows of Ken Barnes, as he detailed in his autobiography: "Bloody hell, I'm no softie, but I can remember Tony Book tearing a strip off one of the Beckfords. The laddie was only seventeen. I said to Tony afterwards, 'Fuckin' hell Tony, you must have been one hell of a player at seventeen. Didn't you ever make a mistake then?'"

4th November. Jimmy Frizzell was rewarded with his first win - albeit in the Simod Cup - (the new sponsors name for the Full Members Cup) at home to Wimbledon. Paul Moulden hit the back of the net for the first time in the first team and added a second later in the game. Kenny Clements grabbed the other in a 3-1 win in front of 4,914 fans.

However, the rank and file support would return for the next game - at home to Aston Villa on the Saturday.

8th November. Billy McNeill brought his new team to Maine Road and everyone was desperate to get one over on him. Frizzell opted for experience, with Moulden being the only starter from the boy Blues, with White remaining on the bench. Frizzell got it right as the Blues won 3-1 with a second successive brace from Moulden and Varadi opening his account too. For Moulden, it was a very satisfactory result in front of his former manager - and a timely reminder of what he was capable of doing given the opportunity. The headline in the *Manchester Evening News Pink* that evening, was the first time the often repeated "Goalden Moulden!" headline was printed.

Adding to his four goals in two games, Moulden was on target along with Paul Simpson the following week in the 2-1 home win against Charlton Athletic and then he hit two goals in the next three games - the only goal of the game at home to Watford in the Simod Cup and in the 3-1 defeat at home to eventual league champions Everton.

The signing of Grealish had pushed Steve Redmond out of the spotlight and the return of Graham Baker meant that White too, would be fighting for his place over the first half of the season, but both would regain their place in the starting line up during the latter half of the season.

2nd December. The reserves beat Sunderland at home 3-1 to start a fourteen match unbeaten run following the trouncing by Everton, winning twelve of the games in a run stretching from 2nd December to 3rd April - when Blackburn Rovers beat City 2-1 at Ewood Park.

13th December. David White grabs his first league goal in a 3-1 home win over West Ham United. Varadi chipped in with a brace. The following week against Coventry, Steve Redmond got his name on the score sheet twice for his first goals in a 2-2 draw at Highfield Road on 20th December, where Redmond, White and Moulden started the game, with Brightwell remaining as the unused sub.

The same three players (with Brightwell again staying on the bench) took a three game winning run to Charlton Athletic on 28th December but were helpless as the blues were thrashed 5-0 at Selhurst Park.

FA YOUTH CUP

City were not expected to go too far in the competition with a relatively new team.

5TH JANUARY. FA YOUTH CUP SECOND ROUND
WIGAN ATHLETIC 2 MANCHESTER CITY 2
(ATTENDANCE 352)

Only Paul Lake and John Clarke from the Class of '86 were on the team sheet, both starting the game. Steve Mills, Steve Macauley and Andy Hinchcliffe were also eligible to play, but were all ruled out through injuries.

Of the incoming players, only Jason Beckford and David Brightwell would graduate into the first team. Paul Warhust did make the bench on one occasion before having a distinguished career with Oldham Athletic, Sheffield Wednesday, Blackburn Rovers and Bolton Wanderers. Colin Small played for Crewe Alexandra after a spell at Hyde United.

The competition now allowed two substitutes to be used in the game.

Match report - courtesy from a City match programme

City: D Williams, Small, Barnes, Cutts, Warhust (D Brightwell), Curry, J Beckford, Lake, Coward, Burns (Wallace), Clarke - Scorers - Curry, Lake.

The twice postponed tie finally got under way in dreadful conditions, City playing into a gale-force wind and driving rain. With only two members of last season's Cup-winning side eligible or available, the inexperienced Blues found life difficult after only ten minutes when Wigan striker Barry Smith hammered home a superb cross-shot. City replied briskly with John Clarke and captain Paul Lake linking well in attack and Steve Coward also unfortunate on a couple of occasions.

The Blues suffered a further setback when central defender Paul Warhurst limped off in considerable pain after 35 minutes, to be replaced by schoolboy David Brightwell, younger brother of Ian. Paul damaged ligaments in making a tackle and to add insult to injury received a booking into the bargain.

The teams took to the field for a still wet second half with Lake continuing to deputise in the back four and playing a full captain's role by his example. It was one-way traffic for the Blues for virtually the whole opening period of the second half and a deserved equaliser came in 55 minutes. Coward centred from the right and following an almighty scramble in the Wigan goalmouth, Lindsay Curry hooked the ball home.

Ten minutes later the Blues went in front when Hall, the Wigan full back handled on the line, and Lake drove home the penalty to the 'keeper's bottom left. City continued to press but as so often happens Wigan snatched an equaliser, with the best goal of the night. After a rare 83rd minute attack the ball was cleared to fullback Jason Banks who, faced with a mass of players, caught the ball exactly right to send it screaming in from 40 yards just under the bar.

Scot Willie Burns limped off 3 minutes from the end to give Mike Wallace, another schoolboy, a taste of Cup football, but the game ended in a 2-2 draw, and was a tribute to the stamina of both teams.

City Star: Paul Lake

10TH JANUARY. FA YOUTH CUP SECOND ROUND REPLAY MANCHESTER CITY 2 WIGAN ATHLETIC 1 (ATTENDANCE 348)

Again, Lake and Clarke started. On the bench as an unused sub was another future City first team player, Ian Thompstone (his only appearance on the team sheet during this campaign)

Match report - courtesy from a City match programme

City: D Williams, Small, Barnes, Cutts, Lake, Wallace (Kelly), J Beckford, Curry, Coward, D Brightwell, Clarke. Sub. Thompstone Scorers – Cutts, Coward

An unusual event, a Saturday morning Cup game at Maine Road, but a fair turn out on a bitterly cold day enjoyed a keenly-contested match. The first quarter of an hour was a nervous period for both teams, neither gaining the upper hand and with passes regularly going astray. Shortly afterwards though, 'keeper Darren Williams began a good move with a throw to Colin Small. The ball progressed to Steve Coward and then to Jason Beckford, who moved swiftly into the Wigan penalty area, but his shot was hit hastily wide.

After 24 minutes a Wigan free kick went safely out after bouncing on top of the City bar, and a minute later the Blues went in front. Beckford hit a corner to the far post, the ball was played out to Robert Cutts, and he hit it through a crowded goalmouth into the bottom corner, Coward having cleverly stepped over the ball.

Athletics' Ian Rennox almost snatched an immediate equaliser but was just wide, and City looked worthy leaders at half time.

Wigan lost the impressive Jonathan Crompton with a cut head early in the second half but continued to press with urgency, and their equaliser came after 65 minutes when, following a free kick, Andy Ainscow hit the ball low into the area and Rennox scored from six yards. A surprising lapse on the part of the Blues' defence who had played well, particularly the commanding Paul Lake. Small and Robert Barnes had also shown considerable skill in their defending.

City sub Paul Kelly came on for Mike Wallace and surprised everyone with a couple of long throw-ins which caused the Wigan defenders problems when they reached the near post. The Blues kept up the strong pressure as extra time loomed, Beckford hitting a post and Lindsay Curry finding the side netting, and their persistence paid off with seven minutes left. Beckford, now playing inside, hit a perfect through ball for Coward to run onto, and Steve made no mistake from 20 yards.

A deserved win for the City youngsters who now face a difficult tie against Newcastle United in the next round.

City Star: Paul Lake

24th January. Paul Lake makes his first team debut at Wimbledon's Plough Lane in a less than thrilling 0-0 draw in front of 5,667 fans. "Steve Redmond had already played for the first team and then slowly but surely Whitey and Ian Brightwell were also getting a taste of it. I couldn't wait for my turn," Lake recalls.

Steve Redmond played alongside Lake, as did Darren Beckford – in what would be his last start in the first team for City - joining Port Vale initially on loan, a deal made permanent in the summer. Also in the team was Peter Barnes, in the second game of his second stint at City - having joined direct from Manchester United. Barnes' return was not a success though, playing seven games this season and just one League Cup game the following season.

The *Manchester Evening News* match report noted, "There was a pleasing debut from Paul Lake who after an initial 20 minute settling in period, splendidly adjusted to the First Division's great demands bringing a pat on the back from Frizzell."

The latest of the Class of '86 to be elevated into the first team was able to reflect on his debut in an interview in a City programme a few weeks later. "It was a great thrill to turn out for the first team and I enjoyed the match. But Wimbledon are one of those hard working sides who tend to cut the midfield out and it wasn't the easiest of games to get into. Still, I think I did my bit." Lake continued in the team for the next three games - the Simod Cup defeat at home to Ipswich and two 1-1 draws away at Norwich (14th February) and at home to Luton Town (21st February).

26TH JANUARY. FA YOUTH CUP 3RD ROUND MANCHESTER CITY 2 NEWCASTLE UNITED 1 (ATTENDANCE 737)

This time, Lake and Clarke were joined by last season's Cup winners Mills and Hinchcliffe in the starting line-up both having returned from injury.

Steve Mills: "The season after winning the Youth Cup was a difficult one. I started the season with a groin problem. I was being treated for an adductor strain. So, I could just about get through a match and then had treatment all week, then play again, treatment and on it went. I won't go on about it but Lakey's book touches on the state of medical care at City. Eventually Paul Moulden pulled me to one side and quietly said he would help but it all had to be hush-hush. He took me to a physio in Bolton, which obviously was against club rules. Anyway this guy spent half an hour prodding away in my groin and told me confidently that it wasn't my adductor, it was something else. He clicked something in both ankles, knees and hips and said matter-of-factly, "OK, don't train for three days then you'll be ok." Amazingly, it worked! That was why I missed the games against Wigan Athletic."

Match report - courtesy from a City match programme

City: Williams, Melville, Barnes, Cutts, Lake, Mills, Clarke, Curry, Jason Beckford, Kelly, Hinchcliffe. Subs: David Brightwell, Small. Scorers - Melville, Lake

City started off brightly, John Clarke winning balls well in midfield, getting Jason Beckford and Lindsay Curry into good positions, and the Blues were taking control of the game when the Magpies struck. In the 23rd minute a free-kick on the City right flank was floated to the far post, where Graham Carter was waiting to head down past Darren Williams. Despite further near misses by the City strikers, United almost snatched a second when a header flashed past a post.

After excellent work by Beckford, a shot from Andy Hinchcliffe cannoned back into play off the bar, and the Blues had penalty claims turned down when Paul Kelly was bustled off the ball. A now lively City forced several corners to no avail, and

Beckford put a shot just over the bar after beating the two central defenders with a diagonal run.

Early in the second half Hinchcliffe cleared determinedly after Williams dropped the ball under pressure following a Newcastle free-kick, and in addition Andy was making some strong runs down the City left.

Newcastle's attacking threats were now sparse, thanks to the excellent work by the City defence expertly marshalled by Paul Lake, fresh from his League debut at Wimbledon, and it was the Denton youngster's forays up front which unsettled the Newcastle defence as they conceded six corners in the last 20 minutes. The Blues had the ball in the net after 72 minutes but it was disallowed for handball.

Kelly's long throws continued to cause problems, and finally the equaliser came. After 84 minutes a clearance fell to Scottish trialist full back Martin Melville, and his shot, taking a deflection en route, flew into the net from 35 yards. A night to remember for young Martin!

Then, with just three minutes left, City grabbed the winning goal.

A Lake drive was tipped onto the bar for a corner, which was cleared for a throw-in. Kelly took it and the ball eventually reached Lake, who was bursting through the middle. He beat keeper Eddie Harrison decisively in the bottom corner to give City a well-deserved victory.

The lads left it late, true, but it was a victory well fought for in a clean and sporting game which entertained an appreciative crowd. Special mention must be made of Lindsay Curry, John Clarke, and also Robert Cutts for his gritty defensive work, but it was Paul Lake who captured the limelight for his superb overall performance.

City Star Paul Lake

7TH FEBRUARY. FA YOUTH CUP 4TH ROUND
MANCHESTER CITY 2 LIVERPOOL 1
(ATTENDANCE 3,186)

Lake, Clarke, Mills and Hinchcliffe again in the starting line up

Match report - courtesy from a City match programme
City: D Williams, Mills, Hinchcliffe, Barnes, Warhurst, Melville (Small), J Beckford, Lake, Coward, Kelly, Clarke. sub. Cutts. Scorers - J Beckford, Clarke

A Liverpool side that had not conceded a goal in this competition this season, arrived full of confidence to face City's Youth team - and left with their tails between their legs.

The Blues opened confidently and gave early notice that they were no push-over, looking the more dangerous team in the early stages. After 14 minutes a super move swept the ball towards the Liverpool goal, involving Andy Hinchcliffe, Paul Lake and John Clarke, which ended with the Liverpool 'keeper punching clear, and within a minute City youngster Paul Kelly hung his head as his blasted shot sailed over an empty net.

City took the lead after 23 minutes when keeper Billy Mercer called for the ball, but it bounced over his head, and Jason Beckford was on hand to score easily. Both Beckford and Clarke had been a constant nuisance to Liverpool down the flanks.

Craig Hignett equalised for Liverpool after 36 minutes, after a move begun by Steve Staunton, continuing through Charlie Boyd, and Hignett scored with a low shot. The Reds then survived a penalty claim just before half time, when a defender appeared to handle a shot from Steve Coward.

Liverpool's forays up front were generally kept in check by a strong back four in which Andy Hinchcliffe and Paul Warhurst - playing his first game since being injured at Wigan in Round 2 - were outstanding.

Four minutes into the second half, John Clarke restored City's lead. Paul Kelly took a throw-in on the left, Paul Lake - having another splendid game - headed it on, and Clarke found the net from close range.

Beckford continued to torment the Merseysiders' defence with superb footwork and he was unlucky not to increase City's lead. Coward, too, had his moments and in the end Liverpool were lucky to get away with a 2-1 defeat.

It was unfortunate; too, that the visitors forgot their manners in the closing moments of the game, and allowed their frustration to boil over in a petulant scene, but Lake did a fine captain's job of ushering the City youngsters away from any confrontation.

An excellent performance indeed from the City Youth team, thoroughly appreciated by the 3,186 who watched it, and the prospect of another home tie versus Mansfield Town or Leeds United in the quarter-final.

City Star: Paul Warhurst

14th February. Ian Brightwell scores his first goal for the first team in a 1-1 draw with Norwich City at Carrow Road.

21st February. Paul Lake scores his first goal for the first team in a 1-1 draw at home to Luton Town. City had only won once so far in 1986 on 3rd January, at home to Oxford United – and wouldn't win until 25th April. In between, there would be six draws and eight defeats as City remained firmly at the wrong end of the table.

Paul Lake: "When I made my home debut, against Luton Town, I wanted to do so well that the nerves got the better of me. I didn't particularly enjoy the occasion because I didn't want to let anybody down. I scored but didn't play particularly well and we drew 1-1. After that I sat down and calmed myself down."

2ND MARCH. FA YOUTH CUP QUARTER-FINAL
MANCHESTER CITY 3 LEEDS UNITED 0
(ATTENDANCE 2,128)

The team was bolstered by the addition of another of the cup winning squad, with Steve Macauley joining Lake, Clarke, Mills and Hinchcliffe in the starting line-up.

Match report – courtesy from a City match programme

City: D Williams, Mills, Hinchcliffe, Macauley, Warhurst (Small), Burns, Barnes, Lake, J Beckford, Kelly, Clarke. Sub Coward. Scorers – J Beckford (2), Clarke

Our Youth team went a stage further in maintaining their grip on the FA Youth Cup when they were hosts to a brisk and lively Leeds United outfit. It was the first time that we had been able to field a Youth XI without missing players out through injury, and as well as welcoming Steve Macauley and Paul Lake back from the treatment table, City's latest signing - Willie Burns from Scotland - also appeared. Willie is the nephew of former United player, Francis Burns.

The Blues gave an early indication that they meant business in the opening minutes when Paul Kelly had a shot blocked and Macauley headed just wide, and after six minutes they drew the first blood. A move flowed from the Blues penalty area and ended with Jason Beckford bursting through the Leeds defence to see his grounded shot hit a post. He then collected and controlled the rebound before calmly hitting the ball into the bottom corner.

Leeds had a chance to equalise after 17 minutes when Peter Maguire went clear on the left and centred to Kevin Noteman. Fortunately for City, his effort was scrambled away for a fruitless corner.

After 24 minutes it was a corner which led to our second goal. The ball went to Irish youngster John Clarke who cut inside and let go a screaming left foot shot that was in the back of the net before startled defenders realised what was happening.

Then, a minute prior to half time, captain Paul Lake embarked on a run down the right wing, and his excellent cross was put away by Beckford at the far post to give City a comfortable 3-0 lead.

There were no goals in the second half but both teams had chances, Lake going near with a header 15 minutes into the half. Warhurst retired temporarily for treatment a little later, just after Robert Barnes almost increased our lead. Leeds went close after 78 minutes when Richard Annan had a shot blocked by Darren Williams' feet and Hinchcliffe cleared the ball off the line.

With five minutes left, Colin Small replaced the hobbling Warhurst and by now the game was clearly City's. They progressed to an away leg in the first semi-final at Coventry and were warmly applauded off the field by a good crowd of 2,128

City Star: Steve Mills

9TH MARCH. LANCASHIRE YOUTH CUP FIRST ROUND
MANCHESTER CITY 4 OLDHAM ATHLETIC 1

Lake, Mills, Hinchcliffe, Macauley and Clarke start as City brush aside the young Latics. Scorers - Lake 2, Jason Beckford, Kelly

25TH MARCH FA YOUTH CUP SEMI-FINAL FIRST LEG
COVENTRY CITY 1 MANCHESTER CITY 0
(ATTENDANCE 1,753)

As with the quarter final, Lake, Clarke, Mills, Hinchcliffe and Macauley started the game. Coventry City had a strong side. Both teams had reached their second successive semi-final, with the Midlander's eventually losing to Manchester United at this stage the previous year.

Match report - courtesy from a City match programme

City: D Williams, Mills, Hinchcliffe, Macauley (Curry), Warhurst, Lake, Barnes, Kelly, J Beckford, Burns, Clarke. Sub. Coward

The Youth team travelled to Coventry for the first leg of their two Youth Cup semi-finals, this one in the national competition, and came away somewhat embarrassed by their inept display.

No excuses; the team which had seen off Wigan, Newcastle, Liverpool and Leeds in the previous rounds was at full strength, and furthermore welcomed back Lindsay Curry as sub after his recent trip home to Northern Ireland.

"It was a disappointing performance" summed up Team Coach Glyn Pardoe later. "We never got anything together in the way we are capable of doing. Too many players were out of touch in the same game. The main fault lay in the passing. Many of our youngsters' moves floundered when the ball was given to the opposition, a gesture of generosity in which the City lads don't usually indulge. We also had a goal by Paul Lake disallowed early on, a mystifying decision at first. On the bench we assumed there must have been a push, presumably on their 'keeper, but the ref said afterwards that it was offside. At the time we couldn't see how."

Coventry shrugged off this irritation and proceeded to take the lead after 15 minutes. Steve Livingstone headed against the bar and City 'keeper Darren Williams was powerless to stop Howard Clark scrambling the ball home. So it was a battle from that point, not helped by our sloppy passing.

There were brief flurries of activity in the Coventry goalmouth but they never came to anything, Jason Beckford and Curry, who had come on for Steve Macauley on the hour, both had shots just past the post, but the Coventry 'keeper was never seriously troubled. Lake marshalled his forces well, however, to prevent any further setbacks.

So the stage is set for the second leg at Maine Road the following week, when the Blues have it all to do to qualify for their second successive Youth Cup Final

City Star: Paul Lake

28th March. City reserves beat United's reserves 3-1 at Maine Road, with goals from Paul Moulden, Tony Grealish and Jason Beckford. For Steve Mills - playing in between the two Youth Cup semi-final ties - it was a night to forget as he picked up an injury that ruled him out not only for the rest of the season, but ended his City career.

Steve Mills: "The reserve match against United was a turning point in my life. I was playing right back. Early on I ruptured my anterior cruciate ligament in my right knee. I don't have to tell you, the curse of footballers. Anyway, City did a patch-up job by just cutting away the split portion – not actually reconstructing it."

2ND APRIL. FA YOUTH CUP SEMI-FINAL SECOND LEG MANCHESTER CITY 1 COVENTRY CITY 0 (AGGREGATE SCORE 1-1 AFTER EXTRA TIME) (ATTENDANCE 3,792)

Steve Mills misses out through injury, with Lake, Macauley, Hinchcliffe and Clarke starting.

Match report - courtesy from a City match programme

City: D Williams, Barnes, Hinchcliffe, Macauley, Warhurst, Burns, Curry, Lake, J Beckford, Kelly (Coward), Clarke. Sub. Small. Scorer – Paul Lake

City's youth team were still in with a chance at the end of this thrilling game at Maine Road, thanks to a splendid goal from skipper Paul Lake.

Unlucky Steve Mills, awaiting a cartilage operation, missed the game through injury, so Robert Barnes switched to the full back berth, allowing stocky Lindsay Curry to return to the side.

The Blues, trailing by a goal to nil from the first leg, soon took up the reigns and attacked strongly in the first half. Both John Clarke and Curry raided effectively down the wings, but a strong Coventry defence prevented an equaliser. Willie Burns, who emerged as a midfield general on the right, went close after 25 minutes, and Paul Kelly hit the side netting after a fine Curry run.

Not that it was one-way traffic. The Midlanders were seeking a consolidating goal and Steve Livingstone had the ball in the net after 14 minutes although he was offside. Both he and Howard Clark were proving to be skilful attackers on the occasions they broke through, but smart mopping up by Andy Hinchcliffe and some alert saves by Darren Williams frustrated the visitors.

Our Blues won a series of corners in the last section of the half, none of which proved fruitful and at the other end Hinchcliffe saved the day by heading off the line after Williams was beaten by a Livingstone header which came down off the bar.

City's pressure continued after the break, Kelly shooting over after a superb run and a move involving Jason Beckford, Clarke, Lake and Curry, and at the other end the visitors wasted chances with Livingstone guilty of a bad miss after 64 minutes when, with only our keeper to beat, he shot wide.

Steve Coward then came on for Kelly, and his runs started to rattle Coventry. Keeper Paul Bostock was lectured for fouling Beckford outside the penalty area. Clarke's free-kick came off the defensive wall, wasn't properly cleared, and Lake hammered in his third goal in the competition to put the sides level on aggregate.

The Blues now had their tails up, Beckford and Hinchcliffe both going close as they fed off Burns and Lake in the middle, and Coward almost prevented extra time with an effort in the last minute as he latched onto Clarke's centre.

With better luck we could have resolved the tie in the extra half hour, as Paul Warhurst hit the bar after 92 minutes and Curry brought a great save from Bostock six minutes later. The Irish youngster also rattled the bar after a beautiful exchange of passes and a burst into the penalty area, while Coventry continued to impress with their attacking movements if not their finishing.

In the dying minutes a Hinchcliffe free-kick gave the visitors some problems, and a Burns-Beckford-Coward move came to nothing when the latter lost control.

There were bookings for Lake, Hinchcliffe (tackles) and for Burns (dissent) but the game was played in a fine spirit throughout. The visitors won the toss to stage the game the following Friday at Highfield Road.

City Star: Willie Burns

Footnote: The rules had changed from the previous season (when City and Arsenal had a penalty shoot-out) to have a third game played if aggregate scores were level after the two semi final legs.

3rd April. City's reserves had been unbeaten in their previous fourteen games (winning twelve), but lost that record, losing 2-1 away at Blackburn Rovers in a side featuring Crompton, Hinchcliffe, Moulden, Redmond and Scott with Clarke on the bench. The unbeaten run of games had taken City to the top of the Central League table.

10TH APRIL. FA YOUTH CUP SEMI-FINAL PLAY-OFF COVENTRY CITY 3 MANCHESTER CITY 0 (ATTENDANCE 2,259)

Lake, Macauley, Hinchcliffe and Clarke carried the Class of '86 flag for the final time in the FA Youth Cup.

Match report - courtesy from a City match programme

City: D Williams, Barnes, Hinchcliffe, Macauley, Warhurst, Burns, Clarke, Lake, Coward (David Brightwell), Curry, J Beckford. Sub. Small

The Youth team travelled once more to face Coventry City's youngsters, having lost the toss for the right to stage the replay.

And what a disappointing outcome on the night once the home side had taken a fifth minute lead through Paul Shepstone. The Midlanders went on to provide a solid, all round performance, eventually proving worthy winners, and reached a Cup Final just two days before their senior side beat Leeds United to clinch a place at Wembley in the 1987 FA Cup Final.

A moment of haphazard play by Jason Beckford, usually so reliable, made him lose possession in the middle of the park, and Shepstone raced forward and curled a 25 yard shot into the top corner to give Coventry that vital first break. Darren Williams atoned for this lapse by making some excellent saves in the first half to keep us in with a chance.

City stuttered along, never seriously threatening the home team and it was no surprise when Coventry increased their lead shortly after the interval through Steve Livingstone, who had impressed the previous week at Maine Road. The ball came over from the wing and Livingstone dispatched it with a precise header.

Poor defensive work generally led to the final goal, again scored by Livingstone, mid-way through the second half.

There were some late efforts from our Blues but they could only be token ones, with Coventry looking as competent as ever. Lindsay Curry kept going but lacked support, while Williams showed promise apart from some lapses.

Let's end the reports on this season's competition on a positive note. The City youngsters have done wonderfully well to get so far in the end, and deserve every credit for their entertaining football and fighting displays. Many of them have also revealed a great potential. Maybe next year....

City Star: Darren Williams

It was a tremendous effort from the Youth team again, with the notion that the side had not been expected to do as well as they did being dismissed.

Steve Macauley: "I had a fair idea we would do OK, there were five of us from the previous year and we had a good group a year younger than us coming through, including Jason Beckford, Paul Warhurst, Rob Barnes and David Brightwell."

21ST APRIL. LANCASHIRE YOUTH CUP SEMI-FINAL
BOLTON WANDERERS 2 MANCHESTER CITY 2
SCORERS - COWARD (2)
(BOLTON WANDERERS WIN 5-4 ON PENALTIES)

Only Macauley, Hinchcliffe and Clarke are in the team as City bow out of the Lancashire Youth Cup on a penalty shoot-out. This defeat meant that it was the last game that any of the Class of '86 would be eligible to appear in a youth cup competition.

3RD MAY. CENTRAL LEAGUE CHAMPIONS.

The reserve side had bounced back straight away from the defeat at Blackburn Rovers the previous month – and in style – winning the next five games (and scoring fifteen goals), the last of which, on 3rd May, was a 4-1 home win against Nottingham Forest which saw the trophy reside at Maine Road for only the second time – first won in season 1977-78.

City had nine of the Class of '86 on the team sheet. Crompton, Brightwell, Redmond, White, Lake, Moulden, Scott, Hinchcliffe and with Clarke coming off the bench. The non Class of '86' players were Andy May, Earl Barrett and Tony Grealish, with Paul Simpson as a sub. The scorers were Scott (pen), Grealish, Lake and Simpson.

9th May. Relegation had been a threat all season for the first team and despite a late rally in two wins and a draw in the previous three games, it all came down to the final game of the season. City needed to win and hope results went their way elsewhere but this was not to be in a 2-0 defeat that saw City return to the Second Division after just two seasons back in the top flight. Redmond and Moulden started the game, with White coming off the bench. Four of the team starting against West Ham United would be playing their final game for City – Clive Wilson (who had actually signed for Chelsea a few months previous and immediately loaned back to City until the end of the season), Mick McCarthy, Kevin Langley and Andy May. Over the previous weeks other players had played their final game for City (Nicky Reid, Darren Beckford, and Tony Grealish) as City planned for the future with one eye on the young players who had followed up last season's Youth Cup with this season's Central League trophy.

"That was a really terrible time for us," Ian Brightwell remembers, "but at the same time the club was having a lot of problems and facing the drop looked more inevitable as the season went on. Our squad wasn't particularly strong and there was no money to make signings, so you have five of the previous year's youth team being shoved into the side. It was just a case of hoping for the best all of the time. All of us young players tried our guts out, but we weren't exactly experienced and result after result went against us."

David White: "To be honest there were too many of us in the team at one time at that level and going down was the best thing for us as players as we could develop better in the Second Division. The fact we won the Central League but got relegated cements the point. We were very good at a lower level but just too young for the First Division. I have some good memories of the Central League run as I was in and out of it all year and I played in the game we won it."

Relegation would hit the club financially, so the emergence of the Class of '86 was very much the preferred option to the board, rather than buying experienced players which was the more expensive option. The club knew that the fans were very supportive of the young Blues and that fans were anxious to see them develop in the first team, so the pressure to spend money they didn't have was not as great as it could have been.

Ironically, Billy McNeill's Aston Villa finished one place below City in the bottom spot – and McNeill was subsequently sacked by Villa chairman "Deadly" Doug Ellis.

13th May. City's 'A' team played away against Alsager College in a 1-1 draw. Ian Brightwell scored City's goal, in a game where he played alongside his younger brother, David, for the first time in a City shirt. Also of note – Tony Book was a substitute in the game at the grand age of fifty-three years old! Also in the side was Steve Crompton – playing what would be his final game in a City shirt.

Crompton had played in twenty-eight reserve team games, sharing the No 1 shirt with Eric Nixon (1 appearance), Alex Williams (1) Darren Williams (2) and Perry Suckling (2). Alex Williams had signed for Port Vale in January, so it was Nixon and Suckling that were ahead of him, with the developing Darren Williams behind him in the youth team and 'A' league and hoping to break into the reserves. Clearly there was no room for four 'keepers on the books. That said, it was news that the 'keeper didn't want to hear. "I was devastated.... but life went on."

16th May. The 'A' team's final game of the season was at Burnley against their 'A' team, a game City won 6-0 (Scott, Coward 2, J Beckford 2, Wallace). Scott, Lake and Clarke are in the line-up – in what turned out to be the final game for John Clarke, who was released soon after the season ended.

John Clarke: "How I was told I was being let go came as a huge surprise because a few weeks before my contract ran out, I went up to ask Ken Barnes if he knew whether I was being kept on or not and he said to me, 'You have nothing to worry about son, you had a very good game against Sheffield United a few weeks ago and the next day they phoned us and offered £100,000 for you and we rejected the offer, so you have nothing to worry about'. So you can imagine the shock a few weeks later when I went to see Jimmy Frizzell and he said to me 'I had a good talk with Tony Book and he thinks you should be at home with your family at the moment as your Mum is so ill', which sounds very nice, but for me it was the final straw with Tony - if I had have known what doing an impersonation of someone was going to cost, honestly, I wouldn't have bothered!"

Steve Mills: "I was actually on crutches when I was summoned to the Manager's office to be told I was being released. It's strange, I can't remember who gave me the news – I think it was Jimmy Frizzell. I can't even remember what he said apart from being gutted at being released, and to make things worse, whilst injured. I was really surprised to be released, I'd played in all the youth team games the year before and quite a few reserve team games that season. I remember hearing Steve Macauley had been offered new terms so I was quite hopeful to get the same - as Steve had also missed a chunk out of that season due to injuries. I have no idea why it didn't happen for me and I didn't hang around to find out."

Paul Lake: "I was particularly gutted to see Millsey leave Maine Road because he and I had become great friends ever since he moved to digs around the corner from me in Denton. On the pitch he was solid and dependable, yet away from football the Sheffield Stallion was a party animal extraordinaire."

Steve Macauley "I was offered a two year professional contract and was naturally extremely pleased with myself. Mick McCarthy was around the office at the same time and congratulated me and offered some good advice, which was a huge boost to me in seeing a senior international player - and fellow centre half - spending time and showing an interest in my career. It was always disappointing when team mates and friends were released - but we also understood that it was the nature of professional football."

Twelve months on from the FA Youth Cup victory, six of the fourteen players had been released by Manchester City and had moved on elsewhere...

2nd - 10th June. Ian Brightwell, Paul Moulden, Steve Redmond and David White travel to South America with the England U-19's side. Brightwell, Moulden and White started in the 2-0 defeat against Brazil in Niteroi (2nd). In Montevideo, Brightwell, Moulden and Redmond started against Uruguay (10th) in a 2-2 draw.

Paul Moulden received the 'Young Player Of the Year' award from Manchester

City's Official Supporters Club at their annual awards ceremony.

PLAYER COMBINED APPEARANCES - 1986-87					
	FIRST TEAM	RESERVES	'A' TEAM	YOUTH CUP	TOTAL
IAN BRIGHTWELL	14 (5 + 8), 1	19, 2	7, 4	-	40 (5 + 8), 7
JOHN CLARKE		11 (4 + 5), 0	23 (1), 6	10, 2	44 (5 + 5), 8
STEVE CROMPTON		28, 0	20, 0	-	48, 0
ANDY HINCHCLIFFE		11 (1 + 1), 0	9, 0	8, 0	28 (1 + 1), 0
PAUL LAKE	4, 1	18 (1 + 1), 4	18 (+1), 6	9, 5	49 (1 + 2), 16
STEVE MACAULEY		5, 0	15, 2	6, 0	26, 0
STEVE MILLS		10, 0	16, 0	5, 0	31, 0
PAUL MOULDEN*	19 (5 + 4), 8	16, 10	7, 4	-	42 (5 + 4), 22
STEVE REDMOND †	30 (1 + 1), 2	16 (1), 7	-	-	46 (2 + 2), 9
IAN SCOTT	-	23, 0	20 (+1), 4	-	43 (+1), 4
DAVID WHITE	24 (6 + 1), 1	15, 9	4 (1), 3	-	43 (7 + 1), 13

* plus 2, 0 for England U-19s
† plus 1, 0 for England U-19s

4. IAN BRIGHTWELL

Born: Lutterworth, 9th April 1968

IAN, AS WE ALL KNOW, is from a sporting family. It is well documented that his parents were international athletes (400 metre specialist Robbie Brightwell & 800 metre Tokyo gold medallist Anne Packer) as well as his elder brother Gary (Athletics) and David (Football).

So it was naturally inborn in Ian that he would become a sportsman, but would it be athletics or football? At school he was a prolific goal scoring centre forward and around the age of twelve he found himself in a formidable junior side (Midas Juniors) alongside what would eventually be members of City's FA Youth cup squad (Paul Lake, Andy Hinchcliffe, David White and a little later Steve Redmond) and began to train with City.

Ian signed schoolboy forms at fourteen and continued his education at Westland's school, Congleton and signed for City on YTS forms, one year into his further education in what he described as "achieving my dream playing for this great club I had supported since boyhood". Jumping at the chance to be made an apprentice despite the pull of athletics in which he had shown tremendous potential at 400 metres he is quoted as saying, "Football has always been my first love and happily my parents backed me all the way. I was never much of a scholar any way".

Ian quickly gained a reputation as a versatile player "I started off in City's juniors as a right back, then moved to centre half, but I enjoyed midfield most of all because it gives you more freedom". He made his Lancashire League debut at Everton on September 22, 1984 and his reserve debut at home to Newcastle United on May 2, 1985. Hard on the heels of the 1986 FA Youth Cup success came his full City League debut on 23rd August 1986 against Wimbledon, a moment Ian describes as "the biggest thrill of my life. But when I was called up for my league debut, I found it hard to adjust to the pace of the game". Though he couldn't have done too badly as he remained with City for a further twelve years, despite spending a year out of football after he snapped his patella tendon.

It was under the leadership of an appreciative Howard Kendall that Brightwell really established himself as a regular for the first team and he deservedly went onto win England under-21 honours. Numerous experts in the game felt it was Ian's versatility that paradoxically cost him the full England cap that his outstanding performance at the highest level for City warranted.

His eighteen year association with the club ended with a testimonial game against Sunderland and a free transfer. He joined Coventry City in 1998 and with his contract due to expire he had planned to go to America to talk to clubs in Denver, San Diego and Charleston, who were all keen on signing him. Instead he answered a call to play for Walsall before moving onto Stoke City.

His next move, would be the beginning in the change of his career path. He joined Port Vale first as a player and then moved on to a coaching position in 2003 and was actually caretaker manager for a period just short of 24 hours. He then followed Brian Horton to Macclesfield as the reserve team coach but also remaining registered as a player. He served the club as caretaker manager before being given the job on a permanent basis, a run of poor results, saw him replaced and although he was given the opportunity to remain as assistant manager to Keith Alexander, he declined and re-joined Port Vale in a temporary coaching capacity.

"I would still love to be in football and hope that an opportunity does appear," Ian says, "I would like to be hands on, but I'm also interested in media work (In 2009, Ian began working at BBC Radio Manchester as a co-commentator). I want to be involved in the game and I still think I have something to offer." Ian is now a business man and has a property investment business.

4. IAN BRIGHTWELL 1984-85 to 1997-98	
FIRST TEAM	337 (45), 19
RESERVES	80, 12
'A' TEAM	43, 12
FA YOUTH CUP	9, 0
LANCS YOUTH CUP	2, 0

One of his younger team-mates, Garry Flitcroft, told him to invest in property (sound advice back in the 1990s when house prices were rising sharply). Brightwell sensibly took note of the tip, so much so that he is now making a career out of the property business himself after finally hanging up his boots.

"It was Garry who originally got me involved. He started investing in property and went into it in a big way with a huge portfolio," recalled Brightwell. "For me it was nice to have an interest outside football, especially when you're involved in the game solidly for 25 years. It was always my long-term aim to concentrate more on the business once I'd finished with my full-time football commitments. Nowadays I'm a lot more hands on and involved in buying and selling, renting and having property built."

Brightwell also has a separate business with a close friend, building squash courts. "We install them for sports clubs and look after the maintenance, whether it is sanding or putting in new floors, cleaning the walls or fixing any problems."

These days involvement with City extends to match day hospitality with Brightwell happily mixing with fans who not that long ago watched him play for the club.

1987-88

THE TENTH IS THERE
FOR THE TAKING

THE 'A' TEAM WAS now becoming a thing of the past for the lads, with the exception of the youngest of the squad, Steve Macauley and Paul Moulden, who used the games when returning from injuries. In fact, the reserves too, had been by-passed as the first team is where the remaining six other FA Youth Cup winners predominantly playing. None of them were now eligible to appear in the FA Youth Cup or Lancashire Youth Cup competitions.

During the pre-season, Jimmy Frizzell had persuaded the coach Mel Machin to join City, with Frizzell becoming 'General Manager', and Machin as 'Manager'. Machin had played for Port Vale (Sir Stanley Matthews was his manager), Gillingham, Bournemouth and then Norwich City. On retiring from the game, he came through the ranks at Norwich City, starting as coach of the youth team, then the reserves before becoming the first team assistant manager alongside Ken Brown.

15th August. There were double debuts from the Class of '86 as Andy Hinchcliffe and Ian Scott play their first games for the first team in the opening 2-1 home victory over Plymouth Argyle in front of 21,046 at Maine Road, with Paul Stewart and Imre Varadi on the score sheet. Brightwell, Redmond and White joined their former youth team colleagues along with the scorers plus Nixon, Gidman, Clements and McNab. Tony Adcock, a pre-season buy from Colchester United, came off the bench for his first City start.

For Hinchcliffe, it was thought his debut would have been a year earlier had it not been for an injury that kept him out until the following January. The sale of Paul Power was said to be on the strength of Hinchcliffe's rapid development, though that is something the player himself didn't allow to go to his head. "I never really took too much notice of all the hype surrounding myself and all City's other youngsters... I just wanted to do the very best for my mates!"

The *Manchester Evening News* match report stated that, "Andy Hinchcliffe earned top marks for a distinguished display that auger well for his future as well" and that "Ian Scott had a creditable league debut."

31st August. On the August Bank Holiday Monday, Ian Scott scores his debut goal for City in a 1-1 draw at Villa Park and also scores City's goal the following Saturday in a 2-1 home defeat against Blackburn Rovers.

8th September. Paul Moulden scores two goals in a 5-1 reserve team victory over Leeds United at Maine Road – but then suffers a fourth bone fracture of his career. It would be almost four months before his next game.

12th September. In the fifth game of the season, away at Shrewsbury Town, six of the Class of '86 started the game – Hinchcliffe, Redmond, Brightwell, Lake, White and Scott, appear in a goalless draw at Gay Meadow.

The following game, a midweek fixture against Millwall, City won 4-0 with Scott again finding the net alongside David White, John Gidman and Paul Stewart in front of just 15,430 fans – the second lowest home attendance of the season (the lowest being 15,172 against Reading in April.)

6th October. Andy Hinchcliffe bags his first City goal in the Second round, Second leg League Cup tie at Wolverhampton Wanderers. A John Gidman free kick in the last minute sent City through to the next round, winning 2-0 on the night, 3-2 on aggregate.

City lost the First leg, 2-1, in a poor performance at Maine Road, where Nixon let in a last minute howler and Peter Barnes came off the bench for his first appearance of the season – in what turned out to be his final appearance for City. The following League game saw Brightwell and White score in a 2-3 home defeat against Sheffield United.

13th October. Taking a step down, six of the cup winning squad appear in a reserve game away at Sheffield Wednesday – White (at right back), Hinchcliffe, Redmond, Lake, Brightwell started the game with Macauley on the bench. Lake scores one of the goals in a 4-1 win.

The reserve team game was clearly used as a dress rehearsal as four days later, at Ipswich Town, White lines up at right back again in the first team, alongside Hinchcliffe, Redmond, White and Brightwell – though the Blues crashed to a 3-0 defeat.

21st October. A run of twenty-one months – and thirty-three games – without an away win since Spurs were beaten at White Hart Lane in January 1986, came to an end at Valley Parade as City beat league leaders Bradford City 4-2. Lake and White scored City's first and third goals with Paul Stewart grabbing a brace in between.

After the Bradford City away win, the following twenty-six days were to be a remarkable period for City, with two First Division scalps in the League Cup and one particular league game attracting national attention. In eight games, City would win seven and draw the other – scoring an amazing thirty-two goals whilst conceding just eight.

27th October. City beat First Division Nottingham Forest in the League Cup 3-0 at Maine Road

31st October. City win 4-3 against Swindon Town at The County Ground

4th November. City are held 1-1 by Middlesbrough at Maine Road

7th November. City thrash Huddersfield Town 10-1 at Maine Road

10th November. City beat Plymouth Argyle 6-2 in the Simod Cup at Maine Road

14th November. City win 2-0 against Reading at Elm Park

17th November. City beat First Division Watford 3-1 in the League Cup at Maine Road

21st November. City win 3-0 against Birmingham City at Maine Road

The game against Huddersfield was the one that brought public attention to City and their young team not just because of the score line but because, thankfully, Granada TV were there to record the game!

There was little indication early in the game that such a score would be achieved – if anything, Huddersfield had the better start and Duncan Shearer could have scored at least twice before City finally broke the deadlock, through Neil McNab in the 13th minute. Three further goals were added before half time, through Stewart (29th min), Adcock (34th min) and White (41st min).

4-0 at half time and Granada's pundit for the game, the great Frank Worthington, was asked if it could be double figures. "There will be goals in the second half, but no, not double figures" came the reply.

Adcock bagged his second in the 53rd minute and Stewart made it 6-0 on 67 mins with a looping header. A minute later Adcock grabbed his hat-trick – as did Stewart on 81 mins. White crashed home his second with five minutes remaining to make it 9-0. The fans spent the final minutes of the game demanding "We Want Ten!" and a tenth goal did appear in the 90th minute but in the City end as John Gidman was judged to have fouled a Town player in the box. It was a harsh decision – even Granada's commentator asks "a sympathy vote, perhaps?" Up stepped former City player, Andy May, to slot the ball past Eric Nixon – and giving the City fans in the Kippax (who were cheering the goal) a wave as he made his way back for the restart.

With injury time being played out, a glorious ball from the left by Simpson through the middle finds David White bearing down on the goal with just the 'keeper to beat, with Town appealing for offside. "The tenth is there for the taking", the Granada commentator stated, as the hapless Brian Cox came out of his box, to be rounded by White - taking the ball to the keeper's left. The striker still had some work to do as he was now at an angle and a defender was running back into the area, but to no avail, as White coolly and calmly slotted in the tenth goal - and his third - into the back of the net in front of the North Stand, sending the City fans amongst the 19,583 crowd wild!

An almost tearful Town manager, the former Newcastle and Arsenal striker Malcolm MacDonald (four weeks into the job), struggled to discuss the game in front of the camera. "We were playing an offside trap... we've never played the offside trap", he said shell-shocked.

Hat-trick hero David White is quick to praise the contribution of one of the unsung heroes of the day who set up many of the ten goals. "The team was supremely confident and in Paul Simpson we had a player right on top of his game on the day. I knew exactly the significance of that tenth goal as I ran at the keeper and will always be grateful that I got it"

"It's just one of those freak games" recalls Steve Redmond, "you know you'll never be in a game like it again. Once we got the first goal, it just snowballed from there - two, three, four... Huddersfield couldn't wait for the final whistle. Everything connected that day. There were three hat-tricks that day - someone gets a hat-trick in a game today and there's mad celebrations, but to get three in one game takes some beating. And my old mate Andy May got their goal too, something I remind him about every time I see him!"

Andy Hinchcliffe: "Quite simply the most extraordinary match I ever played in..."

John Clarke: "Having left City in the summer, I had signed for Huddersfield Town and travelled to Maine Road with the squad that day - it was a bit embarrassing especially as I was sitting with some of my old team mates in the Main Stand as we got hammered - they gave me a lot of stick about not being in the team, but I guess that was the one game I'm glad I missed!"

Footnote: For the record, this wasn't the biggest win in the Football League that season - just four weeks before on 5th October, Gillingham had beaten Chesterfield 10-0 in the Third Division. However, no team has scored ten goals in a league game since.

In the team alongside White was Hinchcliffe, Lake and Redmond, with both Brightwell and Scott remaining on the bench during the game. Hinchcliffe scored in both games either side of the Huddersfield game and White continued his good form with two braces in consecutive games against Watford in the League Cup and Birmingham City in the league.

5th December. An eventful game for Steve Redmond! City were winning 1-0 at home to Crystal Palace when Eric Nixon (who had been targeted by the Palace forwards throughout the game with rough challenges) picked up the ball inside the box. The Palace striker - who had been chasing a 40/60 ball, continued to run towards Nixon, who, fed up with the aggressive stance towards him, struck an arm out towards the Palace player, who hit the deck. The referee awarded a penalty and sent Nixon off to howls of disbelief from the Maine Road faithful. Steve Redmond went between the sticks and his first task was to retrieve the ball out of the net as the penalty became Palace's equaliser. This was Redmond's second stint between the sticks having taken over from Alex Williams in an 'A' team game at Tranmere Rovers. Redmond was on the winning team that day - but not against Palace who took advantage of having an extra man on the pitch and City forced to play an outfield player in goal. Two further goals condemned City to a 3-1 defeat. Hinchcliffe, Lake and White also started in this game, with Scott coming off the bench.

But what of the intrepid, emergency goalkeeper, "I'm not sure [why I went in goal] but it didn't take long until I knew I wouldn't be doing it again! We all just looked around at each other asking what were we going to do and no one wanted to, so I just ended up putting the shirt and gloves on. It was only when I'd done that, I realised that not only had Eric been sent off but the ref had given a penalty too! So my first touch of the ball was picking it up from the back of the net. Every time Palace came forward I was shitting myself - I didn't enjoy it one bit. They say you have to be mad to be a 'keeper and I found out why that day! There was only one sub back then and we never thought about what would happen if the keeper got sent off or injured, there was no one going in goal during training should that happen. The following year Nigel Gleghorn went in twice when Andy Dibble was injured and he was great and he enjoyed it and then there was Niall Quinn - saving a penalty with his first touch - who used to play Gaelic football so he was handy too. But for me - never again!"

There would be three further defeats at Maine Road in December, two in the league to Oldham Athletic and Leeds United as well as a Simod Cup tie against Chelsea. The league defeats left City trailing in their fight to regain a First Division place after just one year - a feat not helped again by another home defeat against Shrewsbury on 2nd January.

Respite from the league would come in the shape of competing in both the FA Cup and League Cup. From 9th January to 3rd February, City would play six cup ties!

5th January. Paul Moulden returns to action – having recovered from his fractured leg – and scores for the reserves in 1-1 home draw against Coventry City.

9th January. All the pre-match talk was about revenge. The FA Cup 3rd round draw had paired City with Huddersfield Town at Leeds Road, just nine weeks after the 10-1 mauling at Maine Road. 18,102 crammed into the old ground as Hinchcliffe, Brightwell, White, Redmond and Scott started the game, with Moulden a surprise inclusion on the bench given that he had played just one full game since his injury.

City were losing 2-1 (Brightwell) with the minutes running down. Paul Moulden was brought on and deep into injury time, was fouled on the edge of the box and the ref blew for the foul. The pumped up Town fans celebrated wildly, assuming the ref had blown the final whistle, with a good number invading the pitch – only to realise the game was not over and City had a free kick! Up stepped John Gidman and – as he had done in injury time in the League Cup at Wolves in the September – he rifled the ball into the net, much to the disappointment of the home fans and to the delight of the City fans packed behind the opposite end!

12th January. The FA Cup replay three days later had home fans very confident of a goal feast – to send City through to play Third Division Blackpool away in the 4th round. A good crowd of 24,565 – five thousand up on the 10-1 league game – turned up. However, despite one hundred and twenty minutes of football, neither side could break the deadlock and a goalless draw meant a second replay. The same five young Blues started, though Moulden was not on the bench (however he was in the reserve team two days later scoring one goal in the 2-0 win at home to Blackpool).

20th January. A 3-2 defeat four days previously away at Plymouth Argyle had hardly prepared City for a tough League Cup quarter final tie away at Everton. Lake had been restored to the team, with Scott on the bench. Brightwell, Hinchcliffe, Redmond and White once again started the game. Everton were 3rd in the First Division, so it was always going to be a tough game for a City side that had former Toffees Gidman and Varadi on the team sheet. Everton won 2-0 with future Blue to be Adrian Heath scoring the second goal in front of a healthy crowd of 40,014.

25th January. A Monday night 3rd round, second replay came two days after City's sixth consecutive home defeat, this time 0-2 against Aston Villa. Huddersfield had won the toss to have the right to host the game and Lake, Hinchcliffe, Redmond and White took to the field, with Brightwell and Scott on the bench. This time City finally managed to shake off the Yorkshire side, in front of 21,510 fans, with goals from Hinchcliffe, White and Varadi, setting up a 4th round trip to the seaside in five days' time.

30th January. The team sheet handed in by City contained seven of the Class of '86 – the highest number it would reach. Out of that triumphant youth team squad, only eight players remained – the seven on show at Blackpool with Steve Macauley playing in the reserves and six having being released – John Bookbinder, David Boyd, John Clarke, Steve Crompton, Steve Mills and Andy Thackeray.

Five of the team started the game – Lake, Hinchcliffe, Redmond, White – and the returning Moulden who now had four straight reserve team games under his belt, replacing the injured Varadi. Brightwell and Scott again sat on the bench, with Brightwell being brought on in the second half.

It was a case of deja-vu for City, heading into injury time a goal down. In a last ditch effort, the Blues – attacking the goal where the City fans were gathered on the open terrace – made one more attempt to break the Blackpool resistance. In an almighty scramble, Moulden hit the bar – but Lake reacted faster to the rebound than anyone else and the ball ended up in the back of the net – cue mad celebrations by both players and fans!

3rd February. The replay, four days later, featured six of the seven on the team sheet for the original tie. Imre Varadi came back in at the expense of Moulden, who took Brightwell's place on the bench. City finally got back to winning ways at Maine Road with former Blackpool striker Paul Stewart, along with Paul Simpson, scoring the goals in a very close run 2-1 victory – the first of five consecutive wins at home.

Bournemouth were dispatched in the league (2-0), followed by the 5th round FA Cup tie against Plymouth Argyle (their third visit to Maine Road this season and third defeat!) with Scott and Moulden scoring one each in a 3-1 success. Two more league opponents went away empty handed – Hull City (2-0) and Ipswich Town (2-0). This put City in a confident mood for their next home game – a quarter final FA Cup tie against Liverpool.

16th February. David White makes his England U21 debut against Scotland at Aberdeen in the European Championship Quarter Final First leg (1-0 win). In the side with White is the former City 'keeper Perry Suckling and future Blues Nigel Clough and David Rocastle. The second leg is a week later at Nottingham Forest's City Ground, where White scored the game's only goal to send England through to the semi-finals with a 2-0 aggregate win.

8th March. 'The Magnificent Seven' are on the team sheet again – this time with a record six in the starting line-up, in the away game at Sheffield United – Brightwell, Hinchcliffe, Lake, Redmond, Scott and White start, with Moulden coming off the bench. Unfortunately, when Moulden came on in the 81st minute, he replaced Lake – so there was never more than six on the pitch at one time. City won 2-1 with goals from White and Morley.

13th March. The visit of Liverpool provided the biggest Maine Road crowd of the season as 44,047 fans came through the turnstiles. Five of the young Blues started – Hinchcliffe, Redmond, Brightwell, Lake and White, whilst Scott was an unused sub. However, the bumper crowd saw the Blues outclassed and beaten 4-0 to a vastly experienced opposition that ended the season as League Champions and runners up in the FA Cup to Wimbledon.

March 19th. In the absence of both John Gidman and Kenny Clements – who had been alternating the captaincy – Steve Redmond is appointed as the captain for the 1-1 draw against Swindon Town at Maine Road, becoming the club's youngest ever captain – a record he would hold for nineteen years, when Micah Richards captained City against Aston Villa in 2007.

13th April. Steve Redmond makes his England U21 debut, coming off the bench in the U21 European Championship semi-final First leg away to France (2-4 defeat). David White started the game, as did fellow City player Paul Stewart (who scored one of England's goals) and former City 'keeper Perry Suckling. Eric Cantona scored one of France's goals.

The second leg was at Highbury two weeks later, when Redmond came off the bench again in the 2-2 draw – Paul Gascoigne was one of the scorers, with Cantona grabbing both French goals.

Back to the league and with just nine games remaining, any lingering hopes of promotion were fast fading – then confirmed with a run in of just three wins, two draws and four defeats – including a 1-0 defeat (out of four previous attempts) by Huddersfield Town! It was time to move the old guard along as Kenny Clements and John Gidman played their final games for the club – as did Eric Nixon and more controversially crowd favourite Paul Stewart. In the last five games of the season, the generation of young players below the Class of '86 were given a chance to impress, with debuts for Jason Beckford, Neil Lennon and Ian Thompstone, while Paul Warhurst was an unused sub. But the disappointment couldn't be hidden that, for all the promise and all the goals, the team ended in ninth position.

Millwall were champions and were promoted along with Aston Villa and Middlesbrough via the play offs. And spare a thought for Malcolm MacDonald, his Huddersfield Town finished firmly at the bottom with twenty-four points, conceding exactly one hundred goals in the process. Not surprisingly, MacDonald was sacked as soon as the season was over.

The season was extended for Steve Redmond and David White into June, on England U21 duty.

5th June. Steve Redmond's full debut for the England Under 21's was in the Toulon Tournament in the 2-1 win over Mexico. Indeed, Redmond featured in all four of England's games, with White starting in the USSR game only:

7th June. USSR 1-0

9th June. Morocco 1-0

12 June. France in the final. The French – as in the European Championship semi-final in April – came out on top, winning 4-2. The starting line-up had future City assistant manager David Platt, as well as future Blues Nigel Clough and David Rocastle, alongside Paul Gascoigne, Nigel Martyn and Michael Thomas. David Ginola was amongst the French scorers.

Steve Redmond received the 'Player Of The Year' for 1987-88 from Manchester City's Official Supporters Club at their annual awards ceremony – the only one from the Class of '86 to receive the award.

Paul Lake collected the 'Young Player Of the Year' Award.

PLAYER COMBINED APPEARANCES - 1987-88				
	FIRST TEAM	RESERVES	'A' TEAM	TOTAL
IAN BRIGHTWELL	38 (4 + 3), 6	9 (1), 3	-	47 (5 + 3), 9
ANDY HINCHCLIFFE	55, 4	2, 0	-	57, 4
PAUL LAKE	40 (3 + 2), 5	7, 0	-	47 (3 + 2), 5
STEVE MACAULEY	-	23 (1), 0	13, 4	36 (1), 5
PAUL MOULDEN	2 (6 + 7), 1	19, 13	4, 6	25 (6 + 7), 20
STEVE REDMOND *	58, 0	2, 1	-	60, 1
IAN SCOTT	24 (7 + 9), 4	11, 0	-	35 (7 + 9), 4
DAVID WHITE †	50 (5), 16	1, 0	-	51, 16

* *plus 4 (2), 0 for England U-21s*
† *plus 4, 1 for England U-21s*

5. STEVE REDMOND

Born: Liverpool, 2nd November 1967

STEVE'S SCHOOLING STARTED at Belle Vale primary where he caught the eye as a very promising footballer. At the age of twelve, City scout George Woodcock invited Steve to Maine Road for a trial and to play in a game against a touring side from the West Coast of America (The Golden Eagles). The date was 26th July, 1979, straight after that game he was invited to stay for the rest of the week at City's expense. He recalls. "Some of the players were staying at the same hotel as me and they gave me lifts to training, it was a great feeling. I remember collecting the autographs of Bobby Shinton, Mike Robinson, Steve Mackenzie and Dragoslav Stepanovic".

At that time Steve was one of the hottest properties in North West football and from the age of eleven he had been capturing the eye with spectacular goal scoring performances. He played for his school team, Our Lady of the Assumption, scoring the grand total of fifty-three goals in sixteen games. He was to carry on scoring almost non-stop for the next few years for Hillfoot Hey comprehensive school and Liverpool schoolboys whilst also playing and scoring freely as an important member of City's nursery side 'Blue Star' and despite being a big Liverpool fan, he overlooked both Merseyside teams to join City as an apprentice on 1st July 1984.

Steve commented "I had played for Liverpool boys and Merseyside boys while at school and this is where Manchester City spotted me. They invited me to have a look around Maine Road and this was the first time that I had been able to see the inside of a major club. I was impressed with the youth policy and quickly agreed to sign. I never regretted the move one bit although my dad was disappointed I did not join Liverpool, as John Benson came round four nights in one week to try and persuade me to join them."

On joining City as an apprentice, he switched roles and his mother was quoted as saying "I would rather still see him scoring goals. We used to love that. We never wanted him to become a defender but I don't suppose we can complain because he went onto to play for England Youth and Under 21's and he might not have done that as a centre forward." Steve first appeared for

City's Lancashire League side against Crewe on 11th February 1984 and that was followed by his reserve debut against Stoke City on 28th August 1984, the same game in which Paul Moulden and Steve Crompton made their reserve bows. He was soon fast tracked to first

5. STEVE REDMOND 1983-84 to 1991-92	
FIRST TEAM	283 (4), 7
RESERVES	57 (3), 12
'A' TEAM	44 (1), 17
FA YOUTH CUP	14, 5
LANCS YOUTH CUP	3 (1), 1

team level and made his debut against Queens Park Rangers in February 1986.

He has won honours as an England youth international and also represented England at under-21 level, whom he captained twice. It was his leadership skills that made him captain of the City youth team that won the FA Youth Cup in 1986 and subsequently being appointed City's youngest ever captain (at the time) as well as being voted player of the season.

In August 1992 he transferred to Oldham Athletic along with Neil Pointon in a deal that brought Rick Holden to Manchester City and spent six years with the Latics before moving to his final professional club Bury, for whom he later became assistant manager.

On retiring from full time football, Steve played one game for Burscough before joining then Conference side Leigh RMI for one season in 2003, becoming a joint caretaker manager there for a short stint alongside former Nottingham Forest player Phil Starbuck – and in his own words has "done a bit of driving for Liverpool Steels and Travis Perkins but got a bit fed up".

Steve now works in customer services and sales for Travis Perkins on Merseyside.

MIDAS UNDER-16'S c. 1984

row (left to right): Ian Scott, Brian Chisnall, Steve Crompton, David White, Ian Brightwell and Anthony Gore
Bottom row: Andy Hinchcliffe, Colin Lannigan, Paul Newton, Matthew McNair and Andy Greaves.

Thackeray, Redmond, Lake, Hinchcliffe and Scott in action for the 'A' Team.

Appearances F. A. Youth Cup '85-86

	Pld	Sub (Unused)	Goals
			3 Clean sheets
Steve Crompton	9	-	3 Clean sheets
Steve Mills	9	-	-
Andy Hinchcliffe	9	-	-
Ian Brightwell	9	-	-
Steve Redmond	9	-	4
Andy Thackeray	9	-	2
David White	9	-	2
Paul Moulden	9	-	9
Paul Lake	9	-	4
Ian Scott	9	-	3
David Boyd	9	-	2
John Clarke	-	2 (4)	-
Steve Macauley	-	1 (1)	-
John Bookbinder	-	0 (1)	-

Steve Redmond holds aloft the FA Youth Cup as Steve Mills joins in the celebrations.

David Boyd's tankard comes out of the loft!
Picture courtesy of Margaret Boyd and Marion Gallagher.

CENTRAL
LEAGUE
CHAMPIONS
1986–87

Top row (left to right):
J. Beckford, Scott,
Lake, Brightwell,
Barrett, Hinchcliffe
Bottom row: Moulden,
Simpson, Redmond
and White.

John Bookbinder practices his skills in the back garden watched by his father David.

John runs out from the Maine Road tunnel to the delight of his father.

Another staged pose with father David. Both pictures were taken for a feature in John's local paper when he signed for City aged 16.

Pictures courtesy of Susan Bookbinder

WEMBLEY '86
PRE-MATCH
FIVE-A-SIDE
GAME
A triumphant Manchester City team stroll from the hallowed Wembley turf:
LEFT TO RIGHT: Brightwell, Book, Bookbinder, Pardoe, White and lagging behind a tired duo of Macauley and Clarke.

HAIRCUT 100
Brightwell Redmond and Hinchcliffe enjoying a Fantastic Day.

CLUB TROPICANA
Whatever happened in Ibiza stayed in Ibiza…
White, Thackeray, Lake, Brightwell (hidden), Mills and Redmond give Wham! a run for theur money.

CITY SUPPORTERS' CLUB YOUNG PLAYER OF THE YEAR - 1987-88.
Paul Lake receives his trophy in his lounge following inj

WHITE EUPHORIA: *David*
is lifted to glory following City
draw at Bradford in May '89 that s
prom

DROWNING IN GLORY:
Lake, Hinchcliffe, White, Moulden a
Redmond from the victorious FA Yo
Cup team, celebrate promotion in th
Bradford changing rooms.

CHANCE AT THE FAR PC
Andy Hinchcliffe heads home duri
5-1 Maine Road massacre in Sep
1989 as Mal Donaghy loc

JL LAKE *training with a clearly visible*
e support at Platt Lane (inset: Testimonial
hure from Oct 1997).

N SCOTT; IAN BRIGHTWELL *sa-*
the crowd before his testimonial (that he
't play in) July 18th 1998 v Sunderland.

VER STARS: *As the players progressed*
became front cover stars for City's match
ramme.

E FIRST DAY AT SCHOOL FOR
Y'S NEW RECRUITS
's YTS players, groundstaff and admin.

KEN BARNES
City's chief scout proudly stands with some of his success stories (left to right): Sheron. Hughes, Redmond, Lake, Quigley, White and Brightwell.

TONY BOOK

GLYN PARDOE

Lake and Brightwell with their mentor 'Skip' (Tony Book)

1988-89

THE MAGNIFICENT SEVEN

THE REMAINING EIGHT Class of '86 players remained with the club for the forthcoming season. A summer of transfer activity saw top scorer Paul Stewart being sold to Spurs (despite chairman Peter Swales maintaining he wouldn't be sold prior to the season ticket deadline!) for a club record fee of £1.7m. That money was used to bring in 'keeper Andy Dibble, Nigel Gleghorn, Wayne Biggins, Brian Gayle and John Deehan – who was signed as player coach, but didn't get to appear in the First team. The signings of experience, to blend in with the existing youth, again saw City installed as one of the favourites to gain promotion the following May.

The fans had been out buying too - stocking up on inflatable bananas and other blow up items! The inflatable banana idea had started the previous season when City fan Frank Newton had the idea of taking a six foot banana to a game wearing a City shirt and sun glasses. It was soon nicked named 'Imre Banana' and had its own chant. Over the next few games more appeared and by the end of the season, the craze had caught on – despite Crystal Palace stewards attempting to ban the bananas from the final game of the season at Selhurst Park for allegedly being seen as racist towards Palace's black players!

By the time the first game of the season came - away at Hull City - there were a huge number of inflatables on the away terrace, as the blow-ups first puzzled opposition fans, but ultimately inspired many of them to design their own club related inflatables as the craze went national over the coming months.

However, two defeats and two draws in the first four games had the natives feeling very deflated and restless - especially the first home game ending in a 4-1 defeat against local rivals Oldham Athletic. Paul Lake scored City's consolation goal, though he also missed a penalty as former City man Roger Palmer banged in three goals to see the game end with familiar cries of 'Swales Out' coming both inside the ground and outside the Main Stand at the end of the game.

Brightwell, Hinchcliffe, Lake, Redmond and White featured in the opening eight games with Moulden on the bench during the third game, joining them from the start of the fourth game onwards.

The fourth game of the season, a 1-1 draw at Leeds United, also saw Ian Scott remain on the bench – making it only the third time those seven players from the Class of '86 had been on the team sheet together. Scott would only make the bench a further two times in the first half of the season.

13th September. Andy Hinchcliffe, Ian Brightwell and Paul Lake make their England U-21 debuts, alongside already capped Steve Redmond, in a 0-0 draw against Denmark in a friendly at Watford's Vicarage Road. It would be Hinchcliffe's solo U-21 cap.

The disappointing start to the league season, which saw City in the relegation zone, soon turned to joy as the Blues went on a fantastic run of eight wins and just one defeat in nine games (including a double win over Plymouth in the League Cup second round). The turn around in form coincided with the inclusion of Paul Moulden into the team – with the six young Blues dominating the team sheet over the next two months. Rumours had been doing the rounds – ever since Moulden came back from injury for the Huddersfield Town FA Cup game the previous season – that Machin didn't fancy Moulden (although the greater rumour that Moulden was dating Machin's daughter can be dismissed). It just seemed to the fans that what ever Paul Moulden did – score in the reserves or the first team – it was never enough, even though the stats were there for all to see in the player's favour.

17 September. City v Brighton & Hove Albion at Maine Road 2-1 (Moulden, Brightwell)

20th September. Chelsea v City at Stamford Bridge 3-1 (Brightwell 2, Moulden)

24th September. Barnsley v City at Oakwell 2-1 (White, Morley)

28th September. City v Plymouth Argyle, League Cup at Maine Road 1-0 (White)

1st October. City v Blackburn Rovers at Maine Road 1-0 (Biggins)

5th October. City v Portsmouth at Maine Road 4-1 (White, Moulden, Lake, Biggins)

8th October. Ipswich Town v City at Portman Road 0-1

12th October. Plymouth Argyle v City – League Cup at Home Park 6-3 (Moulden, Lake, Gleghorn (2) Biggins, McNab)

15th October. Plymouth Argyle v City at Home Park 1-0 (Gayle)

This excellent run of form saw City at one point move up the table into fifth place and November spawned another fine run of three wins and a draw, as Third Division Sheffield United were brushed aside by a Paul Moulden hat-trick in the League Cup 3rd round tie at Maine Road. This was followed by a 0-0 draw at Leicester City and then wins at home to league leaders Watford (3-1 Moulden, Biggins 2), away at Bournemouth (1-0 Moulden) and a last gasp win at home to Oxford. Trailing to a first half goal, Morley equalised with four minutes remaining with an overhead kick and then Redmond hit the winner in the last minute, with a firm header from near the penalty spot. Now City climbed into third place just a point behind leaders Watford.

18th October. Steve Redmond and David White start in the England U-21 home game against Sweden at Coventry City's Highfield Road – White scoring England's goal in a 1-1 draw. Coming off the bench for England was Australian born David Oldfield, who within a few months would sign for City for £600,000 from Luton Town.

26th November. Steve Macauley makes his comeback from injury in the 'A' team away at Morecambe reserves in a 2-2 draw. Playing alongside him would be future first team players Martyn Margetson, Ashley Ward, Mike Quigley and Mike Sheron, with Neil Lennon in the line up too.

For the first team, the month ended on a low, losing the 4th round League Cup tie at Luton Town 3-1 (White), and following a 0-0 draw at Selhurst Park against Crystal Palace, the Blues soon bounced back with Brightwell and Moulden scoring twice each in a home win against Bradford City - that took City to the top of the table.

It was a lead that would last just one week. The following game, at home against Shrewsbury Town, witnessed a memorable brace by Andy Hinchcliffe in a 2-2 draw. Trailing 2-0, to a first half brace by seventeen year old Carl Griffiths (who Brian Horton would sign for City from Shrewsbury in 1993 for £500,000), Hinchcliffe's first was a penalty and he followed that up by scoring direct from a corner! As the full-back explained, "As my career developed, I got into a routine of practicing set pieces more and more. At this early stage all I was looking to do was put a ball in with pace making it difficult for keepers to deal with... sometimes you just get lucky!"

20th December. Steve Macauley starts his only game for the reserve team this season, in a 5-2 home win against West Bromwich Albion. Ian Scott - the only fellow Class of '86 member in the side, scores one of the goals. Macauley, returning from injury, had been on the bench for the previous two games and for the next two games as well – these would be his only appearances on the reserves team sheet all season.

26th December. The year ended in a party mood for players and fans. The inflatable banana craze had gone from City's secret cult to a nationwide phenomenon. The game on Boxing Day had the fanzine Blue Print organising a fancy dress and inflatable party. 12,000 fans made the short trip to the Potteries in all sorts of outfits – and the players came out onto the pitch each holding a six foot banana that was then thrown into the away fans section. Stoke fans replied with thousands of Pink Panthers being waved around! Sadly for City and the fans, the fun ended there as the Blues lost 3-1 (Gleghorn) – but the Blues made it a Happy New Year with a New Year's Eve win away at Swindon Town (2-1 Gayle, Jason Beckford).

The conspiracy theorists gained further ground as Moulden (eleven goals) was dropped to the bench for the Stoke game, in favour of the Biggins (five goals) and Morley (four goals) partnership. Moulden didn't even make the bench at Swindon Town.

2nd January. Ringing in the new, Moulden was again nowhere to be seen, even though Morley was dropped to the bench, in favour of Jason Beckford, in a truly forgetful 0-0 draw at home to Leeds United that saw City drop down to fifth place.

After the Leeds game, the remainder of January saw the start of six consecutive wins. New signing Gary Megson had gone straight into the team (scoring the game's only goal away at Oldham Athletic on his debut) at Ian Brightwell's expense, with Lake, Redmond, White and Hinchcliffe being permanent fixtures in the starting line-up. Brightwell was injured and Moulden, once more (having played in the first three winning games) inexplicably fighting for a place on the bench. An injury to Hinchcliffe gave a debut and subsequent five game run, to youth team player Gerry Taggart, who also covered for a couple of games when Lake was injured too. Fellow youngster Ashley Ward was an unused sub in the same game as Taggart's debut, as Machin delved deep into the club's resources as the season wore on. The six wins on the bounce – from 14th January to 25th February – against Oldham Athletic (away), Hull City (home), Portsmouth (away), Ipswich Town (home) Birmingham City (away) and Plymouth Argyle (home) took City to the top of the league – although the FA Cup campaign came to an end in the middle of the run, with City surprisingly losing to Third Division Brentford 3-1 (Gleghorn) in the 4th round at Griffin Park.

The winning run came to an end with a 1-1 draw on 1st March, at home to West Bromwich Albion – with Machin finally giving in to fans' demand for Paul Moulden to be brought on – and he was rewarded with a Moulden equaliser!

7th February. Steve Redmond plays for the England U-21 side away in Greece in a 1-0 defeat

4th March. Steve Macauley makes his final appearance in a City shirt for the 'A' team in a 1-0 defeat away against Marine reserves. In the league, City were now in second place and away to fourth placed Watford. Once again, Moulden was sat on the bench at the start of the game and even when he was eventually brought on, he couldn't find a way past Watford's 'keeper, man of the match and future Blue Tony Coton – without whom City would have run out winners on the day, instead of losing 1-0.

7th March. Paul Lake and Steve Redmond play for the England U-21 side away in Albania in a 2-1 win.

11th March. Leicester City visit Maine Road for the second time in nine weeks (having been defeated 1-0 in the FA Cup 3rd round by a Neil McNab penalty). A Trevor Morley second half hat- trick should have grabbed the headlines in a 4-2 win, but it was an incident on the field that almost cost one of the players his life, that was the main talking point.

After only four minutes, Paul Lake went up to win the ball from a corner at the edge of the box and clashed heads with the Foxes Paul Ramsey and both went down on the ground - only Lake stayed down. Players from both teams rushed around him as it was clear something was wrong. The City players were gesturing to trainer Roy Bailey to treat Lake. Then the crowd went into an eerie hush as they stood helplessly watching the player's legs twitching up and down as if he was having a seizure. The players then gestured to City's club doctor to come onto the pitch. Dr Norman Luft had been watching the game high up in the directors box and seemed to take forever in getting on to the pitch as the players' desperate plea for him to hurry up got frantic - which cascaded into panicking the crowd even more who began shouting at the doctor to hurry up. The doctor reached Lake and by the time he was taken away motionless on a stretcher, he'd been treated for seven minutes. The game recommenced but hardly a thought was on the game. Fans throughout the stadium thought he might be dead. Debates spread around like wild fire with many assuming that if he was dead they would call the game off and others getting angry when no announcement was made.

On the pitch, the players didn't appear to be in the right frame of mind. City were awarded a penalty towards the end of the First half. The normally very reliable Neil McNab - whose spot-kick had separated the sides in the FA Cup 3rd round tie in January - blasted the ball over the bar. No one in the crowd really cared. Had it gone in, how could they have celebrated, knowing that one of their players could have died in front of their own eyes?

At half time finally, to the relief of the whole stadium, an announcement was made over the tannoy that Paul Lake was OK and on his way to hospital for a check-up. It was the loudest cheer of the day – if not the season. In his autobiography, Lake revealed that he met the match referee years later at Eastlands, who told him that the captains had agreed not to bring the teams out for the second half until they had received word that Lake had regained consciousness.

Interviewed a little later on Granada TV, the physio, the doctor and the player discussed the incident. Roy Bailey: "When I arrived at Lakey, he was obviously convulsing very, very badly, his face was quite blue and obviously his airway was blocked. I immediately tried to clear everybody out of the way, cleared the airway and basically just waited until Lakey began to breathe normally, as I did."

Dr Norman Luft: "I realised it was more than a serious injury when I saw the two lads hit their heads and then hit the deck. Usually Roy and I have a good relationship of injuries. I look at Roy and he gives me a signal to indicate if I am required. By the time I got there, which was, I don't know, fifty, sixty seconds – which I know sounds a long time, when something major is going wrong, thirty thousand fans are watching, Roy had already got there and had started the immediate, necessary treatment. He managed to get Paul into what we call the recovery position, managed to get his tongue forward and clear his airway and everything he did was perfectly correct."

Paul Lake: "There was a corner on the far side and the ball came across, I went out to attack the ball and there was a clash of heads – and the next thing I know I'm on the treatment table seeing Roy Bailey's smiling face. Commenting further, when asked if the incident had affected his play in games he had played in since, Lake added "No, not at all, like I say, I don't remember a thing about it. If I had I would have been struggling, but obviously I knew nothing about it so I was OK and I've put it right out of my mind now."

A direct result of this incident had Dr Luft relinquishing his seat in the director's box, to relocate in the dug out along side Roy Bailey.

The second half commenced and with a relieved crowd now really pumped up and Trevor Morley claimed his first City hat-trick, along with an own goal, as City won 4-2 – all six goals coming in that second half. The victory resulted in City returning to the summit of the league – but it was one of those days when the result of a football match didn't really matter in the greater schemes of things.

In the five weeks until City travelled to Blackburn Rovers, City would play a total of seven times, winning four, drawing once and losing twice and although Lake missed the midweek win at Sunderland, he was back in the side a week later against Chelsea.

14th March. Sunderland v City at Roker Park 4-2 (White (2), Gleghorn, Morley)

18th March. City v Chelsea at Maine Road 2-3 (McNab pen, Taggart)

25th March. Walsall v City at Fellows Park 3-3 (Moulden (2), Oldfield)

27th March. City v Stoke City 2-1 (Hinchcliffe (pen), Oldfield)

1st April. Brighton & Hove Albion v City at Goldstone Ground 1-2 (Morley)

4th April. City v Shrewsbury Town at Maine Road 1-0 (Morley)

8th April. City v Swindon Town 2-1 at Maine Road (Hinchcliffe (pen), Oldfield)

During this period, Paul Moulden made an appearance on Granada TV, being interviewed by Rob McCaffrey. A very cautious Moulden chose his words carefully:

Rob McCaffrey: "Why aren't you playing in every game?"

Paul Moulden: "I don't really know... I don't know, the boss has different ideas, some weeks he leaves me out, I don't know."

RM: "Have you asked him why?"

PM: "I've been to see him a few times as to why I've been left out and I get different things like I've got no pace."

RM: "You must get the feeling that you are not the favourite?"

PM: "I don't know, but he's bought a few players in so it looks like I'm not one of the favourites but at the end of the day I've just got to win him round by scoring goals every time I play. The fans like me and the letters in the local papers must help a wee bit but I'm not a favourite that's for sure."

RM: "Does it undermine your confidence when he signs new strikers?"

PM: "It does for a bit, it's like when he signed David Oldfield and you think 'is it to replace me?' but then I was lucky and scored a couple against Walsall, but yes, it does undermine your confidence when he does sign a new striker"

RM: "Do you feel that every time you go out for City you've got to score to be in for the next match?"

PM: "Yeah I think something like that, I have to score or do really well to make sure I'm in the week after."

RM: "Doesn't it get you down though?"

PM: (laughing) "It does when you don't score!"

The home game against Chelsea was seen as an indication as to where the title would be heading - which is what it turned out to be as the largest crowd of the season, 40,070, saw the eventual Champions Chelsea return to London with all three points.

There was 'keeper drama during the next game away at Walsall, when Andy Dibble went down injured after taking a first half goal kick and had to be replaced. This time the previous 'sub' keeper Steve Redmond kept his Blue shirt on and Nigel Gleghorn went on to perform admirably between the sticks. City were 2-0 down at the time – to a team propping up the rest of the league – but drew level before the interval and scored immediately in the second half to lead 3-2. Gleghorn was finally beaten with five minutes remaining – having been sold short by an Oldfield back pass, for the final score of 3-3.

As a result of Dibble's injury, the vastly experienced former Ipswich Town 'keeper Paul Cooper, was signed and played in all but two of the remaining ten games. Cooper had won both the FA Cup (1978) and UEFA Cup (1981) when at Portman Road and had signed from Leicester City. Cooper had also lined up with Mike Summerbee and Kazimierz Deyna for "The Allies" in the film 'Escape To Victory' (1981). Cooper was the stand-in for the Allies 'keeper, the American POW Robert Hatch – played by Sylvester Stallone!

1st April. A defeat at Brighton was more than noteworthy through the one fact that seven players – the record number it would reach – from the 1986 FA Youth Cup winning squad started a game for the one and only time.

The line-up was Cooper, Brightwell, Hinchcliffe, Lake, Megson, Redmond, White, Moulden, Oldfield, Scott, Morley. Gleghorn and Taggart were the subs.

Although this was the fourth time the "Magnificent Seven" had been on the team sheet (both Blackpool away in the FA Cup 3rd round and away at Sheffield United the previous season and away at Leeds United this season), finally all seven players started a first team game together on the pitch.

For Ian Scott, playing due to Neil McNab's suspension and Brian Gayle's injury, the game would be his first start in the league this season – and his final game in City's first team. Brightwell equalised for City but was then penalised for encroaching into the penalty area too soon – as Cooper lived up to his reputation as a penalty stopper. The retaken penalty was dispatched succcessfully as the Blues went down 2-1.

By the time City had beaten Swindon Town the following week, managed by the former United player and chip shop owner Lou Macari, second placed City held an eleven point lead on the teams chasing them for automatic promotion.

11th April. Ian Scott plays in his final game in a City shirt, for the reserves in a 2-2 draw at home to Blackburn Rovers. Ian Brightwell, who scored one of City's goals, is the only fellow Youth Cup winner in the side that evening.

15th April. City visited 3rd placed Blackburn Rovers at Ewood Park (on the day of the Hillsborough disaster). Despite winning the last two games, Machin opted for Moulden (who started both previous games) to sit on the bench and replacing him with Oldfield - the substitute scoring the winner against Swindon Town. In what was without a doubt City's worst performance of the season, the Blues were torn apart 4 0 by Rovers - a side that included former Blue Nicky Reid - with Gerry Taggart having such a torrid time as full back, it proved to be his final game of the season.

22nd April. For City, there were five games left of the season but a 2-1 home defeat by Barnsley left City looking worryingly over their shoulders at the chasing pack. Hinchcliffe, Lake, Redmond, White and Moulden would start the game - as they would in all of the remaining games. Brightwell was an absentee, but would play in the final four games.

25th April. Brightwell, Lake and Redmond start for the England U-21's against Albania at Ipswich Town's Portman Road. Brightwell scored one of the goals in a 2-0 win, with Steve Bull also on the score sheet.

29th April. The trip to Oxford United's Manor Ground would be tricky. The tight, compact and sloping pitch being the opposite to the width and splendour of Maine Road's surface. This proved to be the case as City went 2-0 down in a dire first half performance, the second goal being scored by former City player Paul Simpson - slotting the ball past surprise goalkeeping selection Andy Dibble. City fans had presumed his season was over and with the more than adequate replacement in Paul Cooper, there appeared to be no rush in bringing him back.

However, the second half was a complete opposite to the previous forty-five minutes with City scoring four times (in front of the delirious City fans) - White, Brightwell, Gleghorn and a Greenhall own goal, completing a remarkable comeback that had surely sealed City's promotion. With only three games remaining City were six points ahead of nearest promotional rivals Crystal Palace. However, Palace had a game in hand - and were the next opponents for City at Maine Road.

1st May. A win for City on this Bank Holiday Monday and they would be a point away from promotion after two years out of the First Division, with two games remaining. Again Dibble retained his place in goal, despite not being able to take goal kicks. Yet any reservations City fans had about their 'keeper were soon forgotten when Nigel Gleghorn slid in to meet a David White cross at the far post to give City a 1-0 lead - in front of 33,456 fans - after only seven minutes. However, Machin's decision to play Dibble soon backfired when the 'keeper went down in agony after an up field punt - just as he had done against

Walsall eight games previously. The goal scorer Gleghorn once again donned the shirt and gloves and performed heroics, along with the defence, as wave after wave of Palace attacks were denied. However, Gleghorn was helpless to prevent a clever turn and shot inside the penalty area from Ian Wright, late on in the game, from hitting the back of the net in front of the delighted Palace fans congregated in the Platt Lane stand. The important point was that City didn't lose and with a superior goal difference, they were still one win (with two games remaining) away from a return to top flight football. Next up was a home game against Bournemouth the following Saturday......

6th May. Bournemouth came to Maine Road for their final away game of the season, in which they had won five games, drawn four and lost thirteen on their travels. They were lying in the middle of the table, on an equal amount of points away from relegation as they were from promotion. Three sides of Maine Road were packed to the rafters - the exception being the 8,000 capacity Platt Lane stand, housing the very small, but nonetheless vocal, Bournemouth following - yet the official attendance given was a laughable 30,564...

The game started in spectacular style for City - going a goal up after just two minutes. A long ball from Hinchcliffe from the left and into the box, was headed on perfectly by a Bournemouth player, into the path of Moulden who made no mistake with his shot. Two further City goals just before half time had the ground rocking; another Hinchcliffe ball into the box was controlled by Morley who then curled a magnificent shot into the back of the net. Moulden grabbed his second after a free kick had been deflected by the 'keeper onto the bar and 'Goalden Moulden' tapped home the rebound. The Blues went off at half time to a rousing cheer from the fans and were now just forty-five minutes from automatic promotion.

What happened next can simply be one of the many entries in the file marked "Typical City". For, whatever instructions Machin had given the team, they simply sat back and defended the lead. This enabled a so far ineffectual Bournemouth side to step up a gear and 'have a go'. Led in midfield by a long haired Scouser by the name of Ian Bishop, Bournemouth scored twice from corners to pull the score back to 3-2. The nerves were setting in and the referee played six minutes of injury time. In the final minute of the six given, Luther Blisset broke free from Andy Hinchcliffe, who then brought him down from behind. No City player challenged the decision to award a spot kick - and Blisset himself fired past Cooper to end the game 3-3.

Even more bad news was given, when it was announced over the tannoy that Crystal Palace had won 2-1 away at Leicester City – the Eagles being four points behind City but with a game in hand. However, within minutes, the fans with the transistor radios were spreading the news that Leicester City had also salvaged a late, late equaliser – meaning that Palace were now trailing the Blues by six points still.

Former City manager John Bond was the guest on Granada Soccer that evening and said that he didn't think City had blown their chances, when asked the question by presenter Elton Welsby, adding "but they are making it very difficult for themselves, but I still have this gut feeling that they won't make it you know – I hope I'm wrong, I really do".

For City's two-goal hero that sunny May afternoon, the bitterness of the Bournemouth game can still be felt years later. "What can I say about Mr Machin that can be put in this book?" recalls Moulden, "I didn't then and still don't blow my own trumpet, but when he brought me off against Bournemouth he nearly blew promotion for all the team, the supporters and the City of Manchester. I just wonder what went through his mind before his decision and certainly at about 8.30pm that night, when the reality of the result had sunk in. It was a good job he had a team of willing, hard working and determined lads – not just the lads that had come through the youth team and had blue blood in our veins but the likes of Trevor Morley, Brian Gayle, Nigel Gleghorn and Neil McNab. He had almost blown it for everybody at Maine Rd and for what reason – to air his new signing? (David Oldfield). I signed for Bournemouth the following June and boy did Luther Blissett and a few of the other boys take the piss out of me for a few days saying that Mel was a double agent with his connections with Bournemouth and to this day I'm still not too sure!"

"Mel's mystifying decision to take off the in form Paul Moulden probably hadn't helped matters," Paul Lake agrees, "but we were all to blame for a pathetic second-half display."

Crystal Palace won their mid-week game in hand over Stoke City, to move within three points of City, with an inferior goal difference. The scenario for City was simple. A point at Bradford would be enough to send the Blues up automatically. A defeat was acceptable – providing a five goal turnaround wasn't achieved by Palace, who were at home to already relegated Birmingham City.

13th May. Tickets for the compact away end at Valley Parade had sold out within the first day of sale weeks before the game. Thousands of Blues would find their way into the other three sides of the ground too, in the 16,000 capacity ground. The Blues line up was: Cooper, Lake, Hinchcliffe, Megson, Brightwell, Redmond, White, Moulden, Morley, McNab, Gleghorn. Oldfield and Taggart remained on the bench throughout the game. A very edgy start saw chances at both ends, before the West Yorkshire side went ahead in the twenty-fourth minute. City increased the pressure on the Bradford goal, with chances from

Gleghorn, Moulden and McNab just off target.

Into the second half and City were attacking towards the goal where the City fans were packed in behind the fences. Gleghorn and Morley both had great efforts just going over the bar. White hit the foot of the post and also shot wide of the right hand post. Morley had another attempt, but shot tamely straight at the keeper. As City pressed further, they left themselves exposed and Cooper had to be alert to block a close shot. Back at the other end and Morley had a shot blocked by the keeper's legs. The crosses from Hinchcliffe and White kept coming over, but to no avail.

Rumours abounded in the away fans section with regards to Crystal Palace's score. Once it reached 3-0 to Palace, it wasn't long before it got to 4-0 and some were saying 5-0. This meant if the scores stayed the same, Palace would gain the automatic spot and City would be in the Play Offs for the first time. The pressure got too much for one fan, with extremely long hair (and instantly nick named Jesus). He ran on to the pitch and before stewards could reach him, he managed to communicate with a good number of City players, holding his hand up, with five fingers spread out, indicating that Palace were five goals up.

With four minutes remaining, Cooper caught a Bradford cross and threw the ball immediately to Gleghorn. He allowed the ball to roll up to him, in the middle of City's half of the pitch and with his one and only touch, moved the ball onto Moulden, who had just crossed the halfway line. Moulden controlled it with his first touch and then half turning; he looked up and instinctively released a through ball to White towards the edge of the penalty box with his second touch. White was ahead of his marker as he nudged the ball a little further into the box before squaring the ball with his second touch, along the six yard line where Morley met the ball under close pressure and turned the ball past the 'keeper's outstretched left hand and into the back of the net. Seven touches from Paul Cooper to the back of the net in 11.66 seconds!

At the final whistle fans invaded the pitch, mobbed the players and celebrated hard as the Blues mission had been accomplished – although as it turned out, Crystal Palace had 'only' scored four goals and as they pushed for a fifth, Birmingham City snatched one back to see the game finish 4-1. City finished one point higher than Palace, who would later gain promotion by winning the play off final 4-3 against Blackburn Rovers over two legs.

In the dressing room, the champagne was spraying everywhere and Ian Brightwell proudly declared that City were "back where we belong". When asked about results elsewhere, Brightwell acknowledged what was going through the players' minds as the game wore on.

"The crowd were saying that Palace were winning 5-0, don't know if that's true or not?" The interviewer asked whether that got through to the players or not – "Yeah, definitely, the crowd pushed us on, it was unbelievable"

The captain Steve Redmond's contribution to the after match celebrations – filmed by Granada TV and obviously missed by the editing team – was his "We're fucking there!" remark to Nigel Gleghorn, who then opened and sprayed a bottle of bubbly over his skipper!

Paul Moulden: "The guy running onto the pitch at Bradford only summed up how frustrated the fans and the players were. Hand on heart I didn't think any one player could've done anymore to get the result we needed. All we really needed again was lady luck to appear which she did. Although I admired him for what he did, he felt frustrated at the lads for not getting the job done at Maine Road the previous week (against Bournemouth) in front of our fans and in our back yard. You ask any of the lads that day – we were going up – it just took us longer than we had anticipated. I often wonder about how that bloke who ran on the pitch is doing – it took guts to do what he did!"

Ian Brightwell: "The game itself was probably the tensest hour-and-a-half of my life. Bradford City had scored in the first half and we had the second half to try to score an equaliser. During the game a City fan ran on the pitch to tell us Palace were winning 4-0. We knew it was now or never and thankfully Trevor Morley managed to score and the bananas went wild!"

Andy Hinchcliffe: "The nerves before the game were ridiculous... all our season's hard work hinged on one game... the relief afterwards was incredible. In the dressing room after the game I was nearly blinded by champagne!"

The end of the season would see three more of the Class of '86 leaving City, three years after the trophy was won.

The Bradford City promotion game would the final City game for Paul Moulden. During the summer he would pack his bags and move to Bournemouth – who he scored his last two City goals against in that penultimate game of the season. It was a decision that was very unpopular with the fans.

Paul Moulden: "I knew my time was up because about six games before the end of the season I was offered a new contract and what I was being offered was an embarrassment – even the club representative who handed me the terms of the contract said 'You're not going to sign that, are you?' Coming out of the meeting, I bumped into Tony Book and Glyn Pardoe and when I told them what I had been offered, they rolled their eyes... I was top scorer despite being in and out of the side all season and that offer was the final act over a season of things going on in the background that I wasn't happy about. So I joined Bournemouth in a move that wasn't connected to the Ian Bishop deal, he was already at City when I joined The Cherries."

Interviewed by City historian Gary James for the City programme in March 2005, Moulden detailed the scenes in the background that occurred over that season. Paul was initially left out of the pre-season team photograph – only to be added at the last minute as the photographer said another body was needed to balance each line out. This followed with a transfer request that was ignored. "I said I wanted to play for City, but if I couldn't I'd have to leave. I didn't want to go but I felt I had no choice at that age. I was angry to be on the bench for the Stoke fancy dress day and then those final weeks of the season were a nightmare."

The exit for Moulden appears to have been sealed by his appearance at the end of season annual supporters club 'Player of the Year' event. "We were all supposed to wear a shirt and tie and I turned up in a tee shirt. He (Machin) didn't like that at all and I think that night he decided I had to go."

The player also revealed to Gary James the offer on the table for him during his new contract talks. "I ended the 1988-89 season as top scorer and my pay was £250 a week and I was offered a half hearted increase of £25 to stay. It felt as if I wasn't valued and I knew I wasn't wanted. Having said that, it was definitely the club that made the final decision."

Ian Scott would also be on the move, remaining with Moulden in the Second Division having signed for Stoke City. Speaking to the authors, Scott remained unaware of the significance of his final first team appearance – seven of the cup winning youth team lining up together in one game – and reflects on what he felt could have been and he also detailed what was going on behind the scenes that ended his City days. "I didn't know any of that info about the relevance of the line up until you told me. It's sad that we never got the chance to develop into the first team as a group because given time, I am sure we would have done OK. However, I fell out with Mel Machin. I had started really well under Mel and thought he was a fantastic coach and he gave us all a chance in the first team. I had scored some goals and everything was going brilliantly.

"I remember getting Man Of The Match at Maine Road against Sheffield United on the Saturday but we got beat. I then was ill midweek and Mel wanted to play the first team in the reserves to try out a new system but I could not play. They won the reserve game and he chose to stay with that team for the Saturday. They got beat on the Saturday so I thought 'OK, I should be back in for the next game', but he left me out again. The team then went on a winning run and I didn't play for weeks. I remember him adding me to the squad to play Chelsea and I said to the other players that I did not want to go all that way and stay over, just to sit in the stands. Unfortunately, one of the coaches overheard me and Mel pulled me from the squad and that was that. He made me train with the reserves and I didn't play regularly again. I just felt that a bit of man management at the time could have sorted that out. I was a young lad being left out when I was playing well and all it needed was a quiet word. I went to see

Mel, to ask for a transfer and he turned it down. I asked him why and he said 'because I am going to fuck you about as much as I can'. A bit harsh, I thought to a twenty-one year old, but there you go.

"During the summer, I went away on holiday, expecting to return to City for pre-season training. On the plane I read in a newspaper that Stoke City were after me and that City were willing to let me go. When I got back I met Mick Mills in the airport and he bought me from City for £175,000."

The season's end was also the end of the road at City for Steve Macauley, who was let go by the Blues. The news of his release, whilst still disappointing, was not unexpected, as Macauley himself admits. "It was no real surprise to me when I was released. By now, I was on a month to month contract as I'd had a bad time with injuries throughout the season, nothing serious, just little niggling injuries here and there and Mel Machin was putting lads before me who I didn't feel deserved it so I pretty much read the script before it happened. The day I was released, Jimmy Frizzell took the time to give me words of encouragement to continue to pursue a career in professional football, words I needed to hear at that time, which I greatly appreciated."

2nd June. Brightwell, Lake and Redmond start for the England U-21's against Poland at Plymouth Argyle's Home Park, in a 2-1 win.

PLAYER COMBINED APPEARANCES - 1988-89				
	FIRST TEAM	RESERVES	'A' TEAM	TOTAL
IAN BRIGHTWELL *	28 (2 + 3), 8	7, 2	-	25 (2 + 3), 10
ANDY HINCHCLIFFE †	43 (2), 5	5 (1), 0	-	48 (3), 5
PAUL LAKE +	41, 4	3, 0	-	44, 4
STEVE MACAULEY		1 (4), 0	7, 0	8 (4), 0
PAUL MOULDEN	33 (7 + 3), 17	6 (1), 3	-	39 (8 + 3), 20
STEVE REDMOND §	53, 1	-	-	53, 1
IAN SCOTT	2 (1 + 3), 0	26, 4	-	28 (1 + 3), 4
DAVID WHITE °	50 (1), 8	2, 0	-	52 (1), 0

* plus 2, 1 for England U-21s
† plus 1, 0 for England U-21s
+ plus 4, 0 for England U-21s
§ plus 6, 0 for England U-21s
° plus 2, 1 for England U-21s

6. ANDY THACKERAY

Born: Huddersfield, 13th February 1968

ANDY WAS SOMETHING of an all-rounder in sport, playing rugby for his school and cricket in his town's under-13 team. It was as a forward that Andy earned a place in the Newsome Junior school team and at the age of ten he was playing against boys who were years older than him. As his schooling progressed so did his football, at Newsome High school he started in the under-12's and kept his place in the grades as the years passed by and he was also a member of the Huddersfield under 13's and then the under 15's. County recognition came with West Yorkshire under 15's and then the under18's, such was Andy's thirst for football he even turned out for a Sunday League teams by the name of Upper Thong and Netherton.

City spotted Andy when scout Len Davies noted him as thirteen year old in an inter town game and he commented: "Andy Thackeray was a lad I saw just once and I was convinced I'd seen enough. He was playing for Huddersfield Boys in September 1981 against Tameside. The boy had a lovely first touch, good control, was two footed and had decent pace; he also had a reasonably accurate shot, stronger with his right. An outstanding prospect I thought"

He was invited to Maine Road at Christmas 1981 for a week's trial and then signed on schoolboy forms. Andy explains "I did have a chance to go to Manchester United and both Sheffield clubs but I preferred the spirit at City and got on really well in the atmosphere at the club, so I stayed and was delighted to sign after I left school."

His first appearance for the Lancashire League side was away at Bolton Wanderers on April 14th, 1984 and seven months later he made his reserve debut when coming on as a substitute in the 1984-85 season against, ironically, Huddersfield Town in a 4-4 draw on November 15th, 1984

Unfortunately Billy McNeill released Andy just weeks after the FA Youth Cup victory. This did not deter him and he went on to play over 500 games in a professional career that took in spells at Huddersfield Town, Newport County, Wrexham and Rochdale. He helped Halifax Town to promotion from the conference and returned to non-league football to play for Nuneaton Borough.

Andy Thackeray

In 2003 he joined Ashton United and for a period of time acted as assistant manager. His final club before retirement was Mossley, where he won the player of the year award.

Andy had always maintained a high standard of fitness and an understanding that life goes on, so along with his football career, he had worked hard and qualified as a chiropodist and this is a field that he is now currently employed in, working at Home Valley Sports Injury clinic in Huddersfield.

6. ANDY THACKERAY 1984-85 to 1985-86	
RESERVES	18 (4), 0
'A' TEAM	41 (6), 5
FA YOUTH CUP	13, 2
LANCS YOUTH CUP	4, 1

1989-90

CHANCE AT THE FAR POST

ALONGSIDE IAN BISHOP (with his new look shorter hair style), City signed former Queens Park Rangers, Palace, Spurs and England striker, Clive Allen, from Bordeaux for £1.1m and Gary Fleming, Nottingham Forest's Northern Ireland international right back.

19th August. It was a baptism of fire for City, facing First Division runners-up and FA Cup winners Liverpool away at Anfield on the opening day of the season. Lake, Hinchcliffe and Redmond started the game along with Dibble, Bishop, Gayle, Oldfield, Allen, Morley, McNab and Gleghorn. White came on as a sub during the game, with Fleming remaining on the bench.

Despite 'the shock' of going a goal up, after a Hinchcliffe free kick was deflected past Grobbelaar, City went into the break full of confidence with the score at 1-1 - but normal Anfield service was resumed and City came home with a 3-1 defeat at a venue where not many clubs would get much of a sniff all season.

Yet four days later, hopes that Maine Road would be where the points are picked up were dashed, when Southampton went home with all three in a 2-1 defeat (Gleghorn).

It would be the fifth game of the season before City would win their first game - at home to Queens Park Rangers with Allen scoring the only goal of the game against his first club. In between there had been a 1-1 draw against Spurs and a 2-1 defeat at Coventry City, with David White scoring both goals. From the day the fixtures were released, City fans had scanned the fixture list for two things: the dates of the Manchester derbies. The first such game was in late September at home, the seventh league fixture, so the win against QPR was proving to be timely in boosting the confidence of both the team and the fans. Yet City lost again on their two journeys into London in the week before the derby at Maine Road. A 1-0 league defeat at Wimbledon's Plough Lane was followed by another defeat at Brentford's Griffin Park, following on from last season's FA Cup defeat. This time though, at least the Blues would be given another chance in the second leg of the second round league Cup tie to overturn a 2-1 deficit, where Oldfield scored City's goal.

It had been a mixed start for the Class of '86. Hinchcliffe and Redmond had started in every game. Lake had missed just the Coventry City game whilst also moving from full back into midfield after the first two games. White had come off the bench in the first two games and was then handed full starts from then on, rewarding Machin's faith with two goals. Brightwell had made just one start, in the fourth game at Coventry, replacing Lake in his one game absence, dropping to the bench for the next three games, appearing on the pitch during the first two of them. Brightwell and Redmond had also started for England U21's in a 1-0 defeat in Sweden on 5th September.

23rd September. The build up to the 111th Manchester derby game was tense for both sides and fans – as both Manchester clubs languished at the wrong end of the table. City's injury list was lengthy with Dibble, McNab and Allen being ruled out of the game. The Reds manager, Alex Ferguson, had assembled an expensive side with Danny Wallace, Paul Ince, Mike Phelan and Gary Pallister being purchased over the summer months.

The injuries at City gave the Famous Five the chance to line up for the first time since the final game of last season at Bradford City. Paul Cooper was once again the replacement for Dibble, Oldfield for Allen and Brightwell for McNab. The rest of the line-up was Fleming, Gayle, Bishop, and Morley. Gary Megson and Jason Beckford kept the bench warm, with Beckford joining in later in the game.

Prior to the game commencing, Machin allowed Tony Book to do a motivational talk to the whole team – before 'Skip' turned his attention to five of the Blues.

"Skip made a beeline for me, Whitey and the rest of the young uns'" Paul Lake recalls, "'his boys' – and shook our hands, his eyes glinting. 'You're ready', he seemed to be saying to us, 'I've prepared you for days like this!'"

The game had barely started when fighting broke out behind Jim Leighton's goal in the North Stand as a large number of United fans had gained entry into it. After three minutes, the players were led off the pitch whilst the police and stewards attempted to regain control and transfer the Reds' fans along the pitch and into the Platt Lane end, where the majority of United fans with tickets for the away end were housed, as well as in the Kippax terrace corner section.

Play commenced after an eight minute delay and City had the upper hand in the early exchanges. From a free kick on the left, Hinchcliffe hit a long diagonal ball to White, almost to the corner flag. White, marked tightly, controlled the ball and crossed low into the box with his second touch. The ball didn't have a lot of pace, yet Pallister – the nearest and therefore favourite to reach the ball first – appeared wrong footed and his stretching right leg missed the ball as it fell to Oldfield who scooped it home, 1-0 to City.

The fans had not had time to draw breath when a White cross into the box was stopped by Mal Donaghy – who appeared to simply freeze on the spot with the ball at his feet. Morley robbed him of possession and then had a clear shot that Leighton did well to save with his right hand. The ball fell to Lake in the box with Viv Anderson coming over to close him down. Brightwell was unmarked and screaming for the ball, but Lake tormented Anderson who was too afraid to tackle in the area. Lake finally moved to the edge six yard line and created the space to have a shot on goal, which Leighton, on his near post, did well to parry to his left – where two hesitant reds stood just in front of the line but failed to act quickly enough as the outstretched right leg of Morley poked the ball home for City's second in as many minutes.

Steve Redmond set up the third, breaking down a United attack, skipping past one challenge and playing a one-two with Lake. Redmond – now on the halfway line by the touchline and in front of the Kippax – aimed a delightful low chip, curling towards the advancing Oldfield. Pallister was slightly ahead of the City man – but slower to react and Oldfield won the challenge, with the United man stretching helplessly on the floor. Oldfield had a free run down the outside of the penalty area and looked up to see the unmarked Bishop running in. The inch perfect cross had Bishop placing a diving header from eight yards out past the helpless Leighton. 3-0 to the Blues.

After half time, future City manager Mark Hughes pulled one back for the Reds but this galvanised City further and when another United move was broken down, Lake ran clear only to see Leighton block his effort. Lake picked up the loose ball and took it beyond Leighton, who was getting back up onto his feet and just before Lake reached the by-line – and seeing the only United defender around covering the near post – he simply passed the ball for the unmarked Oldfield, standing on the six yard line, to tap the ball into an empty net in front of the United fans in the Platt Lane stand. As Clive Tyldesley – commentating for Granada TV – said "and I could have scored that!"

The fifth goal was the icing on the cake. Bishop sprayed a glorious ball from the edge of the centre circle to his right, picking out White running down the wing. White, again closely marked, allowed the ball to bounce once and then crossed the ball into the centre of the penalty box – at that point an excited Clive Tyldesley screamed "Chance at the far post…" – as the ball was met perfectly by the advancing Andy Hinchcliffe who sent a bullet header past the truly dejected, deflated and hapless Jim Leighton. On the replay, Tyldesley added "…What a cross from White…and where did Hinchcliffe come from? He's the left back remember... Bang!".

Hinchcliffe was immediately hugged by Lake and Brightwell before the rest of the team congratulated the left back. Hinchcliffe then made his way back to his position for the kick off, but not before gesturing towards the United fans by raising his hand, with all four fingers and a thumb stretched out, letting them know exactly how many goals City had scored past them!

The *Manchester Evening News* dubbed the game "The Maine Road Massacre", giving each player, including the late sub Jason Beckford, ten out of ten, as the team also became known as Machin's Marvels!

Reflecting on the game, there wasn't a surprise with the victory, but there was with the result! As David White says, "This was before United's dominance of football in this country, but still they were a bigger club than City and with some big name players, but we felt we could do ourselves credit and get a result but never, never in our wildest dreams did we anticipate that we would get the result that we did."

Steve Redmond "I was sitting in the dressing room and the team sheet comes through and I'm looking at the team sheet thinking I'm marking him and you're marking so and so. If the lads were honest, they'll admit on paper we never stood a chance, we weren't doing too well at the time, but it was just one of those games where as soon as we scored the first goal, the belief in the side grew and to get two quick goals, to beat them at Maine Road 5-1, I just don't think any City fan would have dreamt that. We went out that night and had a few shandies - a great day and a great night!"

Andy Hinchcliffe: "You couldn't have dreamed that before the game, everything went unbelievably well." On his goal, he added "During the whole of my career I have played internationally and for two more great clubs as well, but I think that goal, coming back and living in Manchester means more to me than anything else. I don't think I ever remember scoring another headed goal in my career. If you are born and bred in Manchester and you go and watch a Manchester derby, you are very privileged to watch a game I feel. To play in a game, again I feel blessed to have been able to do that and to score in a Manchester derby is just unbelievable, so from every perspective, the game was fantastic, it was in 1989 and I will remember it forever."

Ian Brightwell "It was one of those days where everything that you do works out. We were all over them and the goals just flew in. When I'm an old man and I look back over my career I think that will be one of my favourite ever games, without a doubt."

Paul Lake: (having being substituted late on with an injury and sat on the bench) "Skip leant back in the dugout, dragged on his cigarette and gave me a knowing wink that said 'job well done.'"

For the victors the derby was a springboard for the first of three consecutive wins at Maine Road. The following Saturday had visitors Luton Town heading back down south pointless after a 3-1 City victory, with Oldfield and Bishop scoring again along with Brightwell notching his first top flight goal. The two wins saw City move up to tenth in the league. Brentford were finally brushed aside in the Second Round, Second Leg of the League Cup; a Morley brace coupled with goals from White and Oldfield saw City through, winning 4-1 on the night and 5-3 on aggregate.

10th October. Brightwell, Lake, Redmond and White travel to Poland with the England U21's and all start in a 3-1 win, with Brightwell scoring one of the goals, Steve Bull the other two. It would be the last appearance in the U21's for all four of the City boys – as the age limit was fast catching up with them!

14th October. City's post derby high was soon brought back down to earth with a 4-0 thumping by Arsenal at Highbury, three weeks after the Maine Road Massacre and with exactly the same line up.

22nd October. The following game was live on ITV, who employed the services of former City manager Malcolm Allison to cast his eye on the young Blues. Allison was far from impressed after watching Villa gain all three points with a 2-0 away win at Maine Road, in a game notable for a double sending off (City's Morley and Villa's Gray) and there was a debut from the bench for City from Justin Fashanu.

Allison's verdict began with left back Hinchcliffe, "Andy Hinchcliffe has an excellent left foot, but he doesn't look sharp enough to me and he's got to work terribly hard to me physically. And Redmond is the same; he seems to play like when he was at school. We had a player like that here called Derek Jeffries, with good talent and good ability but doesn't seem to be aware of the situation that's going on around him."

In dismissing Gary Fleming, saying he should be replaced, Allison turned to the centre half pairing of Steve Redmond and Brian Gayle. "They worry me sometimes and I think they probably need another central defender."

He was more praiseworthy in discussing the midfield trio of Paul Lake, Neil McNab and Ian Bishop. "I think those three are as good as any other midfield in the country" and he was more positive in his view on Lake. "Paul Lake has got lovely vision and has got great feet. He could go for goal more than he does but I think the one major thing he needs to improve is his power. At the moment he's like a Rolls Royce with an Austin engine. If Lake played more like in the old inside right position, similar to Colin Bell, he'd have to have more power than he does at the moment. But the most dangerous word about a young player is potential and I think all of these players are experienced and they've all been playing for two years in the first team at Manchester City and they've played in the U21's and that is not a problem with them, the problem now is how to improve their physical condition."

On David White, Allison claimed that although he did one or two runs "his awareness let him down badly... but I think White can be a good player - as can Hinchcliffe who I think will improve if he uses his ability".

Pressed to comment as to whether any of the current Under 21's can go all the way and become regular full England internationals, Allison replied "Not unless they work very, very hard - and that includes Paul Lake".

Maybe Allison's forthright words hit home as City knocked Norwich City out of the 3rd round of the League cup, with a 3-1 win over their fellow First Division team members, with White, Allen and Bishop on the score sheet. City were then tested against both of the clubs they were promoted with - earning a 1-1 draw at Stamford Bridge (Allen) and a 3-0 home win against Crystal Palace, with Allen notching in his third successive game along with White and Morley.

For these three games, Ian Brightwell was back on the bench as McNab had returned from injury, but the remaining four of the Famous Five were still in the starting line up as the four points gained kept City safely out of the danger zone.

The Palace game was on 4th November, yet it would be on Boxing Day when the next victory would arrive - and Mel Machin would not be managing the team that day.

11th November. City travelled to the Baseball Ground to face Derby County. Brightwell started the game in place of the injured Lake, alongside Hinchcliffe, Redmond and White - but City went to pieces - not helped by some questionable refereeing - and were thrashed 6-0. The only notable point of City's game was the second - and final - appearance by Justin Fashanu in a City shirt - not that he was to blame in any way for the debacle. For Machin, the Maine Road Massacre, just seven weeks previous, offered no immunity to the wrath of City fans in the East Midlands town that day.

Following the game, Machin took some of Malcolm Allison's advice and signed Blackburn Rovers' centre half Colin Hendry, partnering him with Redmond and signalling the end for Brian Gayle. Steve Redmond replaced Gayle as captain.

However City - even with Hendry - went on a big slump following the Derby County game, losing successive home games (3-0 against Nottingham Forest and 1-0 against Coventry City in the League Cup 4th round). The only non-defeat, a 1-1 draw away at Charlton (Allen), couldn't keep City out of the relegation zone - and Chairman Peter Swales decided it was time for a change

- Mel Machin was sacked.

Tony Book was given the job in the caretaker capacity but couldn't stop the rot as there was another defeat this time at Nottingham Forest 2-3 (White, Oldfield) in the Zenith Data Systems Cup (the new name for the Simod/Full Members Cup). Liverpool left Maine Road as 4-1 victors (Allen, pen) and Allen was on target again in a 2-1 defeat to Southampton at The Dell on 9th December. City were in deep trouble.

Howard Kendall, the former Everton player and manager as the Toffees won the FA Cup, European Cup Winners' Cup and two league titles between 1984 and 1987 was brought back to England from Athletic Bilbao to join City as the new manager - immediately signing two trusted former Evertonians Peter Reid (as a player and coach) from Queens Park Rangers and Alan Harper from Sheffield Wednesday.

17th December. Ironically, City's first game under the Kendall regime was away at Goodison Park - and live on ITV! Hinchcliffe, Redmond, White and Brightwell started the game. Bishop - an ever present all season - was dropped to the bench in favour of Reid and eyebrows were raised when Megson (another former Evertonian) came in for his first start of the season and his first time on the team sheet since 19th September. Had someone said before the game that City would come away with a point and a clean sheet, many Blues fans would have accepted the gift - but the manner of the draw, playing with only White up front and the rest defending doggedly behind the ball (including Allen) made for a less than spectacular return for Kendall. The watching audience on TV had witnessed 'a scoreless bore draw.' Kendall had a set plan to get City out of the bottom three and to safety - and it involved a none-too attractive game plan. City fans long debated whether they'd rather see the team go back down but in playing football or surviving by shutting the opposition out.

For the Boxing Day game at home to Norwich City, Allen was dropped to the bench in favour of a now fit Morley and tellingly Bishop was dropped completely from the team sheet. Lake was back from injury, so Brightwell joined Allen as a sub. Indeed, it was Allen who scored the late winner, following a glorious move by Lake. Fed by Allen, Lake moved into the Norwich box playing "keepy up" three times, looping the ball over two defenders and laying the ball off for the unmarked Allen to slot the ball home.

If Kendall's four points from six gave the doubters something to ponder over, the new manager's next move shocked fans to the core. Out went Bishop and Morley to West Ham United, with former Everton youth player Mark Ward making the opposite journey. Both had become 'cult heroes' on the terraces. Morley had been a target for the boo boys during his first twelve months at

Maine Road, but his promotion winning goal at Bradford City and his goal in the 5-1 had elevated his standing amongst the fans, while Bishop - playing in every game that season until Kendall's arrival - had endeared himself with his attractive style of play from midfield and, of course, his goal in the Maine Road Massacre. It also emerged that Kendall and Bishop had previous history. Scouser Bishop was on Everton's books as a youngster, signing pro forms the same season Kendall became manager in 1983. Bishop left Everton after only one appearance and (it was alleged) falling out with Kendall after refusing to get his hair cut!

Ward would make his debut in the next game at home to Millwall - his name, when announced in the starting line up over the tannoy, was greeted with derision. It was nothing personal towards Ward himself, he was the unfortunate 'man in the middle' having been swapped for two crowd favourites and was also an ex-Evertonian! The boos soon turned to cheers as a David White brace secured a 2-0 win that saw City climb out of the relegation zone.

Steve Redmond - a Scouser himself - was aware of fans feelings towards the ex-Evertonian's coming in, but had a different take on the subject. "They were winners. They had medals; League, FA Cup, and European Cup Winners' Cup. You couldn't help but feel the benefit of someone like Peter Reid being around you. Even as captain, he would never undermine me, but he wouldn't shy away from giving advice. We did have games against the 'Everton lot' in training, head tennis and things like that, Howard Kendall would join in and they always beat the rest of us. The fact we were bottom when Kendall joined and then we avoided relegation, going on to be fifth the following season shows you he got it spot on."

A New Year's Day trip to Sheffield Wednesday resulted in Kendall's first defeat as City lost 2-0. There then followed a three game marathon against Millwall. Having beaten the Lions in the league the previous week, the pair drew 0-0 at Maine Road in the FA Cup and had a replay three days later at the Den. Colin Hendry equalised with ten minutes remaining, sending the game into a scoreless extra time period. A second replay, again at the Den, took place the following Monday. Millwall proved to be the worthy winners on the night, 3-1, with Paul Lake arguably scoring his finest goal for City - from a weak defender's header away, the ball fell perfectly for Lake, just inside the area to the right side. Without letting the ball hit the ground, he teed himself up for a swerving shot that bent around the outstretched arm of the keeper and into the far side of the net. It capped a fine week for Lake, being called up into England manager Bobby Robson's pre-World Cup get-together the following week.

A level headed Lake was interviewed by Granada TV in his parents Denton home, alongside brother Mike (wearing shorts and with a leg in plaster having broken it the week before playing for Sheffield United). "It's always been a dream for any player to go to a World Cup," the youngster admitted, "you see it on the TV with all the glamour and think 'Yeah I'd love to be there', but I'm in the thirty and there's a lot of good players in front of me so it's going to be very hard for me to get in."

When asked if he thought he could force his way into the final twenty-two, Lake remained optimistic in his reply. "Well I haven't got a crystal ball, but I'd like to think I have a chance."

In the middle of the two FA Cup replays, Kendall raised more eyebrows with his latest acquisition. Wayne Clarke was signed from Leicester City, although fans were very quick to notice that his previous club had been yes, Everton!

The 1-1 draw away at Spurs in north London - played in between the two trips to Millwall's Den - had a team sheet of thirteen names containing only three non "Class of 86" or ex Evertonians! Andy Dibble, Colin Hendry (the goal scorer) and Clive Allen were the "outsiders" in the pack alongside the Famous Five and five former Toffees.

A 1-0 home win the following week against Coventry City (White) had City in a respectable fourteenth place and in a good frame of mind for the following week's game at Old Trafford!

3rd February. The suspension of Peter Reid forced Kendall to shuffle the team around. In came Brightwell in midfield, with Lake reverting to full back to cover for Harper - who had moved into a sweeper role. Clarke started his second game for the injured Clive Allen, in partnering White up front. City fans baited the reds with regular chants reminding them of the 5-1 Maine Road Massacre and the neighbours were desperate for revenge. Following trouble at the last two derbies the strictly all-ticket crowd was capped at 40,000.

A tense first half had City slightly ahead but neither side had broken the deadlock. A similar pattern emerged at the start of the second half and belief was growing that a double over United could be achieved. However, midway through the second period, Clayton Blackmore bravely headed home a low Danny Wallace cross on the six yard line and it appeared that City would rue their missed chances.

But City hit back five minutes later. A throw in by City into the United box was headed out to Ward, who was at the edge of the box on the right hand side. He laid it on for the unmarked Brightwell, thirty yards out and just to the right hand side of the 'D'. In Brightwell's own words, when interviewed at the end of the game, "I just wellied it!"

Granada TV's commentator described it somehow differently. "...the ball laid back for Brightwell to hit it, OOOOOOOOOOOOOHHHHH what a

great goal from Brightwell (pause) ....a tremendous goal from the youngster......
an absolute belter". Detailing the goal on the replay, the commentator added
"Laid back to him, left foot, all the way like an arrow, a beauty!"

Indeed it was a beauty and one celebrated madly by the City fans housed
behind the end in which Brightwell had scored, which was the final goal of the
game. Brightwell later described the goal, "Normally I'd look to cross it into the
box but I heard Steve Redmond scream for me to shoot, so I thought 'why not?'
and connected perfectly from thirty yards out!"

Clearly City had made progress under Kendall - but there were concerns.
From 1st January until the last day of March, City had won only one game - and
although only losing three - there had been six draws. Also worryingly there
had been a lack of goals. In the thirteen games in those three months in all
competitions, City had not scored more than one goal in any game.

In February, Kendall signed Aston Villa's pocket sized striker, Adrian Heath.
Yes, the very same Adrian Heath who played under Kendall at Goodison Park
in the 80's! The team sheet for the 2-1 home defeat against Charlton on 24th
February, contained Dibble and Hendry, the Famous Five and SIX ex-Toffees,
five of whom Kendall had signed - Harper, Reid, Ward, Clarke and Heath -
along with Megson who had been a Machin signing.

The game away at Nottingham Forest on 3rd March was lost to the infamous
Gary Crosby goal - coming from behind the unaware Andy Dibble, holding out
the ball in one hand, only for Crosby to head it out of the keeper's palm and
turn it into the back of an empty net.

With the goals still absent and the transfer deadline approaching, Kendall
went into the transfer market for the final time in late March, in what was
arguably his most successful signing for City - Niall Quinn. To the relief of
the fans, not only was Quinn signed from Arsenal (for £800,000) but he had
absolutely no connections to Everton FC. Quinn scored on his impressive debut
against Chelsea in a 1-1 draw at Maine Road on 21st March.

21st March. Andy Hinchcliffe had missed only one game out of the first thirty-
six - yet he was dropped by Howard Kendall before the home game against
Chelsea - and the subsequent eight games - at first moving Paul Lake to left
back for one game, then switching Alan Harper from right back to left back,
with Lake moving to the right for four games, before Ian Brightwell was right
back for the final four games. Hinchcliffe has a spell in the reserves for the first
time all season, being placed on the bench for the final four games.

27th March. Paul Lake makes the next step up the International ladder after
being called in to England 'B' team for the first time, to play a Republic of
Ireland 'B' team at Turners Cross, in Cork. Lake very much saw this as his

opportunity to impress and stake his claim for a full England call up leading to the World Cup in the summer. Niall Quinn, in a move to get more match fitness, was in the opposition side, indeed he scored twice as the home side won 4-1, with future City loanee Dalian Atkinson scoring England's consolation goal. For Lake, the disappointment wasn't the score, but of his wasted chance. The manager Dave Sexton gave him half a game, the second half, when England were chasing the game – and asked the City man to play high up the pitch on the left wing. A furious Lake did as he was asked, knowing full well that playing there was not going to give him the opportunity to show his full worth by playing in the position he'd been playing all season – either as full back or in midfield – and he could see his chances of a full cap being put back, rather than brought forward.

1st April. On the day Strangeways Prison went up in flames, City – now in the bottom three and without an away win all season – travelled to Villa Park for a Sunday game live on ITV. A Villa win would take them above leaders Liverpool and into top spot. Lake, Redmond and White started with Brightwell on the bench and Quinn partnering the fit again Clive Allen.

After Ward went close, Villa took the lead after a clever run into the City box by future First team coach David Platt. He rounded Dibble twice, before pulling back for Cowans to crash home the opening goal. White and Quinn had good efforts wide and then Ward, given the ball by Reid, shrugged off the close challenge by two Villa players and then on the edge of the box fired in high, past Spink for his first City goal, to have the Blues go in at half time on equal terms.

The second half saw a dominant City have a White shot blocked and Allen striking the bar. But with ten minutes remaining, White was sent running on the left and once in the box and cutting back, he let loose a shot that beat the 'keeper but hit the post and rebounding diagonally across an open goal and running in came the unlikely figure of Peter Reid – and with every Blue heart amongst the crowd and watching back home on TV fearing the worst, Reid calmly placed the ball into the empty net in front of the now celebrating Blues fans. The win for City took them back out of the bottom three.

Statistics can be used for a variety of ways, and now City – unbeaten since the controversial defeat at Nottingham Forest four games ago – went on a further five game unbeaten run, drawing the first game away at Millwall, followed by four consecutive wins – away at Queens Park Rangers (3-1), home to Sheffield Wednesday (2-1), away at Norwich (1-0) and home to Kendall's former club Everton. At Goodison Park, former Toffees Harper, Reid, Ward, Heath, Megson and Clarke (coming off the bench) starred in a 1-0 City victory, the goal scored by Quinn, who scored a total of four goals in City's nine remaining games of the season.

The final two games of the season saw Derby County complete the double over the Blues with a 1-0 win at Maine Road and a 2-2 draw at Crystal Palace in which City had kept their place in the First Division. The Blues finished in fourteenth place on forty-eight points – five points clear of third from bottom Sheffield Wednesday, who were relegated along with Charlton Athletic and Millwall. Also on the same number of points as City were Manchester United, though the reds finished a place higher than City, having a goal difference of minus one compared to City's minus nine.

The Palace game had seen the Famous Five once again appear in a City shirt together, with Brightwell, Redmond, Lake and White starting the game, with Andy Hinchcliffe coming off the bench. However, the Famous Five was about to become the Fab Four as this was the last game in a Sky Blue shirt for Andy Hinchcliffe.

Andy Hinchcliffe: "From the moment Howard walked in the door at City we just didn't get on... these things happen. I was only nineteen and had experienced nothing but success and rapid progress, so having such an experienced manager completely dismiss you as a footballer was a major shock"

There was one final footnote on the season's end and the upcoming World Cup in Italy - Paul Lake had been omitted from the final squad of twenty-two players - but received words of encouragement from England manager Bobby Robson, telling the naturally disappointed player "your time will come, keep playing well and keep yourself fit and I'll be seeing you again, mark my words."

PLAYER COMBINED APPEARANCES - 1989-90			
	FIRST TEAM	RESERVES	TOTAL
IAN BRIGHTWELL *	15 (17 + 11), 1	14, 0	29 (17 + 11), 1
ANDY HINCHCLIFFE	36, (3 + 1), 2	6, 0	42 (3 + 1), 2
PAUL LAKE +	39, 1	1, 0	40, 1
STEVE REDMOND §	46, 0	-	46, 0
DAVID WHITE °	43 (2), 11	-	43 (2), 11

plus 2, 1 for England U-21s
+ plus 1, 0 for England U-21s & (1), 0 for England 'B'
§ plus 2, 0 for England U-21s
° plus 1, 0 for England U-21s

7. DAVID WHITE

Born: Urmston, Manchester, 30th October 1967

LTHOUGH BORN IN URMSTON, David resided for most of his early life in Eccles, where his footballing allegiances were clearly focused on City. Since the age of 10 he had been besotted with the club and was spotted playing for the Eccles Boys team and his performances for them eventually led to an invitation to join City.

Life in football however started as a goalkeeper for the 6th Eccles cub scouts, but then he asked if he could play in a different position so he could have a wider grounding in the game. His career started to take shape as a centre forward and right winger for Godfrey Ermen Junior School and this is when David made his mark for the Eccles boys team when playing in an end of season friendly against Whitehill, his potential was noted by City.

Unsurprisingly, David was also a useful sprinter in his school days and when there was no football to be played, he devoted his time to sprinting sessions. He rotated between games for Whitehill and other City junior sides Midas, Blue Star and Pegasus. Of his first contact with the club, he recalls, "I would call at the City ground every so often to meet people and then from the age of 13, I would report for trials and training during the school holidays. I jumped at the chance to sign schoolboy forms when I had my 14th birthday". His next milestone was the selection for Salford Boys for whom he maintained a regular spot before being called up to play for the Greater Manchester Side.

On leaving school David tied his future up at City by signing on a Youth Training Scheme but continued his education at college and obtained qualifications which would be advantageous to him when his footballing career ended. He made his debut for the Lancashire League side against UMIST in 1983 on the eve of his 16th birthday scored in a 4-0 win and his full reserve debut came during the 1984-5 season in a 0-4 defeat at Notts County on October 23rd.

Having captured the eye as a member of the youth team, he made his full debut in City's first team in September 1986 against Luton Town and became a regular in the side. Having already won England youth honours he went onto play for England under 21's and England's 'B' team before graduating to the full international team, making his sole

7. DAVID WHITE 1984-85 to 1993-94	
FIRST TEAM	328 (13), 96
RESERVES	42 96), 16
'A' TEAM	62 (7), 42
FA YOUTH CUP	13 (1), 9
LANCS YOUTH CUP	6, 5

appearance in September 1992 against Spain. David can claim the honour of being City's first ever goal scorer in the Premier league against QPR on August 17th 1992.

After playing nearly 350 first team games for City, he left for Leeds United in December 1993 as part of a deal that brought David Rocastle to City. On leaving City having scored ninety-six goals, David said his biggest regret was "leaving before scoring one hundred goals, I will always regret not reaching a century. It was not a milestone I thought about at the time, but now it does feel I missed something." After leaving Maine Road, things were never the same. An ankle injury picked up before the transfer needed an operation in the summer of 1994 and just as his full first season with Leeds began more problems arose, not least a broken heel and further trouble with the ankle and as David says "Me and Leeds certainly didn't see the best of each other and the training was poor."

That succession of injuries restricted him to only a handful of appearances for the team from Yorkshire. He eventually joined Sheffield United (managed by Howard Kendall) in November 1995 after an initial loan spell and recaptured some of the form he showed for City. However he continued to suffer problems with his arthritic right ankle and finally admitted defeat and made his final appearance in 1997 in a play-off defeat at the hands of Crystal Palace. He had twelve months left on his contract but had a word with manager Nigel Spackman who agreed it would be best if it were terminated. David says "They made me a very generous offer and I would have been mad not to take it." Despite thinking he had perhaps two years left in the game, he could never regain the right levels of fitness and retired from the game.

After his retirement, his decision to continue his further education came to fruition and the knowledge he gained helped him become managing director of the family business 'White Reclamation' a recycling and waste management company based in Eccles.

"Basically I've been with the White Group. Even when I was at Sheffield United, I spent a lot of time there because I simply was not fit enough to train. It's a family business started by my granddad in the 1940's. It started out with scrap metal, but now it's more of a waste management and recycling company. I was lucky because it was already here for me."

David has also set up his own company called Uniquety Limited, who operate in corporate hospitality, soccer schools, corporate sports tournaments as well as prestigious vacation rentals.

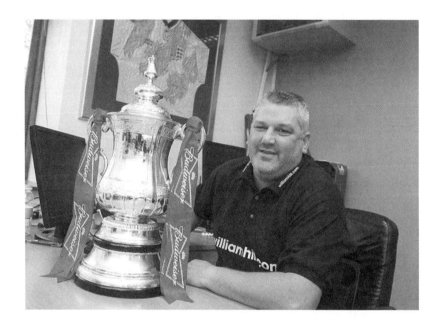

1990-91

WHITE RIOT

HOWARD KENDALL SPENT the summer signing three new players for City - two of whom would further alienate those who were suspicious towards his motives. Tony Coton was without question a top rate 'keeper. But could a million pounds have been spent better elsewhere with Andy Dibble in fine form? And then there was Neil Pointon. Kendall decided to swap Andy Hinchcliffe for Neil Pointon. Pointon played for Everton. City fans felt that the Merseysiders got the best deal and Pointon was soon nicknamed "Dissa" by the City faithful, as they felt he was 'disappointing'. The third signing, Mark Brennan, came from Middlesbrough for £400,000.

Kendall also changed the captaincy - relieving Steve Redmond of the job and giving Paul Lake the armband - he also played Lake in Redmond's centre half position as well.

Kendall explained his decision in the season's first home game programme: "The decision to make Paul the captain is not just for the opening game and I was delighted with him last Saturday. Paul has made splendid progress since I arrived at Maine Road and if he can maintain it, the lad has a great chance of making it at the highest level." Yet Kendall also had words of comfort for Redmond - stripped of the captaincy and his place in the side. "...he must be disappointed at losing the captaincy, he may think back to the beginning of last season when Brian Gayle took over as skipper and Redmond's individual form benefited as a result. Steve has to fight to get his place in the team. I feel that taking away the extra responsibility that the captaincy involves will, in the longer term, be good for him."

Steve Redmond: "I was disappointed to lose the captaincy and my place - who wouldn't be, there was no problem between me and Lakey, he was one of my best mates and I wished him luck, of course, but on a personal level it was difficult as all I had done the previous few seasons was play in every game."

Indeed, after three consecutive seasons as an ever present in the first team, it would be the first time since 18th April 1987 that Steve Redmond didn't start a first team game – a run of one hundred and sixty-two games. However, Redmond would only have to wait two weeks before he regained both the captaincy and his place in the side (remaining an ever present for the remainder of the season) – but not in the manner he would have wished for.

The starting line-up for the first game against Spurs away had Lake, Brightwell and White alongside Coton, Hendry and Quinn – and ex-Evertonians Pointon, Harper, Reid, Heath and Ward. Redmond and Allen sat on the bench.

The nation was on a footballing high following England's semi-final defeat in the World cup in Italy and with England heroes Lineker and Gascoigne in the Spurs starting line-up, the game was as high profile as they come with the media circus in full flow. Unfortunately for City, after only two minutes, Lake miscalculated a back header and Lineker punished the mistake, putting Spurs 1-0 up. Niall Quinn equalised for City, but Lineker scored his second goal as Spurs ran out eventual winners 3-1 at White Hart Lane.

The opening defeat of the season was soon forgotten about as City went on an eleven game unbeaten run consisting of five wins and six draws.

The team containing five former Evertonians beat Everton 1-0 in the season's second game at Maine Road, with Heath scoring the game's only goal and it was the ex-Toffees Pointon and Ward, who scored the goals in the following home win against Aston Villa.

Andy Dibble – playing due to a Tony Coton illness – was Man Of The Match with a remarkable display keeping Villa's attackers, including David Platt, at bay with a series of outstanding saves. The mischievous *Manchester Evening News* reporter, Peter Gardener, issued a "Drop Dibble If You Dare" ultimatum to Kendall in the following day's edition – feeding off the small anti-Coton/pro-Dibble faction, but cynically hiding behind the journalists' own disgruntlement at being removed from travelling on the team coach by Kendall.

Yet ultimately, the game was overshadowed by the cruciate ligament injury to captain Paul Lake that ended his season and his career.

Commentating for ITV, Clive Tyldesley followed the action "…Lake in again…(pause) Manchester City have a problem and it's a real problem at the moment because Paul Lake, probably the game's outstanding player so far, and there's been a few contenders, is in real discomfort". On watching the replay of the incident, Tyldesley concludes "And he just fell awkwardly, there's no malice at all". In summarising – as Lake is stretchered off to the chant of "There's only one Paul Lake" by the Kippax choir – "sometimes the most innocuous incidents in football are the most damaging".

27th October. The eleventh game of the unbeaten run was the season's first Manchester derby – with a lunchtime kick-off at Maine Road. Redmond and

White started, with Brightwell on the bench (indeed, Redmond and White were the only players starting the game that had played in the 5-1 win over United just thirteen months ago).

David White opened the scoring on twenty-one minutes after Ward had played the ball into the box to Quinn, who managed to poke the ball softly onto White, who hooked the ball home. The feeling of another Maine Road Massacre was on the minds of fans (of both sides!) five minutes later when Heath's back heeled flick from a Redmond pass set White running clear on goal – he made no mistake placing his first touch past advancing Les Sealey's left side to make it 2-0. Mark Hughes then climbed above Redmond to head home, leaving Coton rooted on the spot, reducing the arrears to bring the game to 2-1 at half time.

In the second half, White was denied a hat-trick – sending a header crashing against the cross bar. Then, with just twelve minutes remaining, Harper cut out an attack and the ball fell to Colin Hendry just inside United's half. Hendry skipped over a tackle and charged unchallenged towards the penalty area, with only Niall Quinn in support and with three defenders in front of him. On reaching the box, he played a perfect one-two with Quinn, splitting open the defence and slotting the ball past Sealey for City's third goal.

That prompted Howard Kendall to make his by now usual substitution – taking Peter Reid off after the game is thought to have been won. For once, it backfired, as substitute Ian Brightwell, on the pitch for just three minutes and maybe not in tune with the pace of the game yet, lost possession to McClair, who sped away from the chasing Blues to score United's second. Three minutes later, from a corner, Bruce headed goal bound, with McClair flicking on with his head at close range to level matters on the day. Deep in injury time, Tony Coton flung himself to his right as Gary Pallister's shot almost completed an unbelievable comeback.

The following game was City's second defeat of the season in a 2-1 (Allen) loss at Maine Road against Arsenal in the League Cup 3rd round. This was followed by a respectable 1-1 (White) draw away at Sunderland. All seemed rosy in the Blue camp until Howard Kendall decided that the call to return to his beloved Everton was too much to ignore and he left City to go back to Goodison Park, where Everton were struggling at the wrong end of the table.

Ian Brightwell: "That was very upsetting for everyone at Maine Road. I really liked Howard as a boss and as a person and he laid down a hell of a lot of groundwork, which Peter Reid built upon when he took over. We finished fifth in two consecutive seasons under Peter, but a lot of that was down to the sound basis that Kendall had provided the club with. We had no warning signs at all and it came at us like a bolt out of the blue. We felt things were really on the up at Maine Road and this was a real setback."

Paul Lake: "Howard Kendall was definitely the best manager I ever played under. He had fantastic man-management skills, he brought together a squad that was heading for the drop, and steered them to safety. He put a lot of faith in me – he handed me the captaincy in 1990, after all - and I felt ten-feet tall every time I walked on the pitch during his reign at Maine Road. He was a brilliant communicator and was very tactically astute."

Peter Reid was charged with steering the club until an appointment was made and despite a 3-2 home defeat in a live ITV game against Leeds United, the fans gave their backing to the caretaker manager – and the board wasted no time in making Reid City's first player-manager. Reid made a good start - winning three and drawing two of the first five games, including a fighting 2-2 draw at Anfield, where Quinn scored a glorious injury time header. Those five games had Quinn scoring four and White two, continuing their growing partnership. Ward chipped in with two penalties and Redmond scored one at Luton Town. As the year ended, Quinn had scored seven goals in the final seven games of 1990.

The New Year began with City losing 1-0 at home to Arsenal and 2-0 at Everton, with a 1-0 win away at Fourth Division Burnley in the FA Cup sandwiched in between, with Brightwell, Redmond and White starting in each game. There was a quiet confidence that the FA Cup could bring City some success this season and the Burnley game was followed by another trip, this time to the Potteries and Second Division Port Vale.

Before the game at Vale Park, there was the small matter of a double header against Sheffield United. City won both games 2-0 and Mark Ward scored all four goals. The first game at Maine Road in the league was notable for Vinny Jones' setting a new record for being booked after just four seconds! (Jones survived a further fifteen minutes until he was sent off) The second game at Bramhall Lane was in the The Zenith Data Systems Cup, in the 3rd Round.

26th January. The FA Cup game at Vale Park was a sell-out, with 19,132 cramming into the ground. Colin Hendry and Peter Reid were both late casualties and a reshuffled pack saw David Brightwell on the bench for the first time (though he was an unused sub), with his brother Ian starting the game with Redmond and White. Former City player Darren Beckford was in the attack for Vale.

City went ahead early on, when a wonderful cross from Pointon was met by Quinn, who side footed past the keeper. City had further chances from White and Ward, but then from a free kick, floated into the City box, Beckford beat Redmond to flick the ball on to Robbie Earle, whose shot was blocked by

Brightwell - falling to the feet of Beckford who slammed the ball home in front of the City fans, nine minutes before half time.

In the second half, City fans had been calling for the introduction of Clive Allen and with twenty minutes remaining, they got their wish. City won a corner and before the kick was taken, Reid swapped Adrian Heath for Allen, who sprinted into the penalty area. Ward chipped in a near post kick, aiming for Quinn to flick on - only for Robbie Earle to beat him to it, flicking it straight to Allen who headed home from close range! City survived a late fight by the home side to earn another away tie in the 5th round. this time at Notts County.

16th February. Two successive 2-1 wins in the league at Norwich City (Quinn, White) and at home to Chelsea (Megson, White) had City full of confidence for the trip to Meadow Lane. Notts County would have different ideas though. Riding high in the second division, Neil Warnock's side would end the season winning the play offs, gaining promotion to top flight football.

The game started with a host of City attempts on the County goal - yet their 'keeper, Steve Cherry, stopped everything aimed at him. And when he was beaten - the woodwork came to his rescue four times! In the first half Cherry saved a Ward free kick and a close range shot, Allen hit the post and there was a double save from Redmond and Quinn and a one on one from White.

County had their chances to, in a real Cup thriller - Bartlett twice shot over when clean through and Turner placed his effort wide.

In the second half Harper hit the bar from outside the area, with Quinn's rebound hitting the post. Allen headed just over before one of those "Typical City' moments occurred in the last minute when Bartlett raced clear into the box, Coton blocked the shot and Pointon went to clear but his kick was deflected straight into the path of Gary Lund who placed the ball past the stranded Brightwell on the line. There was still time for more drama in injury time with an almighty goal mouth scramble in the County box had Quinn rising above everyone else to head onto the bar! City's FA Cup dream was over for another year.

Four days later City crashed out of the Zenith Data Systems Cup losing 2-0 away to Leeds United and then came three successive home games in the league in which City would win, lose and draw in that order. The win over Luton Town (3-0) took City into 5th place, but then slipped back following a 3-0 defeat against Liverpool and a 1-1 draw with Wimbledon.

A 3-1 defeat at Coventry City was turned around with a seven game unbeaten run (including five wins), which included two very memorable games - the last of which was arguably David White's finest hour in a City shirt.

20th April. There were four games to go - and City were chasing fifth spot, whilst Derby County needed a win to avoid relegation. Brightwell was injured and would play no more part in the remaining four games. Redmond and White were carrying the flag for the Class of '86, nine days short of the fifth anniversary of the Youth Cup victory.

In the first half, Quinn, on the edge of the box, headed forward to Heath, who headed it back for Quinn to fire home. The game then took an incredible twist when Coton was judged to have brought down Dean Saunders in the box. The result was a penalty and the clearly unhappy Coton was shown a red card. Coton threw his gloves at the ref in disgust on his way! Emergency keeper Niall Quinn brilliantly saved Saunders spot kick, diving down to his left hand corner. Ten men City continued to run the game and Quinn was equal to the limited opportunities Derby had, with the Irishman putting to good use his skills gained from playing Gaelic football!

In the second half, White sent the home crowd into raptures, as he seized upon a poor back pass, skipped over one challenge, brushing off another before a thunderous shot hit the back of the top left corner. Quinn's clean sheet was ruined in the last minute when Mick Harford headed home in the last minute, but City won and the day belonged to Niall Quinn.

23rd April. If Quinn attracted the headlines three days previous, then David White was to be the centre of attention after the midweek game away at Aston Villa in which he had ran riot!

The game was only five minutes old when neat passing between Brennan and Quinn sent White clear on the left hand side, firing past Spink on his far side in front of the Holte End. The second goal was a classic route one goal. A huge kick from Coton was flicked on by Quinn, setting up White, who was racing through. The ball bounced just once from Coton's clearance to it hitting the Villa net, as White lobbed the stranded Spink. Coton kept Villa at bay with fine saves and when he was beaten - by David Platt - the future City assistant boss could only watch as his shot trickled inches wide of the post.

In the second half, a swerving Brennan shot from outside of the box rattled the bar. Brennan then added City's third after White, breaking clear on the right wing, squared perfectly for the midfielder to thump the ball in. David Platt scored for Villa from the penalty spot, after Redmond was judged to have handled a Platt shot on the goal line. White then got his hat-trick after Quinn, body sliding on the floor, flicked through for White to run clear and on reaching the middle of the D area, cracked a shot in off the right hand post. And he hadn't finished yet! When Quinn headed on to White, the player was on the corner of the box on the left hand side. Seeming to be posing no threat, White simply blasted the ball between the 'keeper and the near post for his fourth goal – the first City player to score four goals in one game since Brian Kidd at Maine Road against Leicester City in 1977.

White was quick to praise the contribution from his fellow team mates, when interviewed after the game by Granada TV: "We got off to a good start and I got the goal early on and Quinny did superbly for the second one so two was good and that was my fiftieth goal for the club which I was really pleased about and the lads were just saying at half time 'just keep on going and you'll get your hat-trick' and I just tried to be patient and really, as they came forward at the end, chasing the game, I was lucky enough to get the other two."

When asked by the authors for his best City moment of his career, suggesting this Villa game alongside Huddersfield Town and the Maine Road Massacre, White's reply was "Villa Park by far."

27th April. David White makes his debut for the England 'B' team in a 1-0 win over Iceland's full international team at Watford's Vicarage Road. City's Keith Curle played for the entire second half. Future Blue Nigel Clough scored the game's only goal.

4th May. The penultimate game of the season had City travelling the short distance across to Old Trafford. A draw for City would see them finish higher than United for the first time since 1978. Coton was now suspended after his sending off against Derby a week ago - and with Andy Dibble injured, it was a baptism of fire for the young Welsh youth team 'keeper, Martyn Margetson. The game was no classic and although City had protected their rookie 'keeper well, Margetson was helpless to prevent a deflection from Colin Hendry zipping past him. Hendry - understandably - didn't wish to see his name associated with the goal, but how the Football League allowed Ryan Giggs to claim it as his first ever goal for United (having made absolutely no contact with the ball whatsoever) remains a mystery! There were no dubious goals panels in 1991.

11th May. The season finished on a high for City - needing to win (and hope United would drop points away at Crystal Palace) to end the season in fifth place - and higher than United. Sunderland needed to win and hope results went their way too in order to prevent relegation. One of the biggest away followings seen at Maine Road, outside of a United game, travelled down from Wearside to cheer the Roker Park team on.

Niall Quinn opened the scoring for City - who then went 2-1 down as Marco Gabbiadini and former City youth and reserve team defender Gary Bennett had the away fans firmly believing in miracles! However, Quinn once again scored just before half time to even things up.

After the break, the game was a lot less calm, with City's fans cheering as they heard Palace were beating United 3-0 and the Mackems consoling themselves in the knowledge that results elsewhere were going against them. In the final minute, David White headed home the winning goal, sending the Kippax choir into a celebratory "We're the pride of Manchester" chorus!

With the club on a high, the players could look forward to a well-deserved break – all except one, who was battling to save his career.

Having been stretchered off against Villa way back in August, Paul Lake was initially informed he'd be out for six weeks and was soon running up and down the Kippax terrace in an attempt to gain fitness. However, after collapsing during his first training session, it was time for a specialist to take a look at the knee – and Lake was diagnosed as having damaged his cruciate ligaments and underwent investigative keyhole surgery, with the aim of being out for maybe six or so months and fit for the following season. A couple of weeks later, his knee was operated on, in what was then seen as a pioneering operation. After a few weeks in hospital and physiotherapy, Lake was allowed back home and in care of the club. City decided to send him to Lilleshall, in Shropshire, for two out of every three weeks, sharing times with stars from various sporting disciplines. It was far from easy, though there were plenty of scams – according to Lake in his biography – that were acted out amongst the various sports stars, including late nights, alcohol and the opposite sex! In the spring of 1991, the go ahead to step up training was given, only for a further set back to occur – would Lake be fit to start the following season?

PLAYER COMBINED APPEARANCES - 1990-91			
	FIRST TEAM	RESERVES	TOTAL
IAN BRIGHTWELL	37 (5 + 1), 0	1, 0	38 (6 + 1), 0
PAUL LAKE	3, 0	-	3, 0
STEVE REDMOND	44, (2 + 1), 2	3, 0	47 (2 + 1), 2
DAVID WHITE *	45 (1), 17	-	45 (1), 17

* *plus1, 0 for England 'B'*

8. PAUL MOULDEN

Born: Bolton, 6th September 1967

FOOTBALL HAS ALWAYS been in the blood of the Moulden family. Paul's father played for Peterborough, Notts County, Bury and Rochdale, so from about the age of eight football ruled and Paul wanted to play at the expense of everything else. In fact his aunty bought him a City shirt, the one with the Umbro diamonds down the sleeves, and he loved wearing it and that began his association with City. It however did not come without its problems at school. At the tender age of eight he was called into the headmaster's office and told "Just because your dad played professionally does not mean you will", a week later he was in the school team and that began his journey towards becoming a professional player.

Paul started his infant career in football as a centre forward for his school side St Osmund's Primary in Bolton, but they soon switched him to midfield as they had a shortage of players in that position, little did they know what talent they were holding back. Bolton Lads Club however saw him as the answer to their goal scoring needs and for the next five years Paul's finishing flair proved a highlight for them as they stormed away with every prize in sight. In one game Paul scored fourteen times to set a record and at the end of 1981-82 season , having amassed a mammoth two hundred and eighty-nine goals in only forty games, Paul entered The Guinness Book of Records for his goal scoring achievements. This little matter was something Paul was unaware of, "I knew nothing about it until the acknowledgement arrived, a relative had sent it off and it was a big surprise, at the time it was nice but then it became a big embarrassment, and it was one of those things that people would not forget".

His footballing education continued at school as he turned out for St Osmund's church team and was also firmly entrenched in the Thornleigh Salesioan College school side. But in between the glory came agony, as he suffered another one of many injuries that were to hamper his footballing career. At the age of nine he had broken his leg playing for Bolton Lads Club and six years later playing for the same team he fractured his leg against Liverpool Boys.

This was a bitter blow for Paul, because at the time he was at the forefront of playing for the England Boys side, but he soon recovered and was selected to play for the England under-16 side - but disaster struck again on 17th December 1983 when he broke the same leg five minutes from time in a Lancashire 'A' League fixture for City in a 1-1 draw against Chorley reserves (having scored earlier in the game). He had made his debut for the same side as a school boy coming on as a substitute against college side UMIST on 29th October 1983.

Young Moulden had trials at Everton, Leeds, Blackburn and Manchester United but City scout Eric Mullender, had kept a close watch on him and offered a trial. Paul explains "As soon as I walked down the steps (of Maine Road) I felt right at home. Jimmy Rouse, the old caretaker, chatted to me and sold the club to me, from that point on everything felt perfect and I could not wait to sign".

He subsequently joined City signing as an apprentice professional on 4th June 1984, although he almost signed for Bolton Wanderers telling us "My dad had always tried to tell me to stay local and not to go into digs because he knew that would be a distraction and so with Bolton interested I almost joined them but for a managerial change". Paul signed a full professional contract three months later and made his reserve debut as a second half substitute when he scored in the 4-0 hammering of Stoke City on August 28th, 1984. He also played in a full run of ten England under 18's matches, scoring five times.

Ever present in the 1986 FA Youth cup winning team he then went onto make his first team debut on 1st January 1986 against Aston Villa (Paul had appeared as a sub for Gordon Davies in a Full Members Cup tie against Sunderland on 4th November 1985). A fourth fracture of the leg necessitated another long period out of the game and restricted him to just 3 starts in the 1987-88 season. However he was given a clean bill of health, for the City promotion season of 1988-89 and he finished as top scorer with thirteen goals.

He was eventually sold to Bournemouth; however his stay on the south coast lasted only seven months and he was transferred to Oldham Athletic. Paul continued to struggle with injuries and only played 19 matches in three years. He then had short spells with a succession of clubs; Brighton, Birmingham City, Huddersfield and Rochdale before dropping out of League football in 1996. After retiring from full time football he played non-league for Accrington Stanley and Bacup Borough and the occasional Sunday league game in Fog Lane Park, Burnage for 'The Derby' pub side. He then became involved in coaching juniors at Bolton Lads club and for a period back at Manchester City.

Paul can now be seen in the fish and chip shop he runs as part of the family business – 'Paul's Chippy' on Bury Road, Bolton, having previously owned a chippy near to Bolton Wanderers old Burnden Park ground.

8. PAUL MOULDEN 1983-84 to 1988-89	
FIRST TEAM	58 (21), 25
RESERVES	79 (6), 41
'A' TEAM	47 (3), 34
FA YOUTH CUP	14, 12
LANCS YOUTH CUP	4, 2

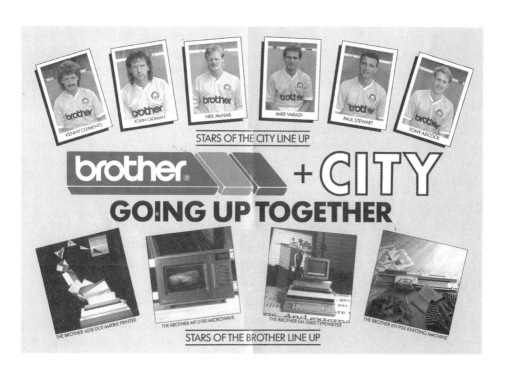

171

1991-92

NOTHING LASTS FOREVER

TWO PLAYERS FROM the previous season were now employed elsewhere - Alan Harper and Mark Ward both re-joined Howard Kendall at Goodison Park. In came Keith Curle from Wimbledon, for £2.5m - then a club record and a UK record for a defender.

After his initial set back towards the end of the previous season Paul Lake spent more time travelling between Manchester and Lilleshall and was given the go ahead to join City's pre-season training - but deep down, Lake knew that something was not quite right. He met Peter Reid for the first time as manager, and Reid reassured Lake that he was very much part of his plans and he would not rush him back too soon. With that, Lake went out onto the training field - but within fifteen minutes, he was on the ground in agony as his knee locked when his heel followed on into the turf after blocking a cross. His season was over before it had even began...

The season commenced with three straight wins to send City to the top of the league. Despite the signing of Curle, it was Redmond, rather than Colin Hendry, who started alongside the new expensive signing - though Curle was given the captain's armband from Redmond. White and Brightwell started the game - as they did for the first eight games

A 1-0 opening day win away at Coventry City (Quinn) was followed with two home wins against Liverpool and Crystal Palace.

21st August. The Liverpool game, in front of a 37,322 midweek crowd, had White in electric form, running Liverpool ragged in the process. After twenty-nine minutes, Quinn set White (who started his run in the City half) clear on the right hand side and as he neared the goal, he shot across Grobbelaar and into his far post. White also hit the foot of the post later in the first half.

In the second half, a sixty-fourth minute kick from Coton was flicked on by Quinn to White who took the ball into the left hand side of the box and then unleashed a shot that hit the bar and bounced back onto the ground and out. The crowd behind the goal in the North Stand celebrated and then went quiet for a few seconds as the linesman and ref signalled to one another before awarding the goal.

White had another great effort tipped over before future Blue Steve McManaman scored his first ever goal in a Liverpool shirt with fifteen minutes remaining. There was more drama with only eight minutes left on the clock when Andy Hill brought down Dean Saunders in the City penalty area. From the resulting spot kick, Saunders crashed the ball against the cross bar and City survived! Saunders miss came just four months after Niall Quinn had saved his penalty when he was playing for Derby County.

When pressed about the controversial goal awarded him, White admits he was lucky. "I don't think it crossed the line, but in my second league game for the club I had one at St. James' Park that crossed the line by over a yard that wasn't given. But that's football!"

White was on the score sheet again three days later against Crystal Palace, poking home a Brennan cross in between two penalties from Brennan, as City went top of the league with a 3-2 win putting them on nine points out of nine.

A goalless draw at Norwich City ended the 100% record, followed by a 2-1 defeat at Highbury - with Brightwell scoring his only goal of the season. That was the beginning of six defeats and seven wins over the next thirteen games (including a double over Chester City in the League Cup). In an away defeat against Leeds United, Peter Reid had a penalty disallowed after his initial shot hit the post and he followed up with the rebound before any other player had touched the ball! Steve Redmond took the next penalty away at West Ham United and with five minutes to go put the Blues 1-0 up - only for the Hammers to equalise minutes later. Colin Hendry had been sent on as a sub to play up front and his injury time winner saw City take all three points. A few weeks later, Hendry would depart City, returning to Blackburn Rovers; Clive Allen left a few weeks after that, to join Chelsea and then West Ham a few months later in the same season.

27th November. David White, playing in the reserves, scored four times as City thrashed West Bromwich Albion 6-1 at The Hawthorns. The other goals came from Mike Sheron and Jason Beckford.

4th December. David White scores in the 2-1 defeat away at Second Division Middlesbrough in the League Cup 4th round tie at Ayresome Park. It was White's first goal in a run that would see him on the score sheet in six consecutive games, scoring seven goals in the process - including a second brace (both memorable lobs over Grobbelaar) against Liverpool this season - as City drew 2-2 at Anfield on 21st December. The final two games of the year, both at Maine Road, had White scoring in his fifth and sixth consecutive games as City beat Norwich

City (2-1) in a game where Steve McMahon made his City debut, five days after playing against the Blues at Anfield, and Arsenal (1-0) to move into third place in the league, within touching distance of pacesetters Manchester United and Leeds United.

Brightwell, Redmond and White, baring the odd game, continued to be regular starters in the first team and on New Year's Day City travelled to Chelsea where Clive Allen joined the club of former Blues scoring against City! A last minute goal by Mike Sheron earned City a point.

City travelled to Middlesbrough again, this time for the FA Cup 3rd round and once again went home with a 2-1 defeat (Reid). The following two games at home to Coventry City and Spurs ended with two solitary David White goals in each game to collect the points for City, before a 4-2 defeat at Sheffield United ended an eight game unbeaten run in the league. Scoring for the Blades that day was Mike Lake – Paul's brother and former reserve team trialist. To rub salt further into the wounds, former skipper Brian Gayle added another. In goal for the home team was Simon Tracey, who would have a short lived – and memorable for the wrong reasons – spell at Maine Road a few years later.

15th February. David White bags another brace in a 4-0 win against Luton at Maine Road, Hill and Heath the other scorers.

18th February. White's scoring run had not gone unnoticed and he was called up into the England B team (along with Keith Curle) against France in the 3-0 win at Loftus Road. White played the entire second half, coming on for Ian Wright.

22nd February. Both Ian and David Brightwell are on the pitch for the first team together, when David came on as a sub, replacing Steve Redmond in a 2-1 defeat away against Wimbledon at Selhurst Park. For the established elder brother, there was never an issue with playing alongside his younger sibling. "It was never a problem, in fact it was quite nice because we've always got on well together and it was something of an achievement for us both to be at the same club - we've never been in big competition with each other because we both played in different positions."

City then went on a bad run that saw them slipping out of the top three. Three successive defeats (away at QPR 4-0, Southampton at home 1-0 and away at Nottingham Forest 2-0) was followed by another goalless performance at home to Chelsea, who thankfully didn't score either. Peter Reid decided it was time to make changes and in came Fitzroy Simpson, a tough tackling midfielder in the mould of the manager himself, but more tellingly for the Class of 86, the Dutchman Michel Vonk was bought from SVV Dordrecht for £500,000. In fairness to Redmond, he hadn't played in the heavy defeat at QPR or at home to Southampton - David Brightwell had covered for the injured former captain, however, the Chelsea game was Redmond's last starting game of the season in the City first team.

Ian Brightwell's place also came under scrutiny. 'Mr Versatile' started January wearing No 2 at right back for Andy Hill and then played in midfield to cover for Adrian Heath in the No 8 shirt. That was then given to Mike Sheron, with Brightwell being an unused sub for two out of the next three games, the other game he was absent from the team sheet all together. Then there was one game at left back, in for Pointon, two more unused appearances on the bench and then wearing the No 9 shirt in Niall Quinn's absence! The final four games had him at No 4 in place of Brennan, right back for Hill and the last two games as left back replacing Pointon. Brightwell would also play in the reserves twice, the first game alongside Steve Redmond, scoring twice in a 3-1 win at home against Bradford City.

Three league defeats and a draw was hardly the preparation for a visit to Maine Road by league leaders Leeds United, who were neck and neck for the title with Manchester United - City's next opponents after the Leeds United game! It was a conundrum that bothered many a City fan. Beating Leeds United and losing to Manchester United could set up the reds to win their first championship title since 1967. It was wrong - but many a Blue quietly hoped Leeds would win at Maine Road.

Either way, arguably City's finest performance of the season saw the title pretenders thumped 4-0, with goals coming from Hill, Sheron, Quinn and Brennan. The Blues then took a point off United at Old Trafford in a 1-1 draw, with Keith Curle's late penalty cancelling out Ryan Giggs' first half strike, in a game which City played the last thirty five minutes with ten men after Pointon had been sent off for serious foul play. Only David White started the game from the Class of 86, with Ian Brightwell an unused sub - which had also been the case against Leeds too.

City then lost the next game away at Sheffield Wednesday, but went on to win the remaining four games (West Ham United at Maine Road 2-0, away at Everton, 2-1, at home to Notts County 2-0 and 5-2 away at Oldham Athletic) to finish fifth place again in the league for the second season running.

2nd May. The final game at Boundary Park had David White score his third City hat-trick - and his twenty-first goal of the season - with the other two goals coming from Mike Sheron and Adie Mike, the youth team player who made his debut the previous week against Notts County. There was also an appearance and a goal from another member of the Class of '86 who was on the pitch that day – with a late consolation goal from Latics' striker Paul Moulden!

Ian Brightwell played the entire game at right back whilst Steve Redmond was an unused sub during this final game of the season – and the final time his name would appear on a City team sheet. Having made way for Michel Vonk, Redmond had been absent from the team sheet for the previous month, though he was recalled for the final two games of the season, where he remained on the bench both times.

Steve Redmond: "I had played in every game bar one all season until we played Aston Villa at home (29th February) and then I was injured, so David Brightwell partnered Keith Curle for the next three games. I was then back in with Curle for the next two games and the manager goes out and buys Michel Vonk. The next game, at home to Chelsea (28th March), Curle was injured so I partnered Vonk. That was my final first team game. There were seven games remaining and the Curle – Vonk partnership played in each one.

"I went to see Reidy and asked him where I stood and he was straight with me, telling me I was no longer in his plans, adding he wouldn't put me in the reserves as I deserved better than that and he would put my name about, making it known I was available. Of course I was shattered, but appreciated his honesty with me. I always imagined I'd be at City forever"

So with another member of the Class of '86 on his way out, that left just a trio remaining from the squad of fourteen – one of whom was fighting to save his career. Paul Lake had spent the entire season not only trying to regain his physical fitness, but his mental fitness too. Straight after the injury in pre-season training, Lake had further exploratory surgery and the results showed that he had re-ruptured his cruciate ligament and would have to undergo a second operation.

Returning to Lilleshall once again, Lake would learn he was the longest serving patient at the FA Centre – a record that did nothing to boost his increasing lack of confidence that he would ever play for City – never mind England – again. His regular returns back to City were met with more self-doubt as the then very small medical team at City were (understandable to some point) more concerned with getting those players who were short term injured back and ready for City's next game. So Lake devised his own training regime when not at Lilleshall, based on what he was doing there, at a local health centre – without any concerns from City whatsoever!

One step at a time, Lake began to regain his fitness and while the rest of the squad enjoyed the summer break, Paul Lake was working hard to join pre-season training in the July.

PLAYER COMBINED APPEARANCES - 1991-92			
	FIRST TEAM	RESERVES	TOTAL
IAN BRIGHTWELL	43 (4 + 1), 1	2, 2	45 (4 + 1), 3
PAUL LAKE	-	-	-
STEVE REDMOND	38 (+2), 1	6, 0	44 (+2), 1
DAVID WHITE	43, 21	2, 4	45, 25

9. PAUL LAKE

Born: Manchester, 28th October 1968

PAUL STARTED HIS SCHOOLING at St John Fishers Primary in Haughton Green, but at an early age switched to St Mary's primary which was also in the Denton area. By then he was already revealing qualities as a footballer and was displaying an appetite to play the game as often as he could. When he was eight years old he was given the opportunity to play for Denton Youth but playing at under 12 level. In his final year at primary school he was selected for Tameside Boys. Even when Paul moved to St Thomas More's secondary school in Denton, the selectors did not lose sight of him and for two years he was a regular in the Tameside team before winning promotion to the Greater Manchester County side.

During all those schooling years, his talents had not been lost on the scouts of Manchester City, in particular Ted Davies and the legendary Ken Barnes, who had noted his potential when he first turned out for Tameside Boys. Consequently he was recruited to play for Blue Star, a side unofficially regarded as City's satellite team for young players. Despite interest from other clubs – Manchester United had invited him for a trial – as a Manchester City fan Lake remained determined to play for the Blues. He was on schoolboy forms in 1983 and on leaving secondary school he signed a contract to become a Youth Training Scheme apprentice on 1st July 1985.

His first appearance for City was when he came on as a substitute in a Lancashire League fixture against Morecambe in August 1984 and his reserve debut came in a defeat at Hull City in August 1985. A member of the FA Youth cup winning side of 1986, Paul made his first team debut on 24th January 1987 against Wimbledon.

Described as Mr Versatile, he appeared as full back, central defender, midfield and striker and was talked about as an England player of the future, he had already gained six under-21 and England 'B' caps, but his career was hampered by injuries in particular, a ruptured cruciate ligament, which kept him out of the game for two years. Paul's struggle with injuries, the ups and downs and the treatment he received, are well documented and are perhaps best summarised in his recent autobiography but he does recall that he owed a lot to the parents of Ian Brightwell who trained him a lot and admits "(Robbie [Ian's father]) got me so fit that I think I could have given Linford Christie a run for his money, I was absolutely flying and felt so strong" but then he suffered another set back when he slipped a disc in his back.

9. PAUL LAKE 1984-85 to 1994-95	
FIRST TEAM	130 (4), 11
RESERVES	36 (1), 3
'A' TEAM	22 (2), 21
'B' TEAM	4, 0
FA YOUTH CUP	17, 7
LANCS YOUTH CUP	2, 5

You simply could not fault Paul's determination and so after a long struggle with injury, which included having to undergo fifteen operations and the prospect of finding himself in pain every single day, Friday 5th January 1996 marked the day he finally announced his retirement from the game. Over the New Year period his knee swelled so badly that he had to go to hospital to have it checked out. Says Paul, "It was then the surgeons noticed that my shin bone was bending alarmingly. They told me that I would have to have serious surgery to rectify it, and it was advised that I should give up football for good. Enough was enough, unfortunately."

On retirement he moved to the other side of the treatment table and became a physiotherapist and had spells with City, Altrincham, Burnley, Oldham Athletic, Macclesfield Town and Bolton Wanderers before leaving to form his own practice.

In March 2010 he was appointed as an Ambassador for Manchester City in the Community, a position he still holds. He also co-presents a City themed programme on BBC Radio Manchester, 'Blue Tuesday', and turned his hand to writing when he released his biography "I'm Not Really Here" in 2011, which went on to become a best seller and is now rumoured to be turned into a blockbuster film.

TAYLOR MADE FOR ENGLAND

THERE HAD BEEN A CULL of players over the previous few months at Maine Road. Jason Beckford had transferred to Birmingham City half way through the previous season. Over the summer, the remaining Evertonians - Neil Pointon, Wayne Clarke, Gary Megson and Adrian Heath, along with Mark Brennan, Michael Hughes and Steve Redmond departed for pastures new. The Fab Four was now down to a Trio.

Steve Redmond: "I went on pre-season training to Italy and one morning at 9am, there's a knock on my hotel room door - it's the manager. He informed me that he had accepted a swap deal involving me and Neil Pointon for Rick Holden from Oldham Athletic. The pair of us are then on a plane flying home that day to discuss details with Joe Royle.

"I never wanted to leave, I wanted to stay at City my entire career, and I'd never really believed it would be anything other than that. But if the manager tells you that you are not part of his plans and wants to sell you, what can you do? The positive things were I didn't need to move house, I'd still be playing in the Premier League and my wages went up from £700 a week to around £1,000 per week - plus a signing on bonus!"

The signing on fee brought back a memory of a conversation that had taken place a few years previous between the much travelled Imre Varadi and a young Redmond. "He told me, 'Steve, never sign for a club for any longer than two years and keep on moving from one club to another'. I didn't understand why, so he explained further. 'You get a signing on fee each time - that's how you make all your money; you won't make it staying at one club, signing three-four year contracts'. And if you look at his career, that's exactly what he did!"

Despite the eight outgoings, Holden was the only signing of the summer, valued at £900,000, with Neil Pointon going to Oldham Athletic for £600,000 and Steve Redmond £300,000.

David White: "Steve Redmond leaving probably signalled the end of an era for me. We were in Italy on a pre-season tour, when one day, without any hint of what was going on, Reddo and Neil Pointon are packing their bags and leaving for the airport to go and sign for Oldham - and the very next day I was lining up alongside Rick Holden. That's how football is!"

Paul Lake: "Unlike in the mid-to-late-1990s, the squad was kept to a minimum and if a player could be sold with a decent replacement, then usually the deal was done, unfortunately. A case in point was Steve Redmond who – along with Neil Pointon – was sold to bring in Rick Holden."

As pre-season training got underway, Paul Lake was back with his colleagues for the first time since the previous season's pre-season training, when he lasted fifteen minutes. This time Lake lasted much longer than fifteen minutes and on the field his training went well, though mentally there were still the doubts and lack of self-confidence. However, a major boost arrived when manager Peter Reid announced the squad who were going to play three games in Italy - Reid deliberately left Lake's name to be the last announced and it was greeted with great cheers by his fellow team mates.

Lake tried to keep a level head, with fan and media expectations now running high, bearing in mind he had not kicked a ball in a competitive game for twenty-three months. Peter Reid, who himself had suffered a serious knee injury during his playing career, was aware of this and gently eased him into the games,

Lake played the second half of the opening game against Brescia and ended up on the score sheet! This was followed up with a second goal against Cremonese, playing just under seventy minutes of the game. The final game, against Verona, Lake featured in the full ninety minutes.

All seemed well on the outside - but on the inside alarm bells were ringing. After each game, whilst the rest of the squad enjoyed a pint or three in a bar, Lake was in his room with an ice pack wrapped around his swollen knee. Meanwhile, manager Peter Reid was all over the media welcoming back his "new £3m signing".

The season started with a bang! It was the first season of the Premier League along with the glamour and razzamatazz of this "new product" (which was the same old product with just a new name and more money thrown at it along with skydivers, cheerleaders and fireworks too!) Football would now be split right over the weekend like never before, including on a Monday night. Ian Brightwell was the City player represented on the billboard posters featuring one player from each club, under the slogan "It's a whole new ball game".

17th August. City v Queens Park Rangers would make history in being the first Monday night game on what was then BSkyB. The three remaining Class of '86 players, - Brightwell, Lake and White lined up alongside Coton, Hill,

Simpson, Curle, Vonk, Quinn, Holden and McMahon.

Lake received a fantastic reception from the Kippax as he tried to focus not on the emotional side of his comeback, but on the game ahead - quite difficult when there was an on pitch camera following his every pre-game move!

In a match that failed to live up to the BSkyB hype, Lake set up White's opening goal, when his initial shot was parried by the keeper. All seemed well, until on the stroke of half time, when a routine tackle on a QPR player had Lake's knee cap feeling the pressure again, causing yet more insecurity and self-doubts in his mind. After sixty minutes Peter Reid replaced Lake with Adrian Heath, with Reid congratulating the off coming player, who tried to hide the feelings inside. Lake went straight down the tunnel for another packet of ice.

After the game, which ended 1-1, Lake attended his first ever press conference, where he smiled - and lied through his back teeth - informing the media that all was rosy in the garden and that he was looking forward to the next game away at Ayresome Park - in just two days' time.

19th August. As City prepared for the away game against Middlesbrough, Paul Lake knew that he shouldn't have been on the field warming up. As excited and expectant City fans chanted his name, he turned his back on them so he couldn't see them. In his own words, his knee was like "a stone in a beer can". He avoided a pre match massage so the physio could not see how swollen it was. The game was eight minutes old when after a pass and sharp turn, the ligament snapped for the third time. Paul Lake's season was over and it was a long trip back home on the coach, sat at the front with his leg strapped up, contemplating the future.

For the record, Mike Sheron came on in place of Lake and City lost to a Bernie Slaven brace.

The next game, away at Blackburn, was another defeat (1-0) that left City in the relegation zone for the very first Premier League table published. Peter Reid's response was to give Wimbledon their second annual donation of £2.5m in return for full back Terry Phelan. Phelan replaced Brightwell as left back, with Brightwell replacing Andy Hill on the right. The following four games saw City shoot up the table with three wins and a draw - with White contributing with six goals, including two braces over that period. The draw in that run had been a 3-3 home game against Oldham Athletic, that saw Steve Redmond and Neil Pointon make a quick return to Maine Road.

9th September. Four days after the fourth game in the unbeaten run, in which City beat Sheffield Wednesday at Hillsborough 3-0 (White 2, Vonk), White became the first of the Class of '86 to pull on a full England strip, when England played a friendly game against Spain in Santander.

The line-up featured two future City players (one also would become a manager) and an assistant coach too: Chris Woods, Lee Dixon, Mark Wright, Stuart Pearce (captain), Des Walker, Nigel Clough, Andy Sinton, Paul Ince, David Platt, Alan Shearer and David White.

The games was only a few minutes old when White went clean through, on the left, but failed to beat the keeper, it was his only chance throughout the game and he was substituted in the 79th minute being replaced by Brian Deane. England lost the game 1-0 to an 11th minute goal. Graham Taylor did not pick David White again for the England squad.

It has been said many times, by many people, that had White's opportunity came a little later in the game, given more time to settle the nerves, the outcome would have been different – something the player himself doesn't disagree with.

David White: "It's probably all true. Graham Taylor never spoke to me after that, but in hindsight my injury had already began to take hold of me so I was never going to get loads of caps." On White's return to City, he failed to score in the next nine games (which included three in the League Cup) until finally getting on the score sheet against Everton on 31st October.

During this nine game run, City only won twice (one of which was a last minute extra time winner away against Bristol Rovers at Twerton Park) as City tumbled back down the table. But City then won the next three - with White scoring in the first two - with wins against Everton (away 3-1), Leeds United (home 4-0, including Ian Brightwell's only goal of the season) and a remarkable comeback away at Coventry City - two goals down at half time to a Micky Quinn brace, City had an amazing twenty-five minute spell with goals from Sheron, Quinn and a penalty from Keith Curle sending City into sixth place.

The remaining six games of 1992 saw three consecutive defeats, the middle game of which was a 2-1 derby defeat at Old Trafford [Quinn] notable for the home debut of Eric Cantona, two draws and a win. The win between the draws came on Boxing Day as a White brace sent Sheffield United back across The Snake Pass pointless.

2nd January. City faced Reading at home in the FA Cup 3rd round, in a game that Ian Brightwell - an ever present all season - snapped his patella tendon (situated in the knee) effectively ending his season. He was replaced by his brother David and a Mike Sheron goal has City heading to Elm Park for a replay after a 1-1 draw.

City - with White returning to fine scoring form - went on to have just one defeat in the following eight games, a run coinciding with a return to City of former player and member of the 1981 FA Cup Final, Ray Ranson, as a replacement for Brightwell. White scored five goals in victories against

Chelsea (4-2 at Stamford Bridge), QPR (2-1 at Loftus Road, FA Cup 4th round), Blackburn Rovers (3-2 at Maine Road) and a brace against Barnsley (2-0 at Maine Road, FA Cup 5th round). In fact, City had yet to lose a game this season, when White was on the score sheet!

This run continued – after successive 2-1 defeats away at Norwich (Sheron) and at home to Sheffield Wednesday (Quinn) – with a goal against Nottingham Forest, with Garry Flitcroft scoring the other, in a 2-0 win at the City Ground. This set confidence high for the following game against Spurs, in the FA Cup Quarter Final.

7th March. The quarter-final tie was to be televised live on BBC1 as City faced a Spurs side that had knocked them out of the League Cup fourth round earlier in the season – and the repeated showing of THAT Ricky Villa goal in the FA Cup Final Replay twelve years previous was another reminder to fans as to why a victory in this game would banish a couple of ghosts from the past.

There was a celebration at the old Maine Road ground too – the Platt Lane stand had been closed for a season, being rebuilt as a result of the inquiry into the Bradford City fire disaster in 1985, when all stands with wood in the structure had to be replaced. Now re-named 'The Umbro Stand' and costing £7m, it would be in use for the first time for this game. The old Platt Lane had housed the visiting fans – they had now been moved into the North Stand, with City fans the new occupiers of the Umbro Stand. As this was a Cup game, Spurs were given a greater allocation and were housed in the entire North Stand.

The game got off to a flying start when Sheron headed home a Phelan cross in the first ten minutes. Everything was looking good, with the exorcist on hand to banish the ghosts – but City went in at half time 2-1 down having allowed Spurs to step up a gear and run the show. Two more Spurs goals in the second half added to City's woes as the exorcist packed his bags and left as he wouldn't be needed that day. With three minutes remaining, Terry Phelan received the ball deep in the City half and simply ran, and ran and ran, running past several Spurs players and finding himself clear on goal before slotting the ball past an advancing 'keeper on the edge of his area and into the empty net in front of the newly opened stand. That sparked a minor pitch invasion from those fans sat in the unfenced former Platt Lane, which then developed into fans from other areas joining in and heading for the Spurs fans in the North Stand, with the players being taken off the field and thirteen police horses plus several dog handlers being brought on to the pitch to help restore order.

When play did resume to see out the last three minutes, Spurs were awarded a penalty in front of their own fans. Teddy Sheringham – maybe conscious of the fact that Spurs were 4-2 up with seconds remaining and that a further goal may cause trouble - blasted over the bar.

The result seemed to deflate the rest of the season and the likely possibility that City could go higher than the previous two season's 5th places quickly evaporated. City won only three of their remaining twelve games, losing four and drawing five. White's record of never being on the losing side when he scored continued with his first goal since the Spurs debacle, notching the winner at the Dell as City beat Southampton 1-0 with three games to go. Yet despite the poor run in, City were somehow still clinging on to sixth place with two home games remaining. A disappointing goalless draw against Crystal Palace (who would be relegated three days later) still had City in sixth place, with just one game of the season left - in what was Howard Kendall's first trip back to Maine Road since returning to Goodison Park.

8th May. David White scored in the final game of the season - but his proud record of City not losing in any game he scored in during the season was blown apart in a totally inept performance at Maine Road. It was so bad that stand in 'keeper Martyn Margetson - in for the injured Tony Coton - was spared any further blushes suffered in a torturous first half, by being substituted at half time with Andy Dibble starting the second half. City lost 5-2 with the other goal being a Keith Curle penalty. With Liverpool, Sheffield Wednesday and Spurs all winning too, City ended up in ninth place - a win would have seen them finish above all three (who tied on fifty-eight points, one point above City) - in sixth place.

To make matters worse, Manchester United had won the very first Premier League title to end their twenty-six year title drought. The prolonged celebrations in the red half of the city made for a miserable summer for blues and piled more pressure on long-time chairman Peter Swales.

12th May. Ian Brightwell makes a comeback in the reserves away at Newcastle United. Lining up alongside brother David. Adie Mike scores the game's only goal as City win 1-0.

For the three remaining Class of '86 players, it had been a different season:

David White had been an ever present in the first team for the first time - scoring sixteen times in the Premier League and three goals in the FA Cup.

Ian Brightwell would miss the entire second half of the season through injury.

AND THEN THERE WAS PAUL LAKE....

Six weeks after being stretchered off against Middlesbrough back in August, via more exploratory treatment, Lake was flying out to Los Angeles in the hope that his next operation would be his final one. Detailed more thoroughly in his autobiography, Lake had an appointment with Dr Domenick Sisto – who had operated similarly on Ian Durrant – who was now back playing for Glasgow Rangers and Scotland – and John Salako, back playing for Crystal Palace. Indeed, it was a supportive phone call from Salako that recommended he go to LA. Manager Peter Reid was supportive of the trip, whilst Chairman Peter Swales – conscious of the cost – was not so supportive. This resulted in a heated exchange in the Maine Road reception area after Lake had spoken to The Sunday People, claiming City had treated him like 'a piece of meat left to hang in an abattoir'

Lake and physio Eamonn Salmon flew business class to Los Angeles and travelled on to San Fernando Valley to meet the world-renowned Dr Sisto in what would be a make or break operation. Dr Sisto's verdict was not necessarily what Lake wanted to hear. He required a double transplantation, one for the inside medial ligament and one for the cruciate. But what specifically hurt the most, was hearing Sisto state that had Lake come to him two years before, he'd be playing now, just as Durrant was Salako were.

After the operation, the over stretched Salmon had to return to Maine Road (via business class) – yet the player needed someone to take care of him in California before being allowed to fly back home. A whip round organised by Niall Quinn and Peter Reid paid for Lake's then girlfriend to fly out to the west coast of America – an act that was appreciated highly, but did little to convince Lake that Swales and his cronies were in any way concerned about their player.

Worse was to follow when Lake checked in to fly home. On claiming to be flying back in business class, he was informed he was to be situated in economy class and with business class full, there was no opportunity of an upgrade. So six foot one inch Paul Lake, on crutches, recovering from major surgery to his knee, returned home via economy class with very little leg room. On arrival at Manchester – in so much agony – Lake requested a wheel chair to take him off the plane and through the airport – all the good work done in LA undone in the time it took to fly back to Manchester.

The rest of the season was a mixture of more constructive sessions at Lilleshall and frustrating times at Maine Road. The club car was recalled and replaced by one supplied via a director – that ended up with the AA being called out on its maiden journey from the used car dealer from where it had been collected. Demands to appear on match days to pick out raffle tickets and smile at half pissed fans in executive lounges, all asking the same well meaning – but wrongly delivered – questions added to the player's agony.

PLAYER COMBINED APPEARANCES - 1992-93

	FIRST TEAM	RESERVES	TOTAL
IAN BRIGHTWELL	26, 1	1, 0	27, 1
PAUL LAKE	2, 0	-	2, 0
DAVID WHITE *	50, 19	-	50, 19

* plus 1, 0 for England

Manchester City F.C.

⭐⭐⭐

SQUAD FROM:
- ☐ Martyn Margetson
- ☐ Ian Brightwell
- ☐ Paul Beesley
- ☐ David Morley
- ☐ Richard Edghill
- ☐ Jason van Blerk
- ☐ Tony Vaughan
- ☐ Kit Symons
- ☐ Gerard Wiekens
- ☐ Kevin Horlock
- ☐ Eddie McGoldrick
- ☐ Ged Brannan
- ☐ Tony Scully
- ☐ Georgi Kinkladze
- ☐ Nick Summerbee
- ☐ Lee Bradbury
- ☐ Uwe Rosler
- ☐ Paul Dickov
- ☐ _____
- ☐ _____
- ☐ _____

MESSAGE FROM FRANK CLARK

"Today's game should serve to remind us all what testimonials are all about, because in the case of Paul Lake we are dealing with a promising young player who was destined for the top, but who instead saw his career destroyed through no fault of his own. I'm only too pleased to be involved this afternoon, as are my players, and I know that we're all looking forward to a very enjoyable match against our neighbours. Let's hope the fan's have a good time, too!"

TODAY'S MATCH OFFICIALS

Referee: Mr L R Dilkes
Assistant referees: Mr E Lomas and Mr J Copeland
Reserve Official: Mr P Eastwood

TODAY'S MATCHBALL SPONSORS

FLIGHTMASTERS

Flight and Holiday Masters

"Would like to wish Paul Lake all the best for the future"

Tel: 0161-832-2444

TODAY'S MASCOTS

Johnjo Walsh,
James Walsh,
Justin Gilbert
and John Tueart.

MESSAGE FROM ALEX FERGUSON

"Manchester United were delighted to accept the invitation to take part in Paul Lake's testimonial game, mainly because we saw it as such a worthy cause. Paul was a player with amazing potential, and it was a tragedy that his career had to end so prematurely. He has showed great spirit in attempting to get back playing over the past few years, so deserves all the support he will no doubt get today. Today's derby should be a great occasion for all of us and I hope it's as entertaining as possible!"

Manchester United F.C.

SQUAD FROM:
- ☐ Peter Schmeichel
- ☐ Gary Neville
- ☐ Philip Neville
- ☐ Denis Irwin
- ☐ Henning Berg
- ☐ David May
- ☐ Ronny Johnsen
- ☐ Gary Pallister
- ☐ David Beckham
- ☐ Nicky Butt
- ☐ Brian McClair
- ☐ Jordi Cruyff
- ☐ Ryan Giggs
- ☐ Karel Poborsky
- ☐ Paul Scholes
- ☐ Teddy Sheringham
- ☐ Ole Gunnar Solskjaer
- ☐ Andy Cole
- ☐ _____
- ☐ _____
- ☐ _____

PRE-MATCH & HALF TIME ENTERTAINMENT

PREMATCH 12.30pm - 1.30pm: A Football match involving the following businessmen and celebrities

Businessmen
Mike Pennington, Ken Williamson and Andy Southern (Bar Cuba), Danny Phillips (Mecro UK), Christian Bakers (Bob Baker Car Sales), Neville Jenning (Gas Care Plumbing & Heating), Ron Chapman and Mike Clarke (Tameside Nissan), Andy Scott and Peter Hensman (Scott Sports & Leisure), Simon Howarth (S R Howarth Building), Dean Maker (SPD), Stuart Wilson (Konrad Limited), Mike Howard (TD Travel), Steve Knight (Bozo), Paul Groome (Mint Corporation), Tony Davidson (Bettin), Simon Jenning (Village Plumbing), Paul Dunford (Neet Feet).

Celebrities
Billy Duffy (The Cult), Mike LeVell, Nick Cochrane, Phil Middlemiss, Kevin Kennedy (Coronation Street), Nick Conway (Bread), Mark Radcliffe and Marc Riley (Radio 1).

HALF TIME Penalty shoot-out between BBC GMR and PICCADILLY RADIO

Team line-ups for Paul Lake's testimonial

10. IAN SCOTT

Born: Radcliffe, 20TH September 1967

I AN'S FOOTBALLING ABILITIES were first noted when he was a pupil at Whitefield County primary school and when he graduated to Whitefield High school, he was quickly recruited by the Bury Boys selectors and nominated as captain of the side. He made such an impression with the town side that he soon progressed to the Greater Manchester County set up but by this time he had already been earmarked by City, when spotted playing for Bury Boys and was asked to play for one of City's nursery sides at the time 'Marauders'.

Ian however adds. "I was first seen and signed for Blackpool at 14 because I thought 'that's it no one else will want me now so I better get signed.' I was with them for 12 months and going to training in the school holidays but then other clubs started showing an interest and so I left Blackpool after that initial period. I was asked to sign by Manchester United and Blackburn Rovers and was asked to go on trial by Leicester City and numerous other clubs which were too far. I went to Blackburn Rovers and Manchester United for coaching sessions but City scout Eric Mullender had been to watch me several times and was the reason in the end I signed for City.

"City's interest came while I was playing for Bury Boys. Eric was quite keen for me to tie up with the Blues and I signed schoolboy forms for them in 1983. Ever since then I was looking forward to being an apprentice. He made me feel so welcome and my mum and dad as well. He was fantastic. When at the club Tony Book and Glyn Pardoe were the same and made us all feel really special and wanted".

Ian signed and arrived at Manchester City as an apprentice in the summer of 1984. Before his arrival, he had in his own words experienced one of the high spots of his career in earning two England Schoolboy caps within a month at Wembley when he was 15 years old… "Wembley was everything I had ever dreamed about". To score against Scotland and put his side one up was even more memorable. "I got possession on the edge of the area and played it upfield to Paul Moulden. He held it very intelligently for a few seconds allowing me time to race up and get into space. He then clipped it over the top and into their area. It was a great chance; I got to it on the left hand side of the box and hit it past the keeper into the far corner. Yes it was a cracking goal and the crowd went wild."

He signed professional forms on September 24th, 1985 and emerged through the ranks following City's 1986 FA Youth Cup win. His Lancashire League debut was in October 1983 against local college side UMIST and he scored one of the goals in a 4-0 victory and he made his reserve debut in March 1984 at home to Chesterfield.

The next step for Ian was progression to the first team and he made his full debut in the opening game of the 1987-88 season against Plymouth Argyle and went onto to stake a claim for a first team spot. After spending the early years of his career at City he joined Stoke City in 1989 before going out on loan to Crewe Alexandra after failing to establish himself in the first team squad. He joined Bury in 1992, where a groin injury effectively ended his professional career and he turned his knowledge and talents to coaching.

"I got what they call Gilmore's Groin at Bury and their Doctor could not diagnose it and as I was on a month to month contract, they let me go. About twelve months later Paul Lake told me to go to the PFA and they would sort it out. They did and it was diagnosed straight away and operated on. I went back playing non-league at Buxton for a pal called Gary Walker. I did my cruciate ligament playing for them on a cold night in Matlock. I remember lying on a hospital trolley in Chesterfield hospital at 2am and telling my dad "never again". From there I started to take my coaching badges, I am level 3 now and got involved with a guy called Alan Keeling at the Manchester FA who introduced me to coach educating for the FA. I had been doing that since 1996. I delivered level 1 courses, first aid courses and Safeguarding courses. I also started working for a college in 1998 working on their football course. They asked me if I would like to do some teaching as they were short and I never looked back. In January 2011 he was appointed as the head coach of the football excellence programme at Cheadle & Marple sixth form college (Cheadle Campus) and was employed there.

"I gained my teaching qualifications and taught in 6th form for over ten years - working for the college and the FA kept me very busy. I played in the local Masters football and the City Old Boys too, which was great meeting some of the old guys three or four times a year." Off the field, Scott is a fanatical Elvis Presley fan - visiting The King's Graceland home in Memphis a number of times when coaching in the USA. However, in January 2013, this casual work in America became permanent when he became a Senior Technical Director at a grassroots club called Westfield Youth Soccer in Indiana, working alongside former City and Buxton colleague Gary Walker. Ian says, "I have finally taken the plunge and things are going really well and as far as I am concerned I will be here for good".

10. IAN SCOTT 1983-84 to 1988-89	
FIRST TEAM	34, 4
RESERVES	93 (5), 11
'A' TEAM	80 (5), 25
FA YOUTH CUP	14 (1), 6
LANCS YOUTH CUP	7, 6

www.allprosoccer.com

1993-94

THE WHITE ROSE OF YORKSHIRE

WITH IAN BRIGHTWELL and Paul Lake still out injured, David White was the only starter from the trio in the new season. Peter Reid had made one addition to the squad, signing a second Dutchman in Alfons Groenendijk for £500,000 from Ajax. The only player to exit the club over the summer was Ray Ranson, playing seventeen times during his second spell with the club.

14th August. The season started with a 1-1 (Flitcroft) draw at Maine Road against Leeds United. The next three games ended up in defeats, with not one goal scored in any of the games - two successive away 0-1's at Everton and Spurs, followed by 2-0 at Maine Road, as Blackburn Rovers returned to Lancashire with the points.

24th August. The defeat against Blackburn Rovers was notable for a three reasons. Firstly, David White missed the game through injury. It was his first absence in a run of eighty-three consecutive League and Cup games, stretching back to 25th November 1991. Secondly, it was the first time since 3rd May 1986 that not one of the Class of '86 had been on the team sheet for a first team game in a run stretching seven full seasons and three games - a total of three hundred and fifty-five games!

Finally, not only did Peter Reid make his last appearance in a City shirt, coming off the bench in the second half, it was also his last game as manager of Manchester City. Peter Swales - feeling more heat from supporters - sacked Reid after just four games, installing Tony Book as caretaker manager once more for a Friday night Sky game at home to Coventry City where a late equaliser by Mike Sheron did little to cheer Blues fans, incensed as what they had heard earlier. Just before the game started, the name of City's new manager was announced. The fans had been hoping for Joe Royle, or Gerry Francis or another 'name' manager. The name 'Brian Horton' coming through the tannoy, left gasps of "Who?" ringing around the old stadium as the appointment left many fans feeling underwhelmed. It was harsh on Horton - and his time at City is now justifiably looked back on fondly by those fans questioning his identity that night.

For the record, Horton had played six hundred plus games for Port Vale, Brighton & Hove Albion, Luton Town and Hull City. He then became player/manager on Humberside, when he was sacked after four seasons. He then became assistant manager at Oxford United, being number two to Mark Lawrenson in his first managerial job. Lawrenson quit shortly after when Dean Saunders was sold without his knowledge to Derby County. The owner of Oxford United was the media tycoon Robert Maxwell – whose son ran Derby County! Horton stepped up and was in charge at the Manor Ground for just under five years, leaving to join City.

Horton got off to a dream start with a 3-1 away win at Swindon and followed up at Maine Road by beating QPR 3-0. There was only one defeat in his first ten games (1-0 away at Wimbledon) with five wins and four draws. White scored his first goal of the season in a 1-1 Second round First leg League Cup game at home to Reading, adding two more in successive home games in a 1-1 draw against Liverpool and a 1-0 win in the 3rd round League Cup game against Chelsea on 26th October - the last of the ten game run.

The honeymoon period quickly evaporated, and with only one win in the following thirteen games - coming on 8th January against Leicester City at home in the FA Cup - Horton began to feel the strain. Including in the slide down the table, was a demoralising 3-2 home defeat against Manchester United. Niall Quinn had put the Blues two up with a first half headed brace - yet the Cantona inspired Reds scored three in the second half - with a late, late winner from Roy Keane sealing the victory.

Bad news was to follow three games later, when Niall Quinn injured his knee against Sheffield Wednesday in a 3-1 home defeat - and would be out for the rest of the season.

18th December. City lose 2-0 away at Blackburn Rovers - the eleventh game of the thirteen game run with only one win - and David White plays his final game for City. The game was City's 26th of the season, including the League Cup games. White had missed five through injury and had only scored three goals in twenty-one appearances - two of which were in the League Cup. Horton swapped White for Leeds United's David Rocastle in a deal valued at £1.2m. The trio was now down to a duo, both of whom were out injured.

Whilst the transfer of White had some fans shocked and others disappointed, the player himself had been disillusioned for some time. "As much as I think Francis Lee is a top guy, I found the 'Forward With Franny' campaign massively unsettling and the 'Swales Out' campaign pretty disgusting. The manager (Peter

Reid) was being undermined. I felt the appointment of Brian Horton (also a top guy) was a step backwards and his assessment that he had a three or four year rebuilding job pretty ludicrous. The day he took the job, I told him I thought it best if we went separate ways, which a few months later we did. When I discovered the extent of my injuries though, I regretted it as I always regret not scoring one hundred goals for City - I was four goals short."

9th March. Paul Lake also had concerns about the new manager's appointment. He naturally worried that in Peter Reid, he had someone who not only believed in him, but who actually wanted him in his side however long it took. With the new regime, he could only hope that it would be the same. However, assistant manager David Moss would, unfortunately, get Lake's back up with probably what he thought was a humorous comment (the usual "sick note" type jibes) that the player did not see the funny side of.

Yet one addition to the training staff lifted the gloom to turn things around. Horton had asked Robbie Brightwell to run some sessions designed to increase fitness and stamina which brought a different approach to the monotony of day to day training. Lake thrived on the new approach that the Olympic Silver Medallist and father to team mates Ian and David had installed and because a lot of the running was in straight lines, Lake could join in with the rest of the team rather than train on his own.

This new routine worked wonders for Lake and his confidence, though for whatever reason, Horton then stopped the sessions run by Brightwell Senior - but Lake knew he was exactly what was needed and the club allowed him to travel to Brightwell's home in Congleton to continue training. Over the months the two became very close as the elder athlete became a confidant for the young footballer, working on the emotional side as well as the physical side. Clearly the player was in good hands - so much so that on 9th March he was ready to play in a competitive game. Former player Neil McNab was now managing City's 'B' team of 16-17 year olds and Lake joined them in a game against Liverpool's youth team at their Melwood training ground. With the game only twenty-five minutes old, Lake clashed heads with an opponent and was knocked out cold - needing twenty-four stitches in his lip and nursing a cracked cheekbone.

This would be Lake's only competitive game of the season, as this interview in the City programme confirms. "I was still getting soreness in my knee. I had been training for around eight weeks and there was no problem in six-a-sides where I was knocking the ball short distances. However, in full scale matches when I had to hit it longer distances it was sore. I had a feeling that some of the staples that had been put in the knee when I had my operation had worked themselves loose and that was the cause of my soreness and irritation. It turned out to be right that it was only the staples so it was decided that I should have them removed which, unfortunately, had to wait because the surgeon was away for three weeks. It meant missing a month's training and between myself, Brian Horton and the Chairman Francis Lee, we came to the conclusion it was no use trying to get in a few reserve matches at the end of the season and I should forget about this term and set my stall for next season."

March 14th. Ian Brightwell makes the first of his two comeback games for the reserves in a 1-0 win at home to West Bromwich Albion. Michael Brown scored the game's only goal, as the Brightwell brothers were central defensive partners, with United star Lee Sharpe's brother, John, also in the City line up. The second reserve game, three days later, is a 4-0 win away at Barnsley, with Adie Mike, Alfons Groenendijk and a Steve Finney brace securing the victory.

26th March. City draw away 0-0 at Oldham Athletic as Ian Brightwell re-appears in the first team after an absence of fourteen months. Following Brightwell's last appearance, there had been many changes – the manager for starters. Since Horton had arrived, just seven moths previous, he had given debuts to youth team players John Foster, Steve Lomas and Richard Edghill. He signed Carl Griffiths from Shrewsbury Town and David Rocastle from Leeds United. Striker Carl Shutt, on loan from Birmingham City, had been and gone with his six appearances (and zero goals) before Brightwell had returned. Outgoing was Rick Holden, back to Oldham Athletic - and long-time pal and – former youth team colleague – David White had swapped places with Rocastle and moved to Leeds United.

There was one other very significant change at Maine Road during this period – Chairman Peter Swales had finally thrown in the towel which enabled former player Francis Lee to take over. Lee, aided by fans movement "Forward With Franny" and Swales had been involved in a bitter fight over the previous months in the power struggle to control Manchester City Football Club. Defeat away in the FA Cup 4th round at Cardiff City on 29th January (the Sunday papers providing the headline "S-Wales Out!") was the last straw for Swales and he conceded defeat - leaving City in the relegation zone of the Premier League table.

Within weeks, Lee had sanctioned the signings of East German striker Uwe Rosler from FC Nuremberg, Paul Walsh from Portsmouth and another East German, Steffen Karl, on loan from Borussia Dortmund. On the day of Brightwell's return at Boundary Park, the jack-in-the-box winger Peter Beagrie made his debut, having signed from Everton.

In the twelve Premier League games played (up to and including the game at Oldham Athletic) in 1994, City had won only two, drawn five and lost five.

More worryingly, City had failed to score in nine of the games – were City missing the White and Quinn partnership? Following the Oldham Athletic game – with eight games to go – the recent signings of Rosler, Walsh, Karl and Beagrie would click into place and the goals would flow in each game – with one exception – and Premier League safety would be assured.

Ian Brightwell would start in six of the final nine games and be a used substitute in one other game, the 2-0 defeat at Old Trafford, the only defeat during his return. The new signings gelled together in a short space of time with Rosler scoring five times, Walsh four, with Beagrie, Karl – and David Brightwell – chipping in with one goal each as City won three and drew five of the final nine games. There was an emotional day for City fans on 30th April, the final home game of the season against Chelsea. Ian Brightwell played the whole game (2-2 draw, Rosler, Walsh) in what was the last ever game for the famous Kippax Terrace at Maine Road. As with other terraces up and down the country in the top two tiers of football in England & Wales, they had to become all seated from the season commencing August 1994, as recommended to the Government via the Taylor Report into the Hillsborough Disaster.

City finished in sixteenth place (out of twenty-two), three points above Sheffield United in the final relegation spot, who went down with both Oldham Athletic and bottom placed Swindon Town. From the previous three seasons finish of fifth, fifth and ninth, it was a disappointment, but hardly surprising given the upheaval the club had endured on the pitch and off, as well as in the boardroom, over the last nine months.

PLAYER COMBINED APPEARANCES - 1993-94				
	FIRST TEAM	RESERVES	'B' TEAM	TOTAL
IAN BRIGHTWELL	6 (1), 0	2, 0	-	8 (1), 2
PAUL LAKE	-	-	1, 0	1, 0
DAVID WHITE	20, 3	-	-	20, 3

11. DAVID BOYD

Born: Robroyston, Glasgow, 21st August 1967

DAVID'S FOOTBALL CAREER really started at the tender age of seven when he was selected to play for the U11 team for his local boys club, in Duntocher. The highlights of this period were when they won the Scottish Cup (he scored a hat-trick in the Final), a year after losing the Final to Celtic Boys club. In addition to also playing for his Primary school (St Mary's) he also played for his District side, but the high school he attended, St Columba's in Clydebank was a non-football playing establishment (probably as a result of a teachers' dispute over extra-curricular hours), so a promising career in athletics developed.

By the end of his first year in High School he had already won the Scottish Cross Country Championship, set the fastest time in Scotland for his age in the 100m and also won the Scottish schools 800m. Selection for the Scottish teams at both Track and Cross Country followed, against the other Home Nations and he even recorded the world's best time for his age group, in the 800 metres. However athletics was getting in the way of his football and he had to make a decision - David himself picks up the story.

"I was actually a better athlete than football player and won numerous Scottish National and Schools, track and cross country titles. I also captained Scottish Schools track and cross country teams. I also competed for British Catholic schools at two European Schools Championships (in Vienna, Austria and Huelva, Spain) winning three golds, one silver and one bronze. Boyd's talent for running was soon to be noted by City's seasoned pro's during pre-season training, as David himself explains. "During long running sessions, myself, Ian Brightwell and Earl Barrett would go off on our own at the front, only to be *ordered* to slow down by the senior players who were being left behind and made to look unfit".

"I knew I could not keep both sports going. I love athletics, but I always wanted to be a footballer. It was not at all easy to make my mind up, but the thought of having to go to university to develop my athletics career did not appeal, so at the age of fourteen I decided to quit the athletics scene."

His desire to become a footballer was well noted. Scottish sides Celtic, Aberdeen and Dundee United were among the regular callers to his home, whilst Manchester United and West Ham were among the people watching him from south of the border

David adds "Prior to coming down to City I was offered schoolboy contracts at Aberdeen (Alex Ferguson was manager) and Celtic, in Scotland. At the same time, I trained at Man Utd during school holidays (Ferguson had now moved down) and also Ipswich Town (Bobby Robson was manager) had offered schoolboy contracts".

City too, were in the hunt for his signature. City's Scottish scout John Ferguson recommended David to City and manager Billy McNeill called at his home - at the time he was confined to bed with Chicken pox so was surprised about the visit - as David recalls "I had fancied joining City because I knew they had a great youth policy (and a great bunch of lads too) possibly the best of all the clubs who were interested. Not only that, the vibrant music scene in the city was a big attraction. I had been to Ipswich and liked their youth scheme, but truthfully didn't fancy living there. After talking to Mr McNeill, I made up my mind it would be City. I actually stayed on at school to sit my Highers (The Scottish equivalent to A Levels) rather than come down to City the year earlier – it turned out to be the right move. Then I was too old to sign YTS forms, so I signed pro forms, but still did the same duties as all the others."

David made his Lancashire League debut on April 21, 1984 in a 9-1 thrashing of Rochdale in which he scored. His reserve debut came in a game at Bradford City on October 16, 1984. David then tells us what happened after leaving City and the path his life took

"John Ferguson, the scout who used to take me down to City, knew people at Hearts. So straight after City, weeks after winning the Youth Cup, I went on Tour with Hearts in an end of season Tournament with their Youth team, to France. I fractured my metatarsal (long before Beckham made it trendy) on the first day of pre-season training. I got myself fit, but it went again during the first week back of training and to compound things it happened for a third time during my first reserve game back.

"I was then told that if it happened again that it would result in permanent damage for life and any subsequent operation at that time had no guarantee of complete success, so I decided to use my qualifications and went to PE College in Edinburgh. However after a few years, I resumed playing again, junior football (semi pro) with Petershill but then was diagnosed with ME. It was a relatively new phenomenon at that time, so that took a couple of years to come to terms with.

"As soon as I qualified, I was offered a job at the British School in Gran Canaria and I worked there for three years as a PE teacher. I then worked a Summer/Fall season with MLS camps in the USA. The

11. DAVID BOYD 1984-85 to 1985-86	
RESERVES	3 (2), 0
'A' TEAM	47 (4), 11
FA YOUTH CUP	13, 2
LANCS YOUTH CUP	3, 4

following year I went back to Las Palmas (Gran Canaria) and worked at another International school (Canterbury School) for four years.

"Since summer 2000 I have been working in America with UK Elite Soccer in New Jersey. During this time my main role has been that of Residential Camp Manager, coaching at numerous levels and being part of our recruitment team who return to UK to interview and hire our coaching staff (the Manchester location is not far from my old digs on Kingsway!) I'm now starting to get more involved in the Tour side of the business."

www.ukelite.com

1994-95

HOTEL CALIFORNIA

WITH THE LATE ADDITIONS to the team towards the end of the previous season, it was no surprise that only one more player was brought in over the summer, with Nicky Summerbee following in his father's footsteps in signing for City from Swindon Town.

Horton had offloaded Kare Ingebrigsten, Alfons Groenendijk, Mike Sheron and, surprisingly, David Rocastle after just twenty games and two goals. Sadly, Rocastle died in 2001 having suffered from the aggressive cancer non-Hodgkin's lymphoma. Steffen Karl's loan period ended too and he spent a year in Switzerland before returning to Germany - in 2004, he was arrested after being accused of fixing a game and was given a nine month suspended prison sentence as well as a ban by the German FA that effectively ended his career.

The season started with a 3-0 defeat at Highbury, with Brightwell - and the returning Niall Quinn - both coming off the bench in a game where City were always chasing shadows after Rosler was sent off early on. Brightwell would then start the next twenty-six games, playing in his customary utility role. He played games at right back covering for Andy Hill and at left back for Terry Phelan. He partnered Keith Curle in central defence when Michel Vonk was injured and partnered Vonk when Curle was injured. And when both Curle and Vonk were out, he played alongside Alan Kernaghan!

The form of the Blues was a great improvement on the previous season and even the absence of the "twelfth man" Kippax Street terrace did not affect home form. For the first half of the season, two games were remembered for opposite reasons.

22nd October. Spurs came to Maine Road riding high with recent signings fresh from the summer World Cup in the USA. The German Jurgen Klinsmann and Romanians Ilie Dumitrescu and Gheorghe Popescu had manager Ossie Ardiles playing attractive football and grabbing the headlines - goals galore flowed, but unfortunately for Ardiles, most of them were in the Spurs net. City too, under Horton, were playing a similar attacking style. City's 5-2 win had

John Motson over-excitedly describing the action as "the game of the century" as City finally get one over the North London side. City's formation was the typical four at the back - with Brightwell partnering Curle - and with only two in midfield, Lomas and Flitcroft. The remaining four outfield players had Beagrie and Summerbee combining a wing role with attacking midfield duties with Quinn and Walsh mopping up any crosses coming their way in a kind of adventurous 4-2-4 formation. City blew Spurs apart and moved up to seventh place. Ardiles was sacked a few weeks later, the Tottenham board presumably not sharing Motson's enthusiasm for his tactics.

10th November. For reasons still not known, the first Manchester derby of the season was on a Thursday evening! City had loanee Simon Tracey from Sheffield United in goal, as Tony Coton had missed the previous seven games due to injury, whilst his stand in, Andy Dibble, was suspended due to being sent off a week before the Spurs game at QPR. For this game Brightwell and Vonk were in central defence, with Tracey and Vonk the only changes from the Spurs game. The first quarter of the game was pretty much even but City went in at the break two goals down. In the second half Andrei Kanchelskis, with help from Eric Cantona, ran City ragged, adding two further goals. City fans had goaded the Red's fans for the past five years over the Maine Road Massacre, and as City fans were praying for the score to stay at four, the reds sensed blood and urged their team on for a fifth, chanting "we want five" - which duly came when Kanchelskis completed his hat-trick in the final minutes. To be fair to Tracey, the second was a deflection and the final three he blocked the initial shots, only for the second attempt to go in when he was still on the floor. But which ever way City fans looked at it, the 5-1 from 1989 was no longer a trump card to be used in debates with their rival fans.

The final ten games of 1994 had City winning four, losing four and drawing two. The final win of the year was away at Newcastle United in the League Cup (21st December), but worryingly, going into the final game of the year City had lost four games on the bounce. Steve McMahon had left to become Swindon Town's player manager and Adie Mike went on loan to Swedish club Linkoping. Incoming was the stylish German midfielder Maurizio Gaudino, from Eintracht Frankfurt on loan for the rest of the season.

Yet in the New Year the Blues fared no better than the old one. City's last League win of 1994 was at away against Ipswich Town on 3rd December and the first win of 1995 was also against Ipswich Town at Maine Road on 22nd February. The slump took City to the wrong end of the table, having been seventh after the glorious win over Spurs back in October. In between the two games against the Suffolk side, City lost six and drew four League games. There was also a demoralising 4-0 quarter final League Cup defeat against Crystal Palace at Selhurst Park and a fifth round FA Cup defeat away at Newcastle United (3-1) after previous round wins against Notts County and Aston Villa.

4th February. Paul Lake plays his first competitive game of the season in the 'B' team at Blackburn Rovers, where he made a scheduled forty-five minute appearance in a 2-1 defeat.

25th February. Lake gets a second appearance in the 'B' team at Preston North End in a 1-0 victory.

11th March. Lake's third game was a 5-0 victory at Platt Lane against Stockport County. The previous 'B' Team's home game had attracted the usual crowd of parents and diehards - but the announcement that Lake would be playing attracted an attendance of over six hundred, the crowd being six deep on the narrow pavement down one side of the Platt Lane pitch, all willing Lakey to produce a performance along the lines he had displayed for the first team and onto the fringes of the England squad.

His presence saw the team produce a display that watching first team manager Brian Horton described 'as the best youth display I can remember ever watching' and when asked about Lake's contribution to the game said 'I was pleased with his performance'. Also included in the City side were Jim Bentley (at the time of writing the manager at Morecambe), Chris Greenacre, Michael Brown and Lee Crooks - the latter three would all go onto to become first team players at Maine Road.

15th March. Ian Brightwell played his final game of the season in a 1-1 draw against Everton at Goodison Park. Brightwell was feeling uncomfortable after the game, but as he was suspended for the next two games and City had a free weekend it was felt ten days rest might cure the problem - as initially it was thought to have something to do with his back or hip. City then travelled to Spain for a friendly against Atletico Madrid and after a bit of training the day before the game, Brightwell could hardly run. It was decided he needed a hernia operation - but it turned out to be a double hernia which kept him out for the rest of the season.

21st March. Paul Lake plays his final game in a City shirt for the 'B' Team in a 2-0 win at Rochdale.

City survived a possible relegation scare - thanks to great (and unexpected) Easter victories over Liverpool at home and away at Champions elect Blackburn Rovers. In the final four games, the first two of which were drawn and the latter two were defeats, City finished in seventeenth place, just four points above Crystal Palace in the fourth relegation spot.

The only statistic worthy of noting over these last four games was that with both Tony Coton and Andy Dibble injured, the much travelled John 'Budgie' Burridge finally got to make an appearance in a City shirt. He'd been on loan for most of the season - warming up enthusiastically in the Platt Lane service tunnel during games (diving on the concrete surface!) and was due to make his debut in January away at White Hart Lane, but the game was called off at the last minute due to a waterlogged pitch. He started in the final three games as well as coming off the bench to replace Coton in the previous game and in doing so, at the grand old age of forty-three years, four months and twenty-six days he became the oldest player ever in the Premier League - a record that still stands!

Rumours had been circulating for months that Francis Lee was to bring his own manager in at the end of the season, having inherited Brian Horton. On the whole, fans were supportive of the manager, whose attractive style of play matched the expectations of what City fans wanted to see, but two successive seventeenth places in the League had Lee thinking differently - and in a move reminiscent of his predecessor Peter Swales, he axed manager Brian Horton and his back room staff.

In the midst of this, Paul Lake had returned to Los Angeles in the spring for a check-up with Dr Sisto. The examination was brief, the verdict even briefer and not what Lake had travelled over to hear. He was advised that the knee was no longer strong enough for the rigours of professional football, but the decision was his. Returning to his hotel, Lake took his painkillers and proceeded to the bar aiming for oblivion that night.

PLAYER COMBINED APPEARANCES - 1994-95				
	FIRST TEAM	RESERVES	'B' TEAM	TOTAL
IAN BRIGHTWELL	36 (1), 0	-	-	36 (1), 0
PAUL LAKE	-	-	4, 0	4, 0

12. JOHN CLARKE

Born: Dublin, 4TH January 1969

JOHN DEVELOPED HIS footballing prowess in the mini leagues back home in Ireland, starting as a 5-year old with Home Farm but three years later he left them to sign for their keenest rivals in the city St Kevin's FC where he stayed until the age of 12. "I then decided to go back to Home Farm because I felt at the time I could do better and St Kevin's had been having a thin time" he reveals.

It was as a 13-year old, playing on the right side of midfield, that Arsenal were attracted to John's talent and invited him for trials. He went over on a couple of occasions, but made no commitment. They asked him over again but he declined the offer, because he felt Arsenal had seen him and other clubs were asking him to England for trials. He had two trips to Leeds, one of them following the week he had spent at City and explained that once he had sampled City, he felt they would be his choice if they wanted him to sign.

"They knew I liked the atmosphere, the friendliness of everyone at City, so the decision was not too hard," he commented

John, who gained his primary school education at St John Vianney and his secondary education at Colaiste Dhulaigh school in Dublin, gained honours with Eire Boys and made his Lancashire League debut for City at South Liverpool reserves in March 1985 before progressing to the reserve side for whom he made his debut virtually a year later in a game at Barnsley. During the nine game FA Youth Cup winning campaign, John was on the bench for the first six games, coming onto the pitch in his first and final games and then playing in all eight of the following seasons FA Youth cup campaign, when City reached the semi-final – losing to eventual winners Coventry City after a play-off.

John was bitterly disappointed to be released by City and here he takes up the story as to what happened to him after leaving Maine Road, "After City I signed for Huddersfield Town. I was there for a six months and it went very well for me as I had played for the first team in the Simod Cup. I travelled with the team to Maine Road for the infamous 10-1 game and a couple of weeks later, Malcolm MacDonald, the manager, said he had wanted to give me my league

12. JOHN CLARKE 1984-85 to 1986-87	
RESERVES	15 (9), 0
'A' TEAM	37 (8), 0
FA YOUTH CUP	8 (2), 2
LANCS YOUTH CUP	2 (1), 0

debut in that game, adding he was glad he didn't as it would have been an awful experience to start with such a bad defeat! He then told me he was giving me a start against Sheffield United (5th December '87) – but on the Thursday I received a dreaded call from home to say my Mam had passed away and six weeks later I walked out on Huddersfield Town and returned to Dublin. It was a decision I regretted afterwards, but it was how I felt at the time as I was absolutely devastated.

"My Mam was only forty-nine when she died and she meant the world to me, it was like switching a light off when she died and I had nothing left to give anymore. A member of the coaching team said to me that I should 'get over it and life goes on'. It was that comment which sent me over the edge. When I said I was leaving, he said 'No John, we don't want you to leave', but I had made up my mind and that was that, I just had to go home and be with my family. You need a lot of luck in football – unfortunately most of mine was bad luck…

"On returning home, I played for Shamrock Rovers - which when you compare to playing professional football in England, well, it doesn't come close

as it was semi pro. So I had to get a job (I've had a succession of driving jobs) and then train in the evenings - Tuesday and Thursday's - and then Saturday morning and then we'd be playing anywhere in Ireland on Sunday, so it was very demanding on you physically with trying to work and (later) have time for my young family. I eventually moved on to Athlone Town. By now I was saving to buy a house so any of the days I wasn't training I was doing overtime in work and still hoping to get a chance to go back to play professionally in England, because for me that was all I ever wanted to do - but the chance never came.

"One great moment at Athlone was when we played Everton in a pre-season friendly and Andy Hinchcliffe was with Everton at the time and we were able to spend some time together over the weekend. After various driving jobs, I now drive a taxi in Dublin. I often thought about doing coaching courses but I never got round to it. I lost touch with all of the lads and what became of them and I'm glad that through this book I've been re-united with a few of them via email. I've since read Lakey's book which was very sad - I had no idea about the torture he went through. I would love to meet up with all the lads again sometime as I loved all of them and even though it didn't work out for me, I have some fantastic memories of my time at Maine Road with a great bunch of lads."

1995-96

ENOUGH IS ENOUGH

CITY FANS SPENT THE summer months anticipating the club's new manager. Chairman Francis Lee had promised one of Europe's leading men to lead the Blues over the coming season and names like George Graham and Franz Beckenbauer were two of those rumoured.

As pre-season training commenced, Lee threatened to take training himself, in the absence of his ability to appoint the promised top manager. Lee delved into the transfer market to sign Georgi (Gio) Kinkladze - a twenty-two year old Georgian international from Dynamo Tblisi for £2m before completely underwhelming the City faithful (even more than when Brian Horton was appointed!) in appointing his old pal Alan Ball, who resigned from Southampton to come to Maine Road. The appointment of former City player Asa Hartford as assistant manager was greeted more warmly.

With the season all set, the players excitedly - with all jokes and laughter - got into position for the annual team photo. Paul Lake once again joined them, not wanting to be there and faking his smile. It is this picture and scenario (stood between Andy Dibble and Uwe Rosler in the centre row) - with Lake's image removed - that explained the front cover of his autobiography "I'm Not Really Here".

19th August. Brightwell lined up alongside debutants Eike Immel, Kit Symons (partnering Brightwell in the centre of defence) and Kinkladze as City drew 1-1 (Rosler) against Spurs at Maine Road. Immel was a former German international 'keeper signed from VfB Stuttgart as cover for the injured Coton. Symons arrived from Portsmouth in a £1.5m deal that saw Carl Griffiths and Fitzroy Simpson heading to Pompey. After three games, the manager dropped - and then swapped - the popular Paul Walsh for Portsmouth's striker Gerry Creaney in a move that did little to endear Ball him to the hearts of fans.

Once again Brightwell would be asked to switch positions over the first half of the season, playing in eighteen of the first twenty three games, at centre half and both full back positions until the end of December.

Asked about his constant switch of roles in the City magazine, Brightwell was philosophical about it. "It works both ways really. On one hand it's good for your career to be known as someone who is able to play in a number of positions, and when I started out as a pro, being versatile meant that you have more opportunities to fill various positions if players were out injured. However, on the other hand it's nice to hold down a position that you can make your own, but over the years I've been played all over the place by various managers". When pushed to reveal his preferred position, Brightwell opted for either right back or central defence.

As events unfolded, the worrying statistic for the first quarter of the season was that City were rooted to the foot of the table after ten games without a win in the Premier League. The only crumb of comfort had been a 4-0 Second round, Second leg League Cup win against Wycombe Wanderers at Maine Road (following a mind numbing 0-0 First leg at Adams Park).

The point on the opening day game against Spurs was the only one gained in the first nine games as defeat followed defeat. Ball gave debuts to young Blues Rae Ingram and Michael Brown (who was sent off on his first game having come off the bench at QPR). Game nine saw the honours for the first Manchester derby of the season at Old Trafford being awarded to the home side as City lost 1-0. Brightwell had to sit out the game having been sent off two weeks prior having received two yellow cards in the defeat at home to Nottingham Forest. He also missed the following game against Leeds United when there was sarcastic joy from the fans as the Blues not only ended a run of eight straight defeats, but also doubled their points tally – to two – after a 0-0 draw at Maine Road. Up next, the mighty Liverpool at Anfield. What could possibly go wrong?

Liverpool 10 Manchester City 0 – although the score line tells two stories!

25th October. City are knocked out of the League Cup in the 4th round in a 4-0 defeat.

28th October. City return to Merseyside in the Premier League and are thumped 6-0. Even more galling for the fans were Alan Ball's post-match comments that he had 'enjoyed' Liverpool's performance.

Brightwell played in both games, taking over from Terry Phelan after the left back was sold to Chelsea for a cut price £750,000.

Yet from the ashes of the Liverpool double debacle came an amazing November when City won three games, drawing one and with no defeats!

Even more staggering for fans to believe, was Alan Ball receiving the Manager Of The Month award! This rush of form took City up two places into the third relegation zone place - though the joy wouldn't last too long with December having a reverse effect from the previous month, with three defeats and a draw.

Paul Lake had continued with his training regime - as Dr Sisto in LA said, it was the player's call to continue. In the gym, he overdid the weights and ended up needing an emergency operation on his lower back. It was during the operation that he met the well-known sports injury specialist Tony Banks, who advised Lake firstly on his back recovery - and secondly on the biggest decision he was to take. In December 1995, a meeting between the two was set up, with Lake - who deep down probably knew the answer - wanting to ask just one question.

After an x-ray examination, the answer was even more severe than expected. A further operation was required - re-straightening the right leg in order to save the knee joint, with part of the shin bone being sliced off, with screws being inserted into the bone. The verdict from Banks was brutal - but honest. The leg couldn't take the strain it was being put through, with a real risk of Lake being crippled for life if he continued. Lake recalls Bank's final words: "I'm so sorry to have to tell you this, Paul, but it's time to call it a day".

Just before the New Year, a meeting was arranged at Maine Road, where Lake announced his retirement to a sympathetic club secretary Bernard Halford, who then discussed informing the media and other financial arrangements. Lake's words to Halford's expressed sorrow was simply "Enough is enough, maybe it just wasn't meant to be".

Tributes to Paul Lake came from three former City managers.

Howard Kendall: "I used to ask for £10m when clubs asked about him but that was in the days when clubs couldn't afford that sort of money. I'd be frightened to put a price on his head these days - he could have gone all the way to the top if he had stayed injury-free. Paul was as good a young player as I've ever worked with. It's a tragedy he has had to retire without being able to prove to people how good he was. He has worked hard to get himself going again. The fact that he has battled for so long shows how determined he was. He was good in the air, strong, brave and quick - he had everything and because he was so versatile, he was used in a lot of different positions."

Mel Machin: 'He looked the all-round player, which is unusual for a lad so young. He had a great arrogance - he was in control of what he did. Without question, he is the best young player I have ever worked with."

Tony Book: "It's a sickening blow for Paul and the club. It's always sad when a player is forced to retire, but when you're cut down in your prime it's especially heart-breaking. You would class Paul in the top bracket. I always likened him to

Colin Bell - he had that great ability to get up and down the park."

In terms of the Class of '86, Ian Brightwell was now the sole member, in what would be the tenth anniversary of the FA Youth Cup triumph.

Commenting in Paul Lake's testimonial brochure, Brightwell reflected on his standing in being the last of the gang at Maine Road. "It was great for all of us lads to be playing together at Maine Road. We were really all good mates, we'd grown up together, and it was like a dream for us all to be playing for City every week.

"It was funny, because deep down, we all thought we would spend the rest of our careers at Maine Road. We couldn't imagine ever leaving. But, realistically, that wasn't going to happen. It was inevitable that some would eventually go elsewhere, but to me it was a real shame when, gradually, we all started to go our separate ways. Had anyone told me in 1986 that in ten years' time I'd be the only one of the lads still at City, I definitely wouldn't have believed them. We'd all been at the club for so long and I couldn't visualise any of us wearing any other team's shirt"

Over the coming weeks into 1996, Ball brought in six players to try and save the club from what was increasingly becoming certain relegation.

Ronnie Ekelund, the former Danish U21 striker, came and went with the blink of an eye with two starts and a further two from the bench. Martin 'Buster' Phillips arrived for £500,000 from Exeter - the tricky winger forever had to live with his manager's claim that "he will be the first £10m player" following any mention of his name. Michael Frontzeck, the former German International left back came on loan from Borussia Monchengladbach. Nigel Clough came in for £1.5m from Liverpool, where he had failed to recapture the form displayed when shining in the midfield at Nottingham Forest. Scott Hiley came in on loan (initially) from Birmingham City - another left back. Giuseppe Mazzarelli - like Ekelund - didn't have time to send a postcard home, when the Swiss international made two appearances from the bench during a short lived loan deal from FC Zurich.

The signings of first Frontzeck and then Hiley seemed to block Brightwell's path into the first team, but his absence from the team wasn't long due to Ball's next foray into the transfer market. Under pressure to balance the books after bringing players in, Ball sanctioned selling the popular young player Garry Flitcroft to Blackburn Rovers for £3.2m. As a result, Brightwell was back in the starting line-up. Tony Coton also left the club - back from injury, Ball mysteriously kept faith with Immel and fans could only watch on in bewilderment as Coton 'defected' to Old Trafford for £400,000.

Yet despite all of the signings, results still did not change for the better. From beating West Ham United at Maine Road 2-1 (Quinn 2) on New Year's

Day until Easter, City only won two games, drawing six and losing four. Those points kept City in and out of the bottom three and with five games to go, Ball's final throw of the dice was to bring in striker Mikhail Kavelashvili for £1.4m from Spartak Vladikavkaz - signed on the recommendation of fellow Georgian, Kinkladze. Fans debated as to whether this was to keep Gio happy or whether he was a genuine player who could help keep City up.

Gio Kinkladze had quickly established himself as the team's star player - or the star player in the fans' eyes. Although there were games when he went missing, there were games when his genius shone through. He ran the show in the 3-3 draw at Maine Road to Newcastle United in February and his second goal in the 2-0 home win against Southampton still remains one of the all-time great Premier League goals to this day. Steve Lomas gave Gio the ball in the middle of the Southampton half, on the right hand side. He cut inside his marker and ran onto the edge of the box, evading a second Saints player. Finally shaking off his initial marker and skipping past a third opponent and the second one again, Kinkladze was faced by 'keeper Dave Beasant and as the City man took his time, feigning his next move, the keeper went to ground as the ball was chipped over him into the net. The standing ovation was still in full motion as kick off was taken.

Yet behind the scenes with the players, all was not well with the star player - as detailed further by Paul Lake in his autobiography. With five games to go, City remained in serious trouble when Manchester United came to Maine Road. Twice City fought back from conceding a goal - the first from debutant Kavelashvili and the second from Rosler. City had played well, especially in the second half - but succumbed to a last minute winner from Giggs, whose long range effort went right into the top corner.

Two days later City lost on Easter Monday at Selhurst Park to Wimbledon 3-0. With three games to go, City were third from bottom, occupying the final relegation place with time running out. Rosler, with the game's only goal, had City victorious against Sheffield Wednesday at home and with two games remaining, City had climbed to joint third from bottom, but with an inferior goal difference to both Coventry City and Southampton. The final two games became a mini league between the three sides, with the bottom placed of the three joining the already relegated Bolton Wanderers and Queens Park Rangers.

27th April. City travelled to Aston Villa, who were riding high in the top five, yet a second half goal by Steve Lomas gave the Blues the points. The celebrations were short lived when both Southampton (1-0 at Bolton) and Coventry City (2-0 at Wimbledon) matched City's win - so all hinged on the final game of the season.

5th May. The game at home to Liverpool commenced after a solemn tribute to former Chairman Peter Swales, who had passed away during the week. The minute's silence was observed without disruption as fans forgot about all the bad times and remembered the man simply for being a City fan.

Ian Brightwell: "We had to win and hope results went our way elsewhere but before we knew it we were 0-2 down. Liverpool were beating us and they weren't really trying too hard as they were in the FA Cup final the following Saturday! After a half time rallying of the troops we came out for the second half and Uwe and Kit scored and we were back to 2-2. The crowd were right behind us; we were obviously up for it and wanting to score the winner as we were well on top of the game. Then for some reason Stevie Lomas ran the ball into the corner trying to run the clock down. This was unusual for Steve as he always played to win and normally would be trying to score the winner himself. The players were wondering what was going on and the crowd were going berserk screaming for him to keep playing for the winner.

"I believe (but you'd have to speak to Stevie) that the manager had told him that we only needed a draw to stay up! Obviously this was wrong and Niall Quinn (who was off the pitch in the dug out) had realised this too and sprinted into the corner where Stevie was holding the ball up to tell him that we needed a win. It was a completely bizarre situation and it turned out we didn't manage to score the winner and ended up being relegated on goal difference as both Coventry City and Southampton also drew.

"We were all devastated but what really screwed us up that season was the poor start we'd had. By the end of the season we'd clawed our way back to a position where it was in our hands to secure Premier League status and we didn't produce. Some people blame that on the alleged call from the manager to Steve to play for the draw but we as players also had a responsibility to win not only that game but more during that season. It was my worst day in football and I still think about what could and should have been to this day. I'd played most of my football with City in the top flight and that is where I (and all players) wanted to play and we now wouldn't be doing that. It really was a hard pill to swallow."

Chairman Francis Lee stood by his manager, maintaining he was the man to take City forward into the next season.

PLAYER COMBINED APPEARANCES - 1995-96			
	FIRST TEAM	RESERVES	TOTAL
IAN BRIGHTWELL	31 (1), 0	1, 0	32 (1), 0
PAUL LAKE	RETIRED		

13. STEVE MACAULEY

Born: Lytham St Annes, Lancashire, 4ᵀᴴ March 1969

FROM A YOUNG AGE, Steve had always dreamed of being a professional footballer. He was a regular choice for Poulton Youth FC in their under 9's team and whilst a pupil at Hodgson Secondary school, he was holding down a regular place with Blackpool Boys team and did such a good job in his original role in midfield that he was also called up for honours with the Lancashire Boys side.

He first came to the attention of Manchester City at the age of 11 and was invited to Maine Road for trials, after that he was a regular visitor to City during school holidays to participate in training schedules as well as watching first team matches.

"I was spotted by a scout called George Woodcock who is sadly no longer with us," Steve explains "he was on holiday at a caravan park and fortunately saw me playing for my local club. He was the same scout who spotted Steve Redmond. My Dad encouraged me to train at different clubs in the school holidays to see which I enjoyed most. I was fortunate enough to train at Leeds, Everton, Blackburn and a few more as a youngster but City was where my heart lay".

This might explain why there was a bit of a delay in him signing schoolboy forms for City as Leeds United invited him for trials and other Lancashire clubs started to make overtures. Word apparently even spread to London and both Arsenal and Queens Park Rangers invited him for trials, but as Steve explains, "I was dead set against the London clubs because it seemed a bit too far to go, so those approaches never entered into it, but I wanted to suss out the other clubs and that's what took the time and that's why I gave City a late decision."

The start to his footballing career at City was hampered by an abdominal problem, but he finally made his debut in a Lancashire League fixture against Tranmere Rovers in November 1985 and scored. His debut at reserve team level arrived in March 1986 against Barnsley. Steve was a member of the FA Youth squad that won the trophy in 1985-86, and gained a winner's tankard for his appearance as a substitute in the First leg of the final, away at Old Trafford.

Steve was the longest serving member of the Class of '86 not to make the first team and on leaving City, he tells us how his career panned out… "My career at City lasted four years - then I went to college to do my 'A' levels whilst playing part-time for Fleetwood Town for the next two years. As I was planning to go to University, Dario [Gradi, Crewe Alexandra manager] persuaded me to give pro football another go, to which I was reluctant at first but obviously succumbed. I had ten great years at Alex under the guidance of respected manager Dario Gradi, and was lucky enough to play with some quality players (including Neil Lennon and Ashley Ward who I had played with at City).

"It was at Crewe when I was given the opportunity to also do a physiotherapy degree at Salford Uni. (the course Paul Lake was to do a few years later). At the end of my Crewe days, I was loaned to neighbours Macclesfield Town but ended up signing for Rochdale managed by former City players Paul Simpson & Jamie Hoyland (I played alongside both in the reserves).

"Then, I once again ended up getting signed by Macclesfield Town by David Moss (ex-City assistant manager) and it was here where I enjoyed my final professional playing days. I also once again crossed paths with Paul Lake, who was the Physio for Macc Town. I played non-league for Bamber Bridge and finally came full circle and ended back at Fleetwood Town as a player coach."

Macauley left Fleetwood Town at the end of the 2007-08 season to concentrate on his physiotherapy practice - only to be appointed caretaker manager a few months later following the dismissal of manager Tony Greenwood. He remained at the club as a part time coach as the club climbed up the non league pyramid from the Conference North to join the Football League with two promotions in three seasons in 2012. Macauley had completed his 'A' licence coaching qualification and in December 2012, he became full time at the club as First team coach, leaving his role at the NHS.

However, this appointment coincided with a managerial change and the new manager brought in his own backroom staff and in March 2013, Steve left Fleetwood Townand returned to work at the NHS.

'I left with a heavy heart', Macauley explains, 'because Fleetwood Town has been a big part of my life but I didn't leave my job with the NHS to do the same job at the club. I wanted to continue coaching because I know that I can add something but there was deemed to be no coaching role available. That's football and we move on.'

Macauley's coaching career may not yet be over as he has just gained his UEFA 'A' Licence badge: 'I passed my final assessment after a two-year period of study in April 2013', added Macauley. 'It's been a hard graft at times, but now I have something in the locker for the future.'

13. STEVE MACAULEY 1985-86 to 1988-89	
RESERVES	32 (6), 0
'A' TEAM	57 (6), 5
FA YOUTH CUP	4 (1), 0
LANCS YOUTH CUP	2, 0

1996-97

CAPTAIN'S CHOICE

THE START OF THE SEASON didn't fill fans with too much confidence as Keith Curle and Niall Quinn departed – with neither being replaced or the squad strengthened elsewhere. And Alan Ball was still the manager.

The season got off to a winning start when Steve Lomas scored the game's only goal at Maine Road against Ipswich Town to send City to the top of the league - courtesy of playing on the Friday evening for Sky, with everyone else playing a day later! Ian Brightwell once again was in the starting line-up, playing at right back.

From there, it could only go down hill and that's exactly where it went. A 1-0 away defeat at Bolton Wanderers the following Tuesday forced Ball to enter the transfer market, purchasing Paul Dickov for £1m from Arsenal.

Dickov made his debut in the next game away at Stoke City which ended in a 2-1 defeat. Ball felt the wrath of both sets of fans – he had taken The Potters down a division in 1990 and was still very unpopular as a result. Ball could sense the growing mood with the fans and resigned as manager, with Chairman Lee placing Asa Hartford as a caretaker manager, which turned out to be for a period of eight games.

Brightwell would miss the next three games due to a strain in his right calf muscle. Making an appearance as a sub away at Crystal Palace, he would be subbed himself thirty minutes later having strained his left calf muscle! Brightwell put the second injury down to "relying too much on the left because of the injury to the right and it soon went on me." That was the only appearance that he made under Hartford - fortunately missing out on the embarrassing 4-1 away defeat and 1-0 home defeat to Lincoln City in the League Cup second round ties.

12th October. Brightwell's return to the side, coincided with the new manager's first game in charge. Former Manchester United and England winger Steve Coppell resigned from his post as manager of Crystal Palace to return to Manchester, bringing Phil Neal, the former Liverpool player and Bolton Wanderers manager as his assistant.

Brightwell's return, in a 2-2 draw against QPR at Loftus Road, was memorable in that he scored his first goal in just under four years! His last coming in a 4-0 home win against Leeds United back in November 1992.

Brightwell managed to play in Coppell's next two games (an away defeat and home win) but missed the next three (Coppell preferring on loan Simon Rodger and Darren Wassall). It was after this final game, (losing 2-0 at Swindon Town), with City languishing in seventeenth place, that Steve Coppell - after just six games and thirty-three days in the hot seat, sent shock waves around the club by resigning, citing being unable to cope with the pressure of the job.

Phil Neal would take charge over the next ten games in which Brightwell would feature in every game - in a worrying run of two wins one draw and seven defeats. Despite this poor run of games, Neal - bizarrely - issued a "back me or sack me" statement to the board, who saw City lying fourth from bottom at the end of the year. The club didn't sack or back Neal as he had requested and as a result, the caretaker resigned and Frank Clark joined from Nottingham Forest - becoming the fifth manager of the season!

Brightwell would only miss two of Clark's twenty four games in charge for the remainder of the season, mostly at right back, with three games partnering Kit Symons in central defence. Clark's early signings were 'keeper Tommy Wright from his old club Nottingham Forest, midfielder Kevin Horlock from Swindon Town and central defender Paul Beesley from Leeds United. Youth product Chris Greenacre was handed a debut and Ged Brannan arrived from Tranmere Rovers, whilst Dalian Atkinson came on loan from Fenerbahce. Leaving Maine Road - and much to the dismay of the fans - was Steve Lomas, on his way to West Ham United for £2.5m.

There was a bit of hope in the FA Cup with an away win at Brentford (1-0) and a home win over Watford (3-1) - but Middlesbrough won 1-0 at Maine Road in the fifth round.

15th March. Ian Brightwell captains City for the first time, away at Blundell Park in a 1-1 draw against Grimsby Town, in the absence of suspended Kit Symons - becoming the third (and final) of the Class of '86 to lead the team, following in the footsteps of Steve Redmond and Paul Lake.

City's form certainly improved over the second half of the season with Clark's record of a total of nine wins, eight draws and four defeats - with City ending the season in fourteenth place (out of twenty-four). Certainly the improvements and stability under Clark gave fans and the board optimism for the coming season.

PLAYER COMBINED APPEARANCES - 1996-97			
	FIRST TEAM	RESERVES	TOTAL
IAN BRIGHTWELL	35 (1), 2	1, 0	36 (1), 2

14. JOHN BOOKBINDER

Born: Derby, 14th September 1968

JOHN, A THIRD GENERATION BLUE, was taken to see City from a very young age, along with his elder sister Susan. So it was a dream come true when he was selected to become a City YTS player under the leadership of Tony Book and Glyn Pardoe. Susan picks up the story.

"He attended Allestree Woodlands School in Derby and always excelled in all sports, was a fast runner and swimmer but from the age of two was passionate about football. He was very good academically too but was really only interested in football.

"Having proved himself as an outstanding left winger with Derby Boys, his signature was much sought after and it was no surprise when – in true Jimmy Grimble style – he rejected Manchester United to sign for the team he supported – Manchester City. John was scouted by Ritchie Williams from Derby County whilst playing for Chesapeake when he was around nine years old."

John's dreams at making it at the top level for his beloved club began when he made his Lancashire League debut at Tranmere Rovers on November 2 1985, where he scored in a 2-1 victory and such were his performances at this level he was soon given his Reserve team debut as a substitute on April 23rd 1986 v Huddersfield Town

John, an unused sub for the second leg of the Youth Cup Final, scored the winning goal at Wembley in a 5-a-side game against Chelsea before the Full Members Cup Final and it came as bit of a shock to John and the family when he was released shortly after such a successful season.

"My Mother tried to persuade him to go to other clubs and she took him to both Leicester City and Derby County," Susan recalls, "but he had lost all his confidence and his burning desire. Instead, he turned to the only other thing he knew about earning a living and that was working in pubs and bars. At that time, apprentices lived in digs and earned £26.50 per week, which they used to make up by doing odd jobs – or in John's case collecting glasses in various smoky pubs in and around his digs in Burnage. Years later, his consultant at University College Hospital London, stated that it was working in such an environment that the mouth cancer - which eventually killed him - may have started."

John carried on playing football on an amateur basis and maintained his fitness for the rest of his short life, at one time playing semi-professionally for Belper Town under Ashley Groves, brother of former Leicester City, Blackpool and West Bromwich Albion player and one time Bournemouth manager Paul Groves.

"He trained as a social worker and was very successful," Susan continues, "I remember meeting him in central London after he was first diagnosed and every street urchin and cardboard box person seemed to know him, coming up to him and greeting him as a good friend and with respect - the same respect John showed them regardless of their background or current circumstance. At the time he was told he had cancer, he was also working as a street performer and had developed quite a following at Glastonbury and the festival scene for an alternative wedding ceremony he'd developed, in which he had "married" Kate Moss and The Libertines singer, Pete Doherty.

"The year that followed John's diagnosis, which was to be his final year, was the most horrifying and unbearable one. John underwent the strongest doses of chemotherapy and radio therapy a man can take. He had to wear a specially made mask for the radio therapy, which looked like something Hannibal Lecter would wear. He went down to five stone and lost all his hair. Throughout the gruelling treatment, he continued to try to work as a street performer, juggler and amateur boxer. All the time he was contemplating how he would make a living if the worst - what he thought at the time would be the worst - would come and he would have to face the removal of his tongue. However the worst was much worse than that…

"As the treatment took its toll, he found it increasingly difficult to eat and ultimately he could only eat baby food as his tongue became increasingly diseased. The suffering and indignity was all for nothing. On 26th October 2005, he was taken into hospital after a projectile bleed from the main artery in his throat. Having watched our mother die from breast cancer some years before, I remember this feeling coming over me and looking at my little brother and realising - 'Oh no, this is it, he's not coming out of here'.

"John had a tracheotomy that day. Eleven operations followed including the removal of his tongue, larynx and voice box as the cancer tried to match his strength and courage. The battle went on until Christmas. Even the ability to cry out in the constant pain was taken away. My brother was so incredibly brave, not only suffering in the silence forced on him but actually, for us, smiling through it.

"I was working half a mile down the road from the hospital at Grays Inn Road for ITN at the time and used to broadcast with my phone on silent, in case I was called to the hospital, where my brother was expected to bleed to death at any moment. I was called there six times and told he had an hour to live. Six times he was given what is known as the rescue package, a cocktail of drugs designed to ease a patient into death. The doctors told me that they had never known anyone survive one of the projectile bleeds John had survived – nor a rescue package. This unbelievable determination and strength earned John the title 'The Cat' at UCL.

"One of the six times I was called into the hospital, I met Martin O'Neill in the lift. While John was fighting for his life on the 14th floor at UCL, Martin's wife, Geraldine, was doing the same on the 13th. Martin had given up his job as manager of Glasgow Celtic to care for Geraldine and I knew him from my previous job at BBC Radio Five Live.

"If I can just explain that this lift is very busy and stops at every floor with people coming in and out in wheelchairs etc. So you can imagine, as I watched the seconds of my brother's life ticking away, I must have been in a terrible state in the corner of this lift. Martin recognised me and came over to comfort me. When I told him about John, he said he remembered him from the City Youth team and that he used to go to Maine Road with Gordon Strachan (when Strachan was at United) to watch the kids and he said he remembered John's superb left foot.

"I was so desperate to get to John, I didn't really take in that he had promised to come up and see my brother one day and if I had, I kind of thought he would have had enough on his plate with his wife being so ill and just dismissed it as a kind thought. So after John survived yet another bleed, I was amazed to walk in to see him on the morning of Sunday December 4th 2005 surrounded at his bedside by Martin O'Neill and Gordon Strachan and our Dad. They were chatting away about the old days and how United had been so worried by the City Youth squad of the day and John was writing notes back to them on his writing board which you could wipe clean, which was his only form of communication.

"Why do I remember the date so clearly? Well, Dad, of course, had tickets for City's game away at Charlton Athletic that afternoon. There was no way John was able to go, of course, but Dad was not going to let Martin or Gordon go without using the opportunity to get John across the road to watch the game on Sky at the Grafton Hotel on Tottenham Court Road. Even though it was literally over the road, the doctors flatly refused to even consider letting John out. He could literally have bled to death at any moment. That was until Dad and I used every political and journalistic power of persuasion we had between us and, as John later put it to me – in writing of course – mercilessly harnessing the forces of Martin O'Neill and Gordon Strachan to shame the various authorities of both the hospital and the hotel to get him across the road to watch City for the last time.

14. JOHN BOOKBINDER 1985-86	
RESERVES	1 (2), 0
'A' TEAM	9 (7), 3
FA YOUTH CUP	(1), 0
LANCS YOUTH CUP	(1), 0

"So with three nurses, two drips, nebulizers, oxygen, two packets of group A minus blood and a wheelchair and the negotiating force that is our Dad, John witnessed a "typical City" game, in which we gave away two soft goals, missed a couple of sitters – but came out with a much needed 5-2 win, with goals from Andrew Cole (2), Trevor Sinclair, Joey Barton (pen) and Darius Vassell. A few days later, John was discharged from hospital to basically die at my home. His suffering hit a new level and to this day, I can't talk, write or think about what he went through...

"All I can say is that, with Martin O'Neill's help, for John, it really was a case of 'City Til I Die'."

JOHN BOOKBINDER

14TH SEPTEMBER 1968 - 9TH JANUARY 2006

★

JOHN BOOKBINDER'S FAMILY are rightly proud of his achievements during his short life – but there was one aspect of his time at City that leaves a lasting sadness with his family. After the Youth Cup win, the following first team programme featured a photograph of the team, Tony Book, Glyn Pardoe and Paul Power in the player's dressing room with the trophy. (*see page 2 of the photo section*). In the bottom right hand corner of the photograph, there was a list of the players who featured in the nine games, with goals scored (or cleansheets kept in the case of Steve Crompton) and substitute appearances. John Bookbinder appears in the picture but not in the text. Therefore, every time the story of the Class of '86 came up in the media, the name John Bookbinder would not appear due to his absence from the text.

The text was indeed incorrect – in that it only included appearances of the substitutes that actually played during each game. Hence John Clarke was listed as only having two substitute appearances (ignoring the four times he was an unused sub). Steve Macauley was acknowledged for coming off the bench in the second leg semi-final against Arsenal to earn his one appearance – but unacknowledged as the unused sub against United in the First leg final at Old Trafford.

Susan Bookbinder was able to address this error and bring John's contribution, as part of the history making youth team squad, to City fans' attention twenty-five years later. The opportunity taken to finally honour John came about when Susan's seven year old son, Zac, was the City mascot against West Ham United at Eastlands on May 1st 2011.

As Susan says, "I will never forget the moment I saw Zac come out of the tunnel holding captain Vincent Kompany's hand. Seeing my son walk out onto the pitch was the single most healing moment in six years of grief for my brother."

The following week's game – at home to Spurs, in which City won and therefore secured a Champions League place for the 2011–12 season, contained a tribute written by Chris Bailey in the match programme officially recognising John for the first time. The tribute contained the following words: "Paul Lake said he had been a pleasure to work with. At his funeral, Lakey said, 'John, or Bookjack – a nickname derived from the fact that as our coach Tony Book was already known as Booky and because John was such a jack in a box on the wing – was a very modest lad, always bulling everyone else up, which made me put him straight one day saying, 'Bookjack…Ability wise, you are probably the most skilful winger in the club with more skill than me! With the opportunity to play games, you can show us all!' At last somebody shut him up! And on the occasion believe you me he did. So yes Bookjack was a good footballer, a ridiculously articulate lad, with far too much to say, but most importantly… a really kind, nice and good man… God Bless you Bookjack"

Four days after the Spurs game, Susan and her son Zac are walking down Wembley Way (now Olympic Way) to watch the FA Cup Final between City and Stoke City.

"Zac" says Susan proudly, "who everyone says is just like John in his looks and cheekiness, also has an amazing left foot and plays for his local side, Watford Town Youth FC. The worry that John's name and achievements would be written out of City's history, had been eased over the previous two weeks and when Yaya Toure hit the winner home, I felt this huge surge of emotion. The waiting was over. City were back and my brother's memory had been honoured at last.

I looked at my son who said "why are you crying Mummy?" Although I am an atheist, I really felt John's spirit come through me at that moment."

City vote in favour of Bookbinder

EVERY schoolboy footballer's dream to play for the team he follows has just come true for one Derby lad.

John Bookbinder (16), Woodlands School pupil and son of Derbyshire County Council leader Councillor David Bookbinder has signed schoolboy forms for Manchester City — the club he, his dad and most of his family support.

"It's like a dream come true but it's going to be really hard work," said John.

Councillor Bookbinder said he was delighted that John was signing for a big club.

"The fact that we have several generations of Manchester City supporters in the family makes it all the more acceptable," he said.

"It means I do not have to face the dilemma of changing clubs in order to support my son!"

John had tried with several major clubs including City's rivals Manchester United and Leicester City, Leeds United, Derby County and Notts County. Their interest stemmed from John's skilful performances with Derby Boys and county and regional teams. And, as he is one of the 'old school' left wingers, interest was that much keener.

"There are not many of us about and we are supposed to be in demand," said John. "But I wouldn't say I had a natural talent. I've worked hard to get better."

John Bookbinder

1997-98

SENT TO COVENTRY

FRANK CLARK BEGAN to shape his own side and out went Peter Beagrie, Mikhail Kavelashvili, and Rae Ingram. Nigel Clough was staying put, his wages too high for any willing suitors and played the entire season in the reserves, save a very short spell on loan, cut short by an injury, at Sheffield Wednesday

In and around the opening games, Tony Vaughan came in from Ipswich, Dutchman Gerard Wiekens from Veendam, Australian Jason van Blerk arrived via Millwall and then Clark smashed City's record transfer fee in signing Lee Bradbury for £3m from Portsmouth.

Ian Brightwell missed only one from the first fourteen games (away at Bury) all as right back. During this time, any hopes of a continuation of last season's good form quickly evaporated. In the first game, Noel and Liam Gallagher took a pre-game lap of honour. Liam, walking over to the visiting Portsmouth fans, gave them a double two fingered salute, rightly predicting a 2-2 draw!

Next up, City were the side show as Sunderland played their first game in their brand new home, The Stadium of Light. The Mackems, now managed by former City player/manager Peter Reid, opened the venue in style with a 3-1 win, with the first ever goal scored at the stadium coming from former Blue Niall Quinn.

5th October. City play Manchester United in a testimonial game for Paul Lake at Maine Road. In a remarkable show of support for Lake, Alex Ferguson agreed to the Reds attending the game, despite both teams playing twenty-four hours previously in their respective leagues – and with many players being called up for international duty with England's final World Cup qualifying game in Italy the following weekend. Given that fans had two games in two days, it was a bigger than expected crowd of 21,262 that turned up – showing the true depth of feelings the fans had towards the player. United had England players Beckham, Butt, Scholes and the Neville brothers starting, as well as Peter Schmeichel. All had approval from their international managers – as long as they were off the pitch within twenty minutes, though that didn't stop Ryan Giggs playing the entire game.

Lake himself kicked a ball in a City shirt for the final time. Being greeted by both sides and of course, the fans, the man being honoured walked over to the Kippax - although no longer a terrace since his final first team game - to acknowledge the support he had received from that part of the ground. There wasn't a dry eye in the ground as the referee blew the whistle to commence the game. Lake kicked off, with a pass to Georgio Kinkladze, and he left the pitch to a standing ovation while the game went on around him as the player acknowledged the fans and the fans the player. For the record, Ian Brightwell captained the City side, which ended 2-2, Kinkladze and Rosler scoring for the Blues.

Other events would continue throughout Lake's testimonial season, such as a gala dinner, golf classic and a cricket match among the fundraisers planned.

26th October. Ian Brightwell was injured during the game against QPR at Loftus Road in a 2-0 defeat that left City occupying the last relegation place. The twelve games to date had yielded just two wins, four draws and six defeats. City had also been knocked out of the League Cup in the second round, losing at home to Blackpool via a penalty shoot-out.

In the following eleven games that Brightwell missed, City would swap Nicky Summerbee with Sunderland's Craig Russell and try to off load Gerry Creaney and Eddie McGoldrick - both transfer listed but with no takers, so they ended up in the reserves for the remainder of the season. Also joining the Blues was defender Murtaz Shelia - another Georgian international - from Spartak Vladikavkaz - but the bad run continued with four wins, two draws and five defeats (including a humiliating 3-1 defeat to Gary Megson's Stockport County at Edgeley Park).

20th December. There were encouraging signs - in the final game without Brightwell, City beat league Leaders Middlesbrough at Maine Road 2-0 - but such games were too and far between. Before the game City were fourth from bottom, but only one point separated the bottom four teams! Brightwell returned, from the bench on Boxing Day as City lost away 1-0 to Crewe Alexandra and two days later he started the game against Nottingham Forest in another defeat (3-2) to send City into the relegation zone. The New Year could only get better.

The New Year started with a 2-0 win in the third round of the FA Cup at home to Bradford City. At half time, captain Gerard Wiekens withdrew through injury and Brightwell led the team out for the second half. Jim Whitley came off the bench for his debut, to play alongside his brother Jeff for the first time.

That win was built on with a great 3-1 win away at Portsmouth which moved the Blues up the table and out of the danger zone.

Brightwell continued as captain, but the following six games produced a total of three draws and three defeats (including a 2-1 FA Cup home defeat to Premier League West Ham United, with former Blue Steve Lomas hitting the winner). During this run, Clark added another Georgian international (also signed from Spartak Vladikavkaz) to the collection, with central defender Kakhaber Tskhadadze – adding to the nightmare local radio commentators already faced!

14th February. The final defeat in that run of six games was a crushing blow to City fans – coming on St Valentine's Day with a 1-0 home defeat against neighbours Bury, dropping the Blues into the bottom two. One fan attempted to end his love affair with City that day, by casually walking onto the pitch during the game and ripping his season ticket into shreds. He was applauded by the thousands of other City fans present that day. Within days, Francis Lee had ripped up Frank Clark's contract and brought in former City player Joe Royle, who had been successful in guiding – and keeping – Oldham Athletic in the Premier League for three seasons and winning the FA Cup with Everton in 1995.

18th February. Ian Brightwell is injured for Joe Royle's first line up, with Richard Edghill taking his place at right back (with on loan Peter Beardsley making his first start) in a 2-1 home defeat against Ipswich Town.

For the following game away at Swindon Town, Jeff Whitley deputised in the No 2 shirt as City win 3-1 at the County Ground (with another loan signing, Lee Briscoe, making the first of his five appearances) as the gloom lifted slightly.

24th February. Ian Brightwell is selected to play against Reading at Elm Park. In doing so, Royle became Brightwell's tenth manager at Maine Road, plus serving under three caretaker managers as well (four if you count Tony Book's double stint as caretaker!) City lost the game 3-0 and the name Ian Brightwell would not be seen on the first team sheet again.

Ian Brightwell: "I'd picked up a hamstring injury just before Joe arrived at the club. I probably in hindsight tried to rush my recovery and was picked to play at Reading when I wasn't 100% fit. I ended up not doing myself any favours because I had to come off after an hour with the same injury – and that unfortunately was my last first team game".

7th April. Ian Brightwell plays his final game in a Manchester City shirt in the reserves against Huddersfield Town. In between the Reading game and the end of the season, Brightwell would appear for the reserves on four occasions, against Leicester City, Port Vale (in which he scored along with Creaney and Clough in a 3-3 draw), Bolton Wanderers - and his final game against Huddersfield Town at Maine Road in a 1-0 win (Horlock).

Ian Brightwell's final City line up:

Nicky Weaver, Scott Hiley, Kevin Horlock, Lee Crooks, Ian Brightwell, Nick Fenton, Ged Brannan, Michael Brown, Nigel Clough, Paul Dickov and Craig Russell.

3rd May. Manchester City were relegated into the third tier of English football for the first time in their history, despite winning the final game 5-2 at Stoke City (who were also relegated).

Ian Brightwell was given a free transfer after the end of the season.

Ian Brightwell: "I didn't know what was happening with regards to a contract before the end of the season. Once the club had been relegated it was obvious Joe Royle was going to have to decide who to keep and who to release. At the time, Uwe Rosler, Kit Symons and myself were all out of contract and the high earners at the time - along with Georgi Kinkladze who was sold to Ajax - and I was told that the club couldn't offer me a similar contract to my previous one. By this time, Coventry City, managed by Gordon Strachan, had shown an interest in me. It was a hard wrench, but Coventry at the time were in the Premier League where I'd played most of my time with City - so I went to Highfield Road after twelve years as a professional and almost twenty years involvement with the club I supported and loved (and still do by the way!)"

Although Brightwell signed for the West Midlands club, City honoured the longstanding commitment given for a testimonial in acknowledgement of his eleven season's service in the first team.

18th July 1998. City play Sunderland (managed by Peter Reid) at Maine Road in Ian Brightwell's testimonial game, which ends a scoreless draw in front of 7,037 fans. Due to signing a new contract with Coventry City, he was prevented from playing in his own game.

The City line up was: Nicky Weaver, Richard Edghill, Danny Tiatto, Gerard Wiekens, Kakhaber Tskhadadze, Tony Vaughan, Paul Dickov, Jamie Pollock, Shaun Goater, Kevin Horlock, Lee Bradbury - used subs Jim Whitley, Michael Brown - unused subs Tommy Wright, Gary Mason, Chris Greenacre.

Ian Brightwell: "Coventry City wouldn't allow me to play, which was understandable as it was pre-season. I came onto the pitch with a microphone after the game to thank everyone for supporting my testimonial and also to thank the City fans for their support over all the years. It was very emotional for me even if I didn't really show it. City was - and still is - a big part of my life."

There was more than a tinge of sadness from many fans present that day, as the final link to the Class of '86 had finally slipped away. From the day David White, Ian Scott and Paul Moulden made their debuts for the 'A' Team on 29th October 1983 through to 7th April 1998 when Ian Brightwell played his final game for the reserves – a run of fourteen years, five months and ten days (or five thousand two hundred and seventy-five days!) had ended.

During this time, City fans had followed the progress of fourteen teenage lads who all wore the Blue shirt of Manchester City with pride and with style and who left lasting memories, not only of their time spent with each other, but also in the hearts of City fans following the club at the time and ever since.

PLAYER COMBINED APPEARANCES - 1997-98			
	FIRST TEAM	RESERVES	TOTAL
IAN BRIGHTWELL	23 (2 + 1), 0	8, 2	31 (2 + 1), 2

THE GREATEST EVER?

CITY IN THE YOUTH CUP FINAL

FROM ITS INCEPTION in 1953, it took City thirty-three years to finally win the trophy. It then took another twenty-two years to win it for the second time! At the time of the publication of this book, in total, City have reached the final on six occasions.

Here are the team line-ups for all six occasions City have been in the final and the players with a number next to their name are those who went on to play at the highest level for City with the number indicating their total appearances (including subtitute appearances) they made in all first team competitions.

Of course, we can only speculate as to who would have come out on top in a head to head game between the six teams. But one thing we can do, is compare the total appearances in the first team made by the players in each team.

In doing so, it is perfectly clear which team comes out on top - the Class of '86 triumph again! Between them they appeared a total of five hundred and seventy-one times more than their nearest rival, the 1979-80 team. And with the greatest respect to Micah Richards (representing the 2005-06 team) he will not be making a further one thousand appearances to overtake the record. Those players from the 2007-08 team still on the clubs books are even less likely to jump from the current fifty-three appearances to become the record breakers!

Interestingly, the record for most players from a team to reach the first team is the 1988-89 team with eight - yet they are the team with the second lowest total appearance record, with Neil Lennon and Ian Thompstone being 'one hit wonders'.

Ian Brightwell holds the most individual appearance record (three hundred and eighty two, forty appearances more than David White in second place) although it is possible for Micah Richards to claim top spot if he remains with City for another four or more years and plays regularly.

So it is official. The Class of 1986 are the greatest ever Manchester City Youth Team.

* *Indicates current appearance figure at time of publication. The name in brackets indicates they only played in the second leg.*

1978-79

v Millwall

First Leg at Maine Road
CITY 0-0 MILLWALL
Second Leg at The Den
MILLWALL 2-0 CITY
Aggregate score
City 0 Millwall 2

Alex Williams 125

Gary Fitzgerald

Richard Cunningham

Nicky Reid 262

Tommy Caton 198

Ross Mcginn

Melvin Mcclure

Mark Leigh

Steve Kinsey 115

Clive Wilson 126

Kevin Glendon

TOTAL APPEARANCES – 826

1979-80

v Aston Villa

First leg at Maine Road
CITY 1-3 ASTON VILLA
Second Leg at Villa Park
ASTON VILLA 0-1 CITY
Aggregate score
CITY 2 ASTON VILLA 3

Alex Williams 125

Andy May 174

Richard Cunningham

Gary Bennett

Tommy Caton 198

Ross McGinn

Keith Parkinson

Steve Mackenzie 76

Gareth Bees

Steve Kinsey 115

Clive Wilson 126

Sub David Fitzharris

TOTAL APPEARANCES – 814

1985-86

v Manchester United

First leg at Old Trafford
UNITED 1-1 CITY
Second Leg at Maine Road
CITY 2-0 UNITED
Aggregate score
CITY 3 UNITED 1

Steve Crompton

Steve Mills

Andy Hinchcliffe 139

Ian Brightwell 382

Steve Redmond 287

Andy Thackeray

David White 342

Paul Moulden 79

Paul Lake 134

Ian Scott 34

David Boyd

Sub Steve Macauley

(John Bookbinder)

TOTAL APPEARANCES – 1,397

1988-89

v Watford

First Leg at Maine Road
CITY 1-0 WATFORD
Second Leg at Vicarage Road
WATFORD 2-0 CITY (AET)
Aggregate score
CITY 1 WATFORD 2

Martyn Margetson 59

Neil Lennon 1

John Wills

Mark Peters

Gerry Taggart 13

Mike Quigley 13

Ian Thompstone 1

Ashley Ward 3

Jason Hasford

Michael Hughes 33

Michael Wallace

Sub Mike Sheron 119

Sub Colin Small

TOTAL APPEARANCES – 242

2005-06

v Liverpool

First leg at Anfield
LIVERPOOL 3-0 CITY
Second Leg at COMS
CITY 2-0 LIVERPOOL
Aggregate score
City 2 Liverpool 3

Laurence Matthewson

Curtis Obeng

Shaleum Logan 3

Sam Williamson 1

Micah Richards 218 (16)

Garry Breen

Paul Marshall

Ashley Williams

Michael Johnson 45

Kelvin Etuhu 15

Daniel Sturridge 32

Karl Moore

Sub David Vadon

Sub Ched Evans 26

(Ashley Williams)

Sub Adam Clayton

(Michael Daly)

TOTAL APPEARANCES = 340★

2007-08

v Chelsea

First leg at Stamford Bridge
CHELSEA 1-1 CITY
Second leg at COMS
CITY 3-1 CHELSEA
Aggregate score
City 4 Chelsea 2

Gregory Hartly

Kieran Trippier

Ryan McGiven 1★

Dedryck Boyata 10★

Ben Mee

Scott Kay

Vladimir Weiss 5

Andrew Tutte

David Ball

Daniel Sturridge 32

(Robbie Mak)

Donal McDermott

Sub Filip Mental

Sub James Poole

Sub Angelos Tsiaklis

Sub Abdisalam Ibrahim 3★

Sub Alex Nimely 2★

TOTAL APPEARANCES 53★

WHAT THEY SAID...

This chapter covers what Ken Barnes thought of 'The Magnificent Seven', what a couple of the lads thought of the rest of the team and for each of the players to pay tribute to Tony Book, Glyn Pardoe, Ken Barnes and other backroom staff.

KEN BARNES ON THE MAGNIFICENT SEVEN

It was extremely rewarding for Tony Book and Glyn Pardoe to see the rewards of their work with the players over the years - and also for Chief Scout, Ken Barnes, who had spotted the potential for each of the players when they were all school boys. There would be no one better placed - nor qualified - to pass judgement on 'The Magnificent Seven' Boy Blues who reached the First team, and that is exactly what Barnes did in his biography "This Simple Game - The Footballing Life of Ken Barnes".

Ian Brightwell: Was a lovely lad with a fantastic attitude. I don't think he was capable of giving less than his best - it just wasn't in his nature. Good defender, strong in the tackle and had a bit of pace about him. He didn't have as much to offer in an attacking sense, but from a manager's perspective, a real asset. His attitude was exceptional and you couldn't hope to meet a nicer man.

Andy Hinchcliffe: Was very fast and a good passer of the ball, especially as a defender. He had a great left foot and that has always been at a premium - as much so then as it is now. For some reason, Howard Kendall didn't rate him and he moved on. But I still believe to this day, that he could have been the first choice left back here for ten years or more. He's not done too badly for himself in the game has he?

Paul Lake: I suppose I have to say Paul Lake was the jewel in the crown. When I first saw him as a young laddie at thirteen, I knew straight away he was a real talent. He was going flat out and had a ball dropping over his shoulder and he set himself up and volleyed it into the back of the net. I remember thinking to myself, right then, that I'd seen enough, he was a player. As he grew up, he reminded me of Colin Bell and I can pay him no greater tribute than that. He could do everything. He could pass and tackle, he was good in the air. He could graft, but most of all he was a smart player. He had vision; he could see things that other players couldn't. Paul could have played anywhere. It was an absolute tragedy that we never got to see the best of him. I'm sure he would have gone on to be one of the true City greats. I really do believe that.

Paul Moulden: Was a goal scoring machine, with great control and a touch and a good football brain. The only thing lacking was a yard of pace. Paul had the talent to achieve a lot more than he did in the game and people always say it was down to that lack of pace. Maybe so, but sometimes you need a bit of luck as well and I still feel that, with a bit of good fortune, things would have been very different for him.

Steve Redmond: Was a good player. But what a lot of people might not know is that, as a youngster, he was a great goal scorer, a real talent. He was so strong and he had two great feet. I felt he had a real future as a front player. Then, bugger me; the next thing is they're turning him into a centre back. I've never understood it – goal scorers are always at a premium. Centre halves, by comparison, are ten a penny. We find a laddie with the talent to play up there and then shove him in the back. Bloody unbelievable really.

Ian Scott: He was one, I thought, who might have done more in the game. He was a decent player with a bit of vision. He saw things early, which I have always liked. Yes, I thought he would be a good player. It didn't quite work out for him and I was sorry about that, because he certainly had the talent.

David White: Had a good career in the game, of course. As a kid he was strong and direct, very quick. He wasn't a tricky winger like we'd seen in the past. He blasted past people with pace rather than licking them with a bit of pure skill. He was a good crosser of the ball. Maybe David lacked a bit of football savvy sometimes but he knew his strengths, he played to them and they served him well.

Probably the best two team members to evaluate everyone else would be Steve Crompton (who spent many hours stood alone guarding the goal whilst a lot of the play - and his team mates - were up at the other end of the pitch) and Ian Brightwell, the longest serving City player of them all. Here are their thoughts on their fellow team mates:

Steve Crompton: Steve 'Reddo' Redmond was the captain. He had the biggest thighs I had ever seen. He was solid all over, not just physically but as a player. He had started out as a centre forward playing for Liverpool Boys, but soon became one of the best centre-half's I had played behind. He could read the game so well, wasn't blessed with the most pace but never seemed to be hurried.

Ian Brightwell: He made the game look so easy, exceptional talent and should really have played for England with his ability.

SC: John Bookbinder was in the squad, and it was really sad to learn about his death not long ago. He was a left footed player, who was on the edge of the squad really, but whenever he came in he did OK. From what I recall he used to get a lot of stick from Skip, but always took it well. His dad was also a bit of a character, not what you'd expect of a typical football dad!

IB: John was a great character as well as being a talented footballer - he will always be remembered as part of City's 'golden age' of youth.

SC: Dave Boyd was the quiet Scotsman, who was a bit of an eccentric dresser, as he followed some weird bands back in the day and dressed a bit like the lads in the band did. Not at all like us with our shiny suits, rolled up sleeves, and red or white shoes!! Proper fashion victims.

IB: The quiet Scot with incredible fitness who used to supply down the left with great effect.

SC: Ian Brightwell, who was just an all-round athlete. Clearly with his background he was odds-on to be a prime physical specimen, and he was quick and could also run all day. He had good football ability too and played the game in a very simple way.

SC: John Clarke, a really nice lad from Ireland with shocking ginger hair. Proper pasty white skin to go with it, but a good footballer.

IB: Good, steady player who had a typical Irish approach to life.

SC: Andy Hinchcliffe was at left back. A brilliant left foot, and strong with it. He was also possibly the poshest footballer I had ever come across. He had attended a grammar school and was obviously bright, and one of my memories from those days was Andy and David White doing the cryptic crossword in the paper every morning! I also picked up Andy and took him to work every day until he could drive. I lived near Lymm and he lived near Timperley, so I would go through Altrincham and pick him up. At the time, he was also my apprentice, so he actually cleaned my boots! That's my claim to fame – the fact that an England international cleaned my boots.

IB: The best left foot I've ever seen (even to this day). Great attacking left back who went on to play for England.

SC: Paul Lake was a brilliant footballer as we all know. Sadly his career was blighted by injury, which goes back as far as I can remember him really and it was such a shame that we didn't see him go on to achieve more than he did.

IB: Everything has already been said about Lakey. Such a waste of talent at such a young age. He'd have gone on to be one of our country's great players. Still gutted for him to this day.

SC: Steve Macauley was another centre half. A tall spindly lad at the time, but was a nice composed player.

IB: Absolutely fearless! Cracking defender, but his weakness was that he was too brave and would end up on the treatment table after most games. People wouldn't believe some of the challenges he'd go in for!

SC: Steve Mills, from Yorkshire was a little boisterous. He had a great friendship with Paul Lake. They used to play out scenes from The Young Ones nearly every day.

IB: "The Looker" of the team, strong as an ox, with plenty of style on the ball.

SC: Paul Moulden was more than just a record breaker. He was like a full grown man by the time he was fifteen and it clearly gave him an advantage at that level. He was a basic, down to earth Bolton lad, who always wanted to own a chip shop once he had finished playing football.

IB: Scored goals for fun. Fit, strong and incredibly dedicated.

SC: Ian Scott was just like Glenn Hoddle. Looked so comfortable on the ball, could hit it on a sixpence from sixty yards, and also had the highlights in the hair to match. He was the playboy of the team, enjoyed his clubbing and his clothes.

IB: Another stylish player (both on and off the pitch) with amazing vision and passing ability.

SC: Andy Thackeray – another Yorkshire man, but the complete opposite to Steve Mills! He was fairly quiet, but really cool with it!

IB: Cool, calm and collected on and off the pitch. Mr reliable and dependable.

SC: David White, as everyone knows, he was tall, blessed with a turn of speed, and had a shot like a thunderbolt. Many a time during shooting practice he would bend my fingers back. A bit frustrating at times, as sometimes his crosses ended up in the back of the stand, but such a good provider and quite prolific at our level. Off the pitch, me, Whitey, Paul Moulden and Ian Scott used to have some good times together. I had a little snooker table, which we would put outside in the garden and have a little competition between us. We couldn't outdo Whitey though, who had a ¾ size slate bed table at his house. I used to love to play snooker and always invited myself to Whitey's to play on his table. His mum and dad were lovely people and always welcomed you.

IB: He could play either right wing or centre forward with equal effectiveness. Quick and strong and one of the best finishers I've ever seen and he went on to represent England too.

SC: And then there was me – Steve Crompton! I wasn't a bad keeper. Probably needed another couple of inches in height. Looking back, I wasn't good enough to make it as a professional. I just don't think I was ready for that at the age of nineteen. The team was brilliant and we just couldn't stop winning – we won the Lancashire Youth Cup, FA Youth Cup, The Lancashire League and The Central League. I was so privileged to play in goal behind those lads. I think looking back, almost anybody could have played in goal for that team because those players were so good. Every time I let one in, Paul Moulden and David White would go down the other end and score three more!

IB: Our goalkeeper and last line of defence – a great shot stopper and organiser.

TRIBUTES

TO TONY BOOK, GLYN PARDOE, KEN BARNES AND THE BACKROOM STAFF

THIS BOOK IS A CELEBRATION of fourteen teenagers who kicked a ball for Manchester City and in doing so, won the FA Youth Cup in 1986 – for the first time in the club's history. What came out in researching the book and speaking to 'the lads' was their affection for those charged with guiding them through their YTS days, into the reserves and beyond – be it with City or elsewhere. We both felt that it was more than appropriate for personal tributes from the players to be recorded at the end of the book.

DAVID BOYD

"I remember Lakey nutmegging Tony Book in practice and being told in no uncertain terms what would happen if he tried that again! Needless to say Lakey took this as a challenge and next time they came face to face, Lakey gave a swivel of his hips – but Tony dived into the tackle and caught him. Lakey ended up having to go off – I think he may have missed training the next day and maybe even the next game!

"Glyn was the joker to Tony's straight man. They were invincible as a pair at head tennis in the old gym under the Main Stand. Also, in practice neither of them hardly ever gave the ball away, whether it was against us youngsters buzzing around, or even against the first team when the reserves played them and they were in the team! Both of them fostered a great camaraderie amongst us all.

"Ken Barnes was a real gent and I'm sure you'll find that no one has a bad word to say about him. He was the ideal man from the club to deal with the school boys and their parents. The personal touch went a long way and made everyone feel 'special"

IAN BRIGHTWELL

"After my family, Tony, Glyn and Ken were the biggest influences not only on my career – but on my life. They instilled discipline, respect and hard work alongside teaching me football in a simple, uncomplicated but highly effective way. Whenever I coach today, I use the same principles and the same goes for my business life too. I have the utmost respect for all of them and am proud to be associated with them and also lucky enough to be friends with Tony and Glyn to this day."

JOHN CLARKE

"Ken Barnes he was an absolute gentleman and a big reason why I chose City over other clubs, he was always there if you needed him with encouragement and positivity - I was very sad to hear of his passing.

"I really loved Glyn, he could always make you laugh - especially with his own infectious laugh and his famous line at half time of 'How do you expect to play if you can't pass the ball?' Tony Book was very good coach, knew the game very well, hard as nails and sometimes when he joined in practice games with us you could see why he was such a good player. He would never give the ball away."

STEVE CROMPTON

"Tony Book was a brilliant man. Not only was he a brilliant football person, but he also instilled a discipline into us that lives with me to this day. Scotty used to take the piss out of him when his back was turned, and did a brilliant impression of his West Country accent. He had a few sayings that used to make us laugh. I don't know how old he was when he was coaching us, but he could still play the game, and was still fit for his age, even with his bandy legs. I owe so much to Skip for those early days.

"Glyn Pardoe was a top bloke. You could have a proper laugh with him, but he got serious when he needed to. Glyn was a brilliant player and a great coach. In practice matches he would ping the ball around, and never seemed to give it away. His saying that always stuck with me was 'How do you expect to play if you can't pass the ball?' Simple, yet so true. And he always used to tell us about the day he scored five goals at Wembley!

"Ken Barnes was a great man, and such a gentleman. Ken was the first person, other than the scout Eric Mullender, to talk to me when I went to City, and he was the one who told me that they wanted to sign me on schoolboy forms. I wasn't aware at the time that he had been such a great player. To me he was more the father of Peter Barnes, the legendary winger. Ken was an honest person and I don't recall him ever having a bad word to say about anybody. Once I had signed, I didn't really have a lot to do with him. We would see him at some of the games and we would always have a chat with each other. Ken was also the person that I spoke to shortly after I had been released by the club. He gave me a lot of good advice at the time, none of which, I can remember!"

ANDY HINCHCLIFFE

"My over-riding feelings about winning the Youth Cup then (and still now) was that Tony Book and Glyn Pardoe really deserved it. They worked us incredibly hard but they did it because they knew the talent they were coaching"

PAUL LAKE

"Ken Barnes, Tony Book and, to a lesser extent, Glyn Pardoe were the greatest influences in my football career. Bookie and Glyn seemed to have the good cop - bad cop routine off to perfection. Tony was quite strict and set very high standards and for the most part that was fine, but if Ken thought he was being too hard on a youngster, he'd have a blazing row with Tony. 'Hey, did you never make a mistake then? What the fuck do you know anyway? You were only a full back.'

"Tony was more one for detail and more analytical maybe, but Ken just had a way of making you feel ten feet tall. Tony rarely missed a game but I can remember he did miss one once and Ken gave us the team talk. He walked in with his usual fag on the go and said: 'Go out and play. Express yourselves, you're better than them, so get out there and fuckin' enjoy it.'

"That was it. We came in at half time winning 3-0 and he just walked in and said, 'Do the same again. I told you that you're better than this lot. Enjoy yourselves.' Team talk over. We won about 5 or 6 nil. We were only kids, but we could have given Real Madrid a game that day, or at least Ken had us believing we could. We all had immense respect for him. I think I was in the first team before I stopped calling him Mr Barnes. He told me to call him Ken. I can't explain how good that made me feel. It was like I had been accepted as a player."

STEVE MACAULEY

"Tony Book - 'Skip' the disciplinarian! He demanded the best and didn't tolerate anybody who 'shirked'. He would often join in five-a-sides on the bowling green at Platt Lane and if any of the lads had pissed him off during the week, sure enough they would be on the wrong end of one of Skip's infamous scissor tackles! He was firm, but fair with good old fashioned values, it was his job to make men out of us and sculpt our personalities to that of a professional footballer. Skip was also the most mimicked man in football (John Clarke, Andy Hinchcliffe, Lakey, Eric Nixon, to name but a few of the better ones!)

"Glyn Pardoe was very much the good cop with a happy outlook on life. He would often put an arm around you and get you smiling again. Glyn would also join in the five-a-sides (in fact he'd often be one of the first picks!) Glyn would ask us all if we'd finished cleaning up the dressing rooms (the duties of old fashioned apprentices! Now they don't lift a finger!) We were all desperate to go home when Glyn would ask, he'd then go and tell Skip who would come back and run his finger along the top of the door only to find a speck of dust! "I'll come back in half an hour when you've finished!" smirked Skip. This was a little charade Skip & Glyn would play with us all from time to time to instil discipline and teamwork. I can see Glyn's face now, a huge grin from ear to ear."

"Ken Barnes was a true gentleman. This man was class. He would always make time to chat and give advice. I do remember being in his room once with Ken, Denis Law and Tony Book and the conversation was littered with profanities to the point of me barely understanding the thread of the conversation! In walked a lady and it was as if someone had flicked a switch - three perfect gentlemen (a true art!) However, Ken, as nice as he was, once left me standing outside his room for what seemed like an eternity, after physio Roy Bailey had sent me for a 'long stand!' All part of the life experience I suppose. Ken was an old school gentleman who had time for everybody - a legend."

STEVE MILLS

"I don't think I need to go on about Tony or Glyn too much - I think Lakey covered it perfectly in his book to give you an idea of what they were like. I do believe though, if your face didn't fit with Skip, then you were on your way out. He also had a way of dishing out a bollocking that some kids couldn't handle."

PAUL MOULDEN

"I had then and will always have a great respect for Billy McNeill and all the people that gave me my football education at City - Tony Book, Glyn Pardoe, Ken Barnes, Roy Bailey and many more even down to Joyce Johnston, the laundry lady who educated me in turning my match kit and training kit the right way out to make life easier for her! That stayed with me for the rest of my career."

STEVE REDMOND

"Tony Book - 'Skip' - was just a different class. He was very hard on us but also fair too. As young kids we looked at each other wondering what we had signed up for – this was the same person who before we signed was very calm and polite to me and my family! We didn't realise it at the time, of course, but looking back we all fully understand what he was instilling in us and how he moulded us into what we became and what we achieved.

"One thing he didn't like was 'Fancy Dan's' in training – especially people doing nut megs. John Beresford was always up to these kind of tricks in training and would regularly find himself on the receiving end of one of Skip's scissor kick tackles as a result! I have total respect for Skip and still see him at games and always greet him with a hug.

"Glyn Pardoe was the opposite to Tony. If Tony had the hard touch, Glyn offered the softer touch. After a Skip bollocking, Glyn would follow up, arm around the shoulder and say "All he's trying to say is...." and he would build you back up having been knocked down a peg or two. He had a great distinctive laugh which I have never forgotten. The pair of them really bounced off each other and were superb together.

"Ken Barnes for me is on the same level as I see the likes of Bill Shankly and Brian Clough – he had such a great aura about him. I could listen to Ken all day long. He would say to us 'It's a simple game, pass the ball from A to B, why complicate it? Just go and express yourselves and enjoy it'."

IAN SCOTT

"Tony Book and Glyn Pardoe were like good cop, bad cop. Tony or "Skip" as we called him, was the task master. He made us do all the dirty jobs in the summer, like painting the ground or making sure the toilets were cleaned and floors swept – but what a grounding it was and what a great team spirit it helped build. We were in it together and that meant everything. He shouted at us and kept us in line and kept our feet on the ground. We would not have changed that for the world and I still treat my students with the same kinds of discipline that he installed in us. I was with Skip recently when he visited the college where I used to work, to do a talk and I was telling the students all about his discipline and why I was like that with them.

"Glyn was the good cop. The one we would sound off to and moan about Skip to. We didn't mean it; we just needed to sound off. Glyn was the joker as well, although Skip was often involved. He was and is a really good bloke who had a lot of time for us all and would take the mickey out of us in a fun way.

"Ken Barnes was like the Grand Master. He would sit in his office full of smoke and on the occasional times we went up there, usually before we had signed, he would tell us stories of his time at City. A great man, but I did not spend much time in his company after signing. I recently had the pleasure of going to a fundraising event at City's stadium in honour of Ken – it was a privilege to be there and a great night was had by all."

ANDY THACKERAY

"Skip and Glyn, they were hard but fair, always encouraging but always demanding your best. I remember training at Platt Lane and Skip called us over and said we were going to play the first team in a practice match. In the dressing room with all the apprentices he went through a full team talk as if it was your first team debut – with a few expletives thrown in. His belief was there are no such things as friendlies, he said 'get your pads on, get your studs on and get out there and show the first team how good you are, take no prisoners because if you want to be in that first team you have to prove your worth'. They are two fantastic football men."

DAVID WHITE

"Ken Barnes was a great guy who every now and again would get his kit on and join in a practice match. He would be in his mid-fifties and was a different class even then.

"The Skip/Glyn partnership was superb. Skip had done every job at the club but took his role very seriously. He was hard as nails both on and off the training pitch and would think nothing of cutting you in half in training if he thought you needed bringing down a peg or two. We also won the Lancashire League in the Youth Cup winning year and having lost just one game to South Liverpool (Skip was not there), we never dropped a point after that as far as I remember – yet we got a bollocking after every game. When you got in the first team, Skip was so proud and he would challenge you to go and keep your place and suddenly you were the best player at the club. He was and still is a top man!

"My biggest memory was after training each day, we would be left to shower at Maine Road and then put our 'afternoon kit' on – which even then were pretty much rags. Our jobs included cleaning all the boots including our own, the pros and the staff, sweeping and mopping all the floors in the changing areas, coaches' room, refs' room, physio room etc. We had to get all the kit up to Joyce in the laundry room to be washed and ironed for the next day. We also had to scrub forty training balls in the bath before scrubbing the bath and shower areas. The whole process took a couple of hours and when we finished Steve Redmond would go up and tell Skip that we were done. It would then be up to an hour before Skip came down. He would just leave us in the changing room to have a crack and 'bond'. He would quite often come down to find us in pitch darkness leathering balls around at each other. If we had trained or played badly he would find some dust in a remote part of the changing room and tell us to wipe down again - and leave us for another hour. It was so frustrating and we called him like mad for it but looking back it was all part of the growing up process and all part of getting us together.

"Glyn was the good cop, the one who would put his arm around you after you had got a bollocking. He was a great player and nine times out of ten if you were on his side in the five a sides your team won. Again Glyn is a top guy. In football you need to grow up very quickly and need to be at the height of your profession by the time you are say twenty-three. You don't get that without having strong leaders around you. The partnership was perfect. The days when Skip kept us back, Glyn would be laughing his bollocks off."

EPILOGUE

THE MAKING OF "TEENAGE KICKS"

IF THIS BOOK HAD BEEN A DVD, it would come with 'extras' and one of them may have been how the book was initially planned and then eventually put together a decade later. A directors' commentary if you will...

The idea first came about after 'Morrissey's Manchester' had been published in 2002. Receiving great reviews and with sales to match – I was hooked on the 'drug' of writing and decided 'Teenage Kicks' was to be my next book.

The 1986 Youth Cup team has always had a place in my heart. I had followed the youth team from around in 1984, attending all of the home games and being present at Springfield Park when City won the Lancashire Youth Cup Final in 1985 at Wigan Athletic. I was present at all of the home FA Youth Cup games in the season City won the cup in April 1986, as well as the away leg of the final at Old Trafford. I know I'm not the only City fan of that era to have a special affinity with the Class of '86.

This may bring out the 'trainspotter' in me, but the names "John Bookbinder", "David Boyd" and "Andy Thackeray" had always been at the back of my mind. I clearly remember the day reading the *Manchester Evening News* – around two to three weeks after the FA Youth Cup was won – announcing that the three aforementioned players were being released and thinking "But they've just won the Cup, Boyd scored the first goal. Why are they being released?"

And I'm sure I wasn't the only City fan who had hoped that the whole team would go on and become the major force in English football – if not Europe – for years to come!

Seventeen years after lifting the FA Youth Cup, I met Paul Lake at a supporters club meeting in early 2003. I gave him a copy of 'Morrissey's Manchester' and sounded him out about 'Teenage Kicks' and he was very receptive towards the idea (as well as the name!) – as was Andy Hinchcliffe at another supporters club meeting. And that's about as far as it got. I changed jobs in March 2003 and, well, let's just say I was supervised a little more closely in the new job than the previous one – so being paid to write a book, rather than do actual work, was out of the question!

A year later, I was contacted by Ian Cheeseman. He had the idea of writing the same book and speaking to Andy Hinchcliffe about it, he was pointed in my direction. I was happy to hand the project over to Ian, jokingly adding that it was on the condition that he must call the book "Teenage Kicks"!

Fast forward to September 2011. I'm in the City Store on Market Street, three days before emigrating from Moston, Manchester to Boston, Massachusetts, USA. I'm standing in line to get Paul Lake to autograph a copy of his book. On signing, I reminded him that I wrote the "Morrissey's Manchester" book (which I was delighted to hear he still had on his bookshelf) and that I was moving abroad that very week.

On the plane flying to my new home, I read Lake's book with tears in my eyes - and I'm very certain I wasn't the only one to have done so. This re-ignited "Teenage Kicks" in my mind, knowing there was a great story to be told. But again, the idea got no further than my mind as I settled into life in Boston.

Then, in April 2012, on the City fans forum "BlueMoon", someone posted a message looking for contact details for the 1986 FA Youth Cup winning team. I sent the individual a personal message, asking if he was planning on writing a book about the team, as that's what I had in mind too. Thankfully he replied that he was just interested in attempting to get the match programme from the second leg of the final signed by the entire team. Nevertheless, it spooked me into finally taking action. I still had not received my authorisation to work in the USA - so figured it was now or never with a few months to spare.

I contacted Ian Cheeseman via Facebook to ask if he still had plans for the book - he didn't. Like me, other things had got in the way, so he was happy to hand it back to me. I then contacted football historian and author Gary James, asking if he had plans to write on the subject. He personally had no plans, but someone he knew had suggested they were interested the previous year, to tie in with what would have been the 25th anniversary of the Youth Cup triumph in 2011.

I decided to carry on regardless of whatever someone else was planning to do. The main problem I had though was being three thousand five hundred miles away from Manchester, with no access to any information from that era I was planning to write about - never mind the ability to actually go and interview anyone. Despite this major issue, I sat down and wrote my introduction to the book. When that was finished I realised it was time to accept the fact that I could not write this book without the help of a fellow fan back home. It was then when I thought of Andrew Waldon. I had known Andrew from the Family Stand at Maine Road. We sat next to each other - although separated by the isle at the end of our respective row of seats - and through our different writings for fanzines, we got to know each other. I was among the many contributors to

Andrew's first book, "Maine Road Voices".

The move to Eastland's cast both of us and our kids far and wide in the new Family Stand and our paths didn't cross again until a few weeks before I moved to the USA, when I was eating a cheese & onion pie, chips and curry sauce outside Tony's Stadium Chippy, when we bumped into each other, had a brief chat and exchanged email addresses. This proved to be a very lucky chance meeting as it was my first "chippy tea" from that establishment and I only went there as it was the Monday night game against Swansea and I had come straight from work with nothing to eat.

I emailed Andrew, explaining the idea of the book, asking if he would like to co-write the book with me and also providing copies of relevant match reports from old programmes etc. and also being my "man on the street" in the UK. Andrew proved to be far more resourceful than I had ever imagined - straight away he provided me with an email with an attachment that had spread sheets containing every 'A' team, youth team and reserve team starting line up throughout the 80's and 90's, as well as links to a website (www.mcfcstats.com) showing the same information for every City first team game during the same period as well as before and beyond. I had everything I wanted at the click of a mouse! I printed off season by season pages for the 'A' team and reserves (6 pages per season for each team), stuck them up on the kitchen wall one season at a time and highlighted each player in a different colour so I could see how many games each player appeared in and the goals they scored. Gradually the story of each individual player was built up so their respective debuts, goals, final appearances and everything in between could easily be charted into dates to become a diary of the team. Then their first team debuts (where applicable) and other details such as England Youth and Under 21 appearance statistics were slotted into the relevant date.

This process took the best part of three weeks (with a four day gap of no activity as City won the Premier League, resulting in a four day bender!) by which time I had received in the post photocopies of match reports of the youth cup games and relevant interviews with players from old programmes from Andrew. These match reports and interviews were then placed in their chronological order into the text.

The next step was to contact the players themselves. Some would be easier than others - Paul Lake worked at the club, Paul Moulden has his Chippy in Bolton and David White has his business in Salford. But where would we find David Boyd, John Clarke, Steve Mills, Steve Crompton etc?

Then Andrew, who had been digging away seeking contacts, sent me an email suggesting that he thought John Bookbinder had passed away a couple of years ago but wasn't 100% sure. He also thought - but again wasn't fully certain, that John's sister is Susan Bookbinder, the well-known broadcaster – and staunch City fan. A day or two later, Andrew confirmed that John had sadly died of cancer and that his sister was indeed Susan Bookbinder.

I contacted via electronic means both Gary James and Ian Cheeseman who both knew Susan and both of them encouraged me to contact her, insisting she would be supportive of the book and consented to me using their names as a reference should she want validation as to who I was, bearing in mind the very personal nature I would be enquiring about.

I found Susan on Facebook and composed around four different messages – deleting them all, before finally being comfortable with the one I sent. I introduced myself and my City credentials and also my literal credentials and then gave the details of the book, asking if she or members of the family were willing to contribute with John's story. I also gave a little of my own personal background away – I too, had a brother, David, who had died unexpectedly in 1980 – he was twenty-one and I was seventeen. I wasn't too sure whether I should have done that, but I guess I was trying to say "Please trust me, tell me John's story and I will get it published, I'm not here to stitch anyone up, I'm here to tell the tale you give me". I sent the message late at night and went to bed worried that a random private message from someone wanting to ask rather emotive, personal questions to a high profile individual may have been the wrong way to go about gaining information.

In the morning, there was a message waiting for me from Susan Bookbinder. I was excited, yet apprehensive at the same time. It was either going to be "yes I'd love to help" or "please don't contact me again". Nervously I opened the message to be greeted warmly by Susan – clearly delighted that her brother's contribution to the Youth Cup winning side was going to be written about. Susan's openness, honesty and trust from the off – to a complete stranger – was amazing. Over the coming weeks – with Susan enjoying a late night glass of wine and myself enjoying an early evening beer – we shared stories of our brothers' and between us reached for the tissues quite a few times. We also discovered other similarities between ourselves and family in terms of skeletons in the closet – the topics of which will remain strictly between the two of us! I also discovered that Susan and John are related (second cousins) to Elkie Brooks (Elaine Bookbinder) and that one of Elkie's brothers was in the 60's Manchester band The Dakotas with another brother opening the 'Bookbinders' club that was on Bloom Street (at the back of Chorlton Street bus station) for over four decades. With my Manchester music loving hat on, I was fascinated and at this point I offered to write the Bookbinder family book! But my lasting memory of Susan is chatting on Facebook around 7pm my time – midnight UK time. Susan would write "I have to go now, got to be up in four hours for a broadcast" and would then repeat this about every ten minutes for the best part of thirty minutes – as actually leaving the discussion proved harder than saying it!

I was also able to sound ideas off Susan too. She actually saw early stages of the text before I had let Andrew see it. Although personally attached to the book, as a City fan too, she was able to judge the content and her words of encouragement were greatly appreciated in those early days in that I knew I was using the right formula in bringing out each player's individual story within the context of the greater story.

At the same time as contacting Susan, I also sent an email off to the secretary of Fleetwood Town FC, as Steve Macauley was the first team coach there. I gave a brief outline as to who I was and asked if he could forward the email onto Steve. Within six or seven hours an email from Steve popped up in my inbox and like Susan, he was willing to contribute to the book – although he did warn me he had slept quite a few times since 1986!

We thought it would be best to initially contact the players who were less high profile, on the basis that we pretty much knew how to contact the others. Andrew then set about in search of three of the squad.

He knew Ian Scott worked at Cheadle & Marple College and after an internet search he sent the college administrator an e-mail and she forwarded it to Ian who subsequently responded. Another search for Steve Crompton online came up with a name on a business website and looking at the profile for the person, it mentioned he had played for Manchester City. A quick e-mail confirmed it was *the* Steve Crompton and he too was willing to come on board. Finally, Andrew knew that Andy Thackeray had become a physio and was from the Huddersfield area, a further search and a message left on an answer machine resulted in Andy also pledging his support.

We began to feel confident that no one else was writing the book, based on the fact that none of the four players we had contacted – or the family of John Bookbinder – had been approached by anyone else.

The next stroke of luck – especially for me – happened on 6th June 2012 in New York! Paul Lake was coming over as a follow up to community work City had set up the previous summer when playing in New York – and was bringing the Premier League trophy with him to the Mad Hatter bar in Manhattan. Off I went on an eight hour/four hundred mile round trip to have my picture taken alongside the trophy – and more importantly, to have a chat with Paul Lake. This I did, he offered his support, adding if I dropped him an email he would be able to supply contact details for David Boyd (who he said lived not far from New York) and Steve Mills who was now in South Africa! However, he had no idea as to the whereabouts of John Clarke – other than "he returned to Ireland". Sure enough, the following Monday after he had returned from the States, an email from Paul contained the email addresses for David and Steve and he said he would try and find out about John via an old scout he knew in Ireland.

I sent David and Steve an email and within an hour David had replied positively. Steve did the same the following day. Interestingly, David was the only one of the gang who actually asked for a bit of background as to who I was – which I was happy to do and as soon as I mentioned my books on Manchester music we began exchanging emails not about football, but about our love of music from Manchester in the 80's, with David being a big New Order fan. As with Susan Bookbinder, a friendship via email grew with David, and I don't think a week has gone by without some form of communication taking place that had nothing to do with football as we discussed music, films, travel, wine, Hurricane Sandy and winter snow storms! David only lives down the road from me (OK, admittedly two hundred and fifty miles away, but straight down Interstate 95 into New Jersey nonetheless) and I hope our paths will cross one day soon.

None of the lads' we had contacted had any details regarding the whereabouts of John Clarke. "Finding John Clarke" became our Holy Grail. I have a friend, Fergus, who lives in Dublin and he contacted the Dublin branch of the City supporters club on my behalf, asking if members of the branch could maybe help out with any information. Andrew was trying to find out from Home Farm FC if they had any details. All came to nothing. I then posted a request on the weekly City fans email newsletter 'MCIVTA' and also on the Bluemoon forum – again, with no reply. Each time I would email David Boyd, or the two Steve's with a question, they would reply and then enquire "Any news on John yet?" It got to the point where I was seriously thinking of placing an advert in a local Dublin newspaper seeking information on John. However, three weeks after the message was placed on Bluemoon, a reply was posted. The message was short but to the point. "Hello, I'm Sarah Clarke. My dad is John Clarke, the player you are looking for. We live in Dublin, just saw your post and hope I can help you."

My immediate thought was a mixture of celebration and uncertainty. Bluemoon – like all internet forums – has it's fair share of wind up merchants and trolls! So I sent a private message off to Sarah who replied within the hour with an email address for John. I sent an email to him, explaining about the book and asking for a landline number that I could call him on and a convenient time to do so. I received a reply and a time was set to for me to call. Andrew had given me the names of the two schools he attended as questions to ask to prove his identification! The call was made and there was no need to ask the questions as from his first words I could just tell this was the one and only John Clarke - without prompting he was asking me what the other lads were doing and telling me how he had lost contact with everyone. John explained that he was a taxi driver in Dublin and he had picked up an old friend of his who was also with his young son. His friend told his son that 'John used to play for Manchester City' and the young awestruck lad then went home and googled John to find out about his career at City – and the only thing he could find on the search was my message on Bluemoon asking for any information about John! The lad told his dad, who passed the request onto John and his daughter Sarah replied to the post.

I quickly spread the joyful word to the other players that the most elusive of them all had been found and John's email address was forwarded on and friendships reunited. I said to Andrew 'well if the book doesn't see the light of day, at least we have got the team back together'. I felt like Cilla Black!

It became a common theme every time we informed those we had been in touch with that someone else had been 'found' to enquire "what are they up to now?" We would reply teasingly "You'll have to wait until the book comes out", before passing on the details.

By now, the text, match reports and quoting old interviews was practically finished and it was time to start firing off questions to each of the players, based on what was written about them in the text. I sent questions off, two individuals at a time, starting with Susan Bookbinder and Steve Macauley, with Andrew contacting the three players he had been in touch with too.

Once the answers came in (which usually resulted in follow up questions about their answers being returned!) these were all inserted to fit in the relevant text to the story, whilst Andrew was putting together all the information given relating to pre and post City questions in producing an individual biography for each of the players. Some of the players had fantastic memories – Steve Crompton sent in an amazing amount of info back. Paul Moulden was also very sharp around dates and games: – He questioned my listing of his 'A' team debut being against UMIST in October 1983, insisting it was against Stockport County reserves at Platt Lane. I checked the stats on the spread sheets and there it was – listed as a pre-season friendly in the August!

Obviously time had caused one or two memories to fade and when this occurred, Andrew and I would refer to it as a case of "Macauley-itis" taken from Steve's regular "I've slept since then" term for saying he couldn't remember!

With this complete, it was now the time to contact the rest of the players. I looked online for the phone number for Paul Moulden's Chippy and made a call, timing it to be around 30 minutes before I imagined the Chippy would open! After a brief chat, Paul "signed up" for the book and gave an email address where to send questions to. Then I got the phone number for David White's business and gave them a call and explained to the receptionist the nature of the call. She gave me her email address and said she would forward my email to her onto David. The following morning there is an email from David in my inbox, offering his full support.

Steve Redmond had recently appeared on a video film on City's official website in a "Where Are They Now" series. A quick search on the internet found the phone number of the company he currently works at and on the day I called, Steve was not in. His work colleague gave me his email address and he said would pass on the info to Steve on his return. Steve was the only one who was interviewed over the phone as he doesn't have a computer! A suitable time was arranged for me to call and for forty minutes we reminisced about his time at City together.

Andrew called Paul Moulden at his chippy one day to clarify an answer and ended up with Ian Brightwell's phone number, who in turn supplied Andy Hinchcliffe's number. The set was complete! They were the last two to be contacted and on receiving their answers, the book was completed. Almost! A late rally saw John Clarke and Ian Brightwell (who Andrew bumped into before the home game against Spurs on the 11th November 2012) adding further anecdotes for inclusion.

Even then, there were a few late scares as we both spent weeks during February to April pouring over the facts, spellings and grammar. It was in March when we heard Ian Scott had emigrated to the US and with just five days before the book was dispatched to the printers, news came through that Steve Macauley was no longer at Fleetwood Town! That was added just in time – as was a nice quote from Paul Lake about John Bookbinder on BBC Radio Manchester when talking to Susan Bookbinder in April on the 'Blue Tuesday' show.

Taking a step back a little, in September we were discussing who could write the foreword. The immediate thought (and I again sounded the idea off with Susan Bookbinder as well as Andrew) was Tony Book - but I wanted someone who was from 'outside of the team set up' - but with inside knowledge! The answer lay in the middle of the picture of the team in the changing room with the trophy. Paul Power. Susan offered to contact Paul on my behalf during a conversation we had on a Thursday evening. The following morning, I received an email from Paul, who eventually agreed (after initially suggesting it be Tony Book!) to write the foreword. Later that very same day, the foreword was in my inbox. Now that gave me a buzz for a few days!

Amongst all this, Andrew had completed the fourteen profiles and was also collecting all the photographs that could be used for the book too.

It was with immense pride - yet with a hint of sadness for me when the book was completed. As a writer, I love to write! But this was completely different to any other book I'd written. I'd never had to interview anyone before – never mind interviewing former players of Manchester City FC who I had spent many years travelling all over the country to watch. It had been an incredible journey for me, over an eight month period – in capturing the lives of fourteen teenage lads in a specific period of time and turning it into a book.

I could never have made the journey without the tremendous support and commitment from Andrew, Susan Bookbinder and those thirteen lads. Upon receiving each and every email, it was an amazing feeling to be the first to read the anecdotes enclosed, knowing they would fit perfectly into the text of the book. We were also privy to a few stories under strict instructions that they were not for inclusion in the book! (What happened in Ibiza stays in Ibiza!) – such is the loyalty that still remains between them all.

Looking back, I'm glad that I didn't write the book in 2003 – it would have been too early – Ian Brightwell, Steve Macauley and Andy Thackeray were still playing! So thankfully for me no one else did write the story and thankfully for me I bumped into Andrew outside that Chippy that night and thankfully for me the US Immigration office took an unbelievable length of time in issuing me with a work visa. All these little things conspired together to create the opportunity to bring the story of Manchester City's 1986 FA Youth Cup winning team into print.

To everyone who has contributed towards the book, many thanks – the pleasure, the privilege was definitely mine.

PHILL GATENBY
MARCH 2013

ENGLAND   SWEDEN

TONIGHT'S SQUAD   TONIGHT'S SQUAD

No.	Name	Club	No.	Name	Club
GOALKEEPERS:			**GOALKEEPERS:**		
☐	Nigel MARTYN	Bristol Rovers	☐	Anders ALMGREN	Djurgarden
☐	Kevin PRESSMAN	Sheffield Wednesday	☐	Lars ERIKSSON	Hammarby
DEFENDERS:			**DEFENDERS:**		
☐	Colin COOPER	Middlesbrough	☐	Jan AHLBOM	Västra Fröhlun
☐	Brian STATHAM	Tottenham Hotspur	☐	Jan ERIKSSON	AIK Stockholm
☐	Andy HINCHCLIFFE	Manchester City	☐	Magnus KARLSSON	Norrköping
☐	Steve REDMOND	Manchester City	☐	Pontus KAMARK	Västeras SK
☐	Stephen CHETTLE	Nottingham Forest	☐	Mikael NILSSON	IFK Gothenbur
MIDFIELDERS:			**MIDFIELDERS:**		
☐	Paul LAKE	Manchester City	☐	Sulo VAATTOVAARA	Norrköping
☐	Vincent SAMWAYS	Tottenham Hotspur	☐	Kenneth ANDERSSON	Eskilstuna
☐	Steve SEDGLEY	Coventry City	☑	Klas INGESSON	IFK Gothenbur
FORWARDS:			**FORWARDS:**		
☐	Ian BRIGHTWELL	Manchester City	☐	Jan JANSSON	Osters Vaxjo
☐	Jason DOZZELL	Ipswich Town	☐	Ulrik JANSSON	Osters Vaxjo
☐	David SMITH	Coventry City	☐	Stefan SCHWARTZ	Malmö
☐	Paul MERSON	Arsenal	☐	Thomas BROLIN	GIF Sundsvall
☐	David WHITE	Manchester City	☐	Hans EKLUND	Osters Vaxjo
☐	Stuart RIPLEY	Middlesbrough	☐	Martin DAHLIN	Malmö

UEFA UNDER-21 EUROPEAN CHAMPIONSHIP

GROUP TWO QUALIFYING MATCH
England v Sweden, Highfield Road, Coventry
Tuesday, 18th October 1988

MANCHESTER CITY IN THE FA YOUTH CUP - 1985-86

DATE	ROUND	OPPONENT	SCORE	SCORERS
5th November 1985	First Round	Tranmere Rovers (a)	7-1	White (2), Redmond, Scott, Boyd, Moulden, Lake
28th November 1985	2nd Round	Blackburn Rovers (h)	7-1	Moulden (3), Lake, Scott, Thackeray, Willis (o.g.)
7th January 1986	3rd Round	Blackpool (a)	1-0	Scott
30th January 1986	4th Round	Leicester City (h)	4-1	Moulden (2), Redmond, Thackeray
8th March 1986	Q-Final	Fulham (a)	3-0	Lake, Redmond (2)
16th April 1986	S-Final First Leg	Arsenal (a)	0-1	
22nd April 1986	S-Final Second Leg	Arsenal (h) AET	2-1	Moulden (2)
	Aggregate score 2-2 - Manchester City won 5-4 on penalties			
24th April 1986	Final First Leg	Manchester United (a)	1-1	Lake (pen)
29th April 1986	Final 2nd Leg	Manchester United (h)	2-0	Boyd, Moulden
	Manchester City won 3-1 on aggregate			

AUTOGRAPHS